Season the Preaching

**Inspiration from the
Common Lectionary**
Years A, B and C

Paul Canon Harris

**kevin
mayhew**

**kevin
mayhew**

First published in Great Britain in 2017 by Kevin Mayhew Ltd
Buxhall, Stowmarket, Suffolk IP14 3BW
Tel: +44 (0) 1449 737978 Fax: +44 (0) 1449 737834
E-mail: info@kevinmayhew.com

www.kevinmayhew.com

9 8 7 6 5 4 3 2 1 0

ISBN 978 1 84867 931 3
Catalogue No. 1501565

Cover design by Rob Mortonson
© Image used under licence from Shutterstock Inc.
Edited by Virginia Rounding
Typeset by Angela Selfe

Printed and bound in Great Britain

Preach the Word; be prepared in season
and out of season; correct, rebuke and
encourage – with great patience and
careful instruction.

2 Timothy 4:2

They … are to unfold the Scriptures,
to preach the word in season and out of season,
and to declare the mighty acts of God.

The Church of England Ordination Service

Contents

YEAR B

YEAR C

About the author

Paul Canon Harris is an Anglican priest, writer and poet. He draws on over 30 years' experience of preaching in local churches as well as conferences in the UK and abroad. He is a regular contributor to BBC Radio 2's Pause for Thought and other radio stations. He is a Canon Emeritus of Gloucester Cathedral. He is married to Catherine; they have four adult sons and a gaggle of grandchildren. They live in Bournemouth with their dog called Hope.

Other books by Paul Canon Harris published by Kevin Mayhew:

- Overturning Tables – *Subversive poems for Christian worship (2016)*
- Jump Leads and Bump Starts – *A year's worth of unusual conversations with God (2016)*
- Leading for a Change – *Practical tips and challenging questions for leaders (2016)*

Invitations to preach can be sent to paulcanonharris@gmail.com

Introduction

Season the Preaching has been so-named deliberately. It is not the preaching equivalent of a ready-meal, more an assembling of some of the main ingredients. I am writing preacher to preacher but with half an eye on people who like to meditate on the weekly Gospel reading. Over the last 40 years I have been fortunate to receive encouragement and practical help from many other preachers. I tried to follow their advice and frequently borrowed their illustrations and insights. When it comes to preaching, there is 'nothing new under the sun'. As a preacher, I do not aim for novelty; all sorts of pitfalls lie down that road, but I do aspire to freshness. In my experience, that requires God's grace during preparation and in the delivery. I hope that you find the thoughts I share on the Gospel reading week by week helpful, as you prepare to feed those who will hear your sermons. Use them as seasoning and garnish on your own preparations!

I have never been one for keeping my sermon notes and re-heating them later. We are all different, and in any case my handwriting is so bad that it would have been hard to read them! In writing this resource, I have sat down with my old preaching Bible and returned to the texts afresh. It has been good to be reminded that, no matter how often we return to familiar Bible passages, there are new insights to be found. I have not set out to write a light-weight commentary on the Gospels – there are plenty of proper commentaries available. I have tried to offer clarification on tricky aspects of the meaning or confusing factual issues.

The Common Lectionary does not provide a theme for each Sunday, although some weeks do have an obvious theme. Consequently, I have chosen to focus primarily on the principal Gospel reading and draw in the other readings and Collect for the day to a greater or lesser degree.

Over the years, various well-meaning church members would buy me books and resources as 'presents'. Some I recognised as kind gifts and was grateful for the thought, if not always for the choice. Others I knew were thinly disguised corrective attempts to make me more/less charismatic/reformed/liberal/conservative according to the penchant or prejudices of the donors. If this has been bought for you as such a gift, I hope you can make good use of it despite the intent. If you have bought this as a resource for yourself, I hope you find it useful.

One of the best pieces of advice I received in my training was this: when you think you have finished your preparation, look at the text or outline notes and ask yourself: 'Where is the Good News in this?' If you cannot find it – revise your sermon. This does not mean that as preachers we serve up sugar-coated fluffy whimsy. I am of the school who believe that we should comfort the uncomfortable and discomfort the comfortable.

Each of these reflections is between 300 and 400 words long. I have worked in commercial radio and still broadcast regularly. Sometimes contributors and interviewees were taken aback to be told their piece was only going to be two or three minutes long. I know that if we use our words carefully, we can communicate a significant amount in such a time. I imagine your own sermons will grow to something longer! The wise preacher under whom I served an 'apprenticeship' regularly reminded me that 'the best blooms grow on pruned bushes'.

YEAR A

First Sunday of Advent

MATTHEW 24:36-44

Isaiah 2:1-5; Romans 13:11-end

Use in conjunction with a full Lectionary or Table of Readings. Obviously, there are not always the same number of Sundays before Lent and after Trinity every year, depending on variables such as the date of Easter and the day of the week on which 25 December falls.

Introduction

The Old Testament reading from Isaiah chapter 2 paints *a picture of hope and world peace* in the last days. The greeting 'Good will to all and peace on earth' will feature in the Christmas readings and celebrations in a few weeks' time. That message is fleshed out here as being a feature of the last days. The reading ends with *an invitation to walk in the light of the Lord.* There has always been much speculation, misunderstanding and even fear surrounding the so-called last days and end times. Preachers may want briefly to remind congregations that apocalyptic writing, like other forms of prophecy, usually have two and sometimes three points of focus. (Imminent events, e.g. exile or the Fall of Jerusalem, messianic application, unknown end times.) The advice and call to be ready also apply to individuals preparing for the end of their life on earth.

The Epistle, Romans 13:11-end, is a *wake-up call.* Paul was warning his readers against complacency. In households preparing for a day at work and school, someone often exclaims: 'Goodness, is that the time? We need to get a move on!' Essentially his message, and that of the Advent season, is 'Do not get caught out, sort your lives out now!'

Tales of the Unexpected (Matthew 24:36-44)

This is part of Jesus' extended discourse in which he prepared his disciples for his impending death and for the future Fall of Jerusalem in AD 70. Sudden natural disasters and cataclysmic political upheavals often come with little warning. They are shocking and devastating to all aspects of normal life. They also have the potential to divide families and other groupings. Jesus referred to the days of Noah. He reminded his disciples that life was going on as normal, and people ignored the signs and warnings to their cost. He did not want his followers to be complacent or caught out by events. They needed to be alert on every level, conscious of current affairs and personal matters, with lives as ordered and godly as possible.

Illustration

Security-conscious businesses and homeowners install elaborate systems with cameras and monitors relaying pictures back to a security control room. It does not matter how sophisticated the equipment, it is rendered useless if the person whose job it is to watch the monitors dozes off in the middle of their night-shift.

Final Thought

Advent is a season of preparation, of readiness on many levels.

Second Sunday of Advent

MATTHEW 3:1-12
Isaiah 11:1-10; Romans 15:4-13

Introduction

The Epistle (Romans 15) begins by speaking about the purpose and value of scripture; teaching, endurance and encouragement. It then goes on to make an appeal, based on this encouragement, for unity and mutual acceptance. This acceptance extends to Gentile followers of Christ. Finally, it links and refers to the Root of Jesse, the Messiah prophesied in Isaiah 11.

John the Baptist – 'last of the Old Testament prophets' (Matthew 3:1-12)

John the Baptist, Christ's herald on earth, is in the spotlight today. It is almost wrong to speak in those terms since John was clear that he was preparing the way. He was under no illusions; he was the warm-up act (verse 11). Matthew, writing for a predominantly Jewish audience, states categorically that words in the book of Isaiah referred to John (verse 3). His appearance was wild and unkempt (verse 4), his message was clear and uncompromising. It was a message of repentance because God's Kingdom was near (verse 2). Although such a message may not sound like an immediate 'vote-winner', it seemed to strike a chord with many people who were prepared to go out to the wilderness and submit to baptism (verses 5, 6). He was less welcoming and consequently less popular among the religious leaders and establishment figures (verse 7). He was unimpressed by their position and saw them and their actions for what they were. He struck at the very root of their belief system and tradition, warning that appealing to their lineage from Abraham was fruitless in the face of the reckoning that was shortly to befall them (verses 8-10, 12). He declared that he would be followed by someone altogether more powerful, who would bring a baptism of 'the Holy Spirit and fire' (verse 11).

Illustration

In William Boyd's novel, *Sweet Caress,* two of the main characters have a long-running game of describing other people they meet with just four adjectives. Invite the congregation to try describing John the Baptist (either privately or aloud) in four words.

Third Sunday of Advent

MATTHEW 11:2-11
Isaiah 35:1-10; James 5:7-10

John the Baptist – the sequel! (Matthew 11:2-11)

Matthew introduced the next episode with a bridging summary verse. There was a rhythm to Jesus' ministry, public demonstrations of power followed by retreat for personal space (not always achieved). Teaching the multitudes followed by more detailed instruction for the disciples (verse 1). Now John the Baptist had been imprisoned for speaking out publicly against Herod who had married his brother's wife. News of Jesus' ministry got through to John and he in turn could communicate with some of his own disciples.

Still haven't found what I'm looking for (verses 2, 3)

Just as Jesus' own disciples struggled to accept the thought that Jesus would be arrested and killed, perhaps John the Baptist wondered if he had got it wrong in some way. 'Should we expect someone else?'

If in doubt, read the signs (verses 4-6)

People have speculated whether John's question represented a loss of faith, a spiritual crisis or simply a request for further clarification. There is a clear lesson for any Christians who face uncertainty or have doubts. With hours on his hands and with almost too much time to think in prison, he did the logical and right thing: he directed his question to Jesus. The messengers are told to go back and tell John what they had heard and seen – namely, powerful teaching and miracles that were signs of the coming Kingdom of God, that John had prophesied (verses 4, 5). Verse 6, 'Blessed is anyone who does not stumble on account of me,' should almost certainly be taken as an encouragement to John as opposed to an insensitive warning.

Speak well of others (verses 7-11a)

It is hard for leaders in the Church to voice doubt or uncertainty. Word of John's questioning would have quickly spread. Jesus wasted no time in addressing any gossip or speculation head-on. He reaffirms John's standing and status. As if in response to John's question, 'Jesus, are you the real deal?' he goes out of his way to say that John himself was an authentic prophet and herald. Jesus then characteristically took the opportunity of adding a post-script. In the Kingdom that was to come – even the least would be greater than John. This was not about putting John in his place or denigrating him. Jesus was teaching by comparison for effect. He was expressing how great the reality of the Kingdom would be for ordinary people (verse 11b).

Application

Life seldom runs smoothly all the time. Disappointments come, things take longer than we hoped or take an unexpected turn. This can lead to doubt or uncertainty. Consciously taking hard questions back to God and recalling what he has done in the past is a tried and tested way forward.

Fourth Sunday of Advent

MATTHEW 1:18-END
Isaiah 7:10-16; Romans 1:1-7

The Birth of Jesus

Matthew set out the family tree, Jesus' earthly lineage (Matthew 1:1-17). He used the Exile as the fixed time-point in his dating scheme. In the first instance this was for the benefit of his Jewish readers. Then he made the birth announcement.

The main characters

Mary, the mother of Jesus – is there anyone more Jesus-focused than she is? Joseph – arguably one of the most under-estimated men in the New Testament. He was an outstanding man, resourceful, kind, faithful. Despite his shock and pain, he did not want to shame Mary publicly (verse 19). It is one thing to have a remarkable dream from God (verses 20-23) – it is something else to act on it (verses 24, 25).

The Journey

We read about Joseph and Mary journeying to Bethlehem, to Jerusalem, to Egypt and to Nazareth, but the most significant journey was surely their mental and spiritual one. Bewildered, their world turned upside-down, they must have wondered if they were going mad before faithfully accepting God's will and purpose.

Matthew was at pains to emphasise the holy, divine nature of the Incarnation. He stresses the fact that Mary and Joseph did not have sexual relations at any point before the birth of Jesus (verses 18, 25). The conception was 'of the Holy Spirit' (verses 18, 20). God entering life on earth in human form was the greatest miracle of all. It makes sense of every subsequent miraculous event in the life of Jesus, including the Resurrection. Matthew rarely missed an opportunity to show how Old Testament prophecy was being fulfilled (verse 23).

The Baby

It would be wrong to call Jesus a post-script in this account but the final two sentences (verse 25) are understated. God had come to earth, among his people. He had come to 'save his people from their sins' (verse 21) – to end the great exile.

Christmas Day

(See also Years B and C)

LUKE 2:1-14 [15-20]
Gospel reading from Set 1

Introduction

This Christmas Day Gospel reading from Luke 2 reads rather like a second start to the story. It does not refer to the events preceding Jesus' birth in chapter 1 where Luke set the scene in greater detail.

The Historical Context (verses 1-3)

Luke the physician and historian was at pains to nail the historical context of this great event and for Jesus' subsequent ministry. Typically, he related it to characters (Caesar Augustus, Quirinius) beyond the Jewish community. People and events that could be cross-referenced for historicity. That said, there has been debate among scholars over which census is being referred to – a point probably not for detailed examination on Christmas Day!

The Home Context (verses 4-7)

 In the space of four verses, Luke covers Jesus' royal Davidic lineage, the relationship of Joseph and Mary, the fact she was pregnant, the journey to Bethlehem and the birth itself at an overcrowded inn. It is enough to take one's breath away! People's understanding of the Christmas events often owes more to Christmas card scenes than to the biblical texts. Given the upheaval caused by people returning to their home towns, space was at a premium. It is highly likely that the space where Mary gave birth was the ground floor of a house which typically was used to house animals at night or in extreme weather. The manger was available and put to great use. (See poem 'Manger Danger' below!)

The Heavenly Context (verses 8-14)

The very down-to-earth account of the birth itself is countered by a heavenly announcement to nearby shepherds (verses 8, 9), complete with special effects (verse 12). The appearance of heavenly messengers was not an everyday occurrence and the shepherds were understandably afraid. The encouragement not to be afraid and the declaration of peace are like the post-Resurrection words of the angel and of Jesus himself at the end of this life story (verses 9, 10). The message is one of 'good news that will cause great joy for all the people'. It has been a tragedy of Christian mission through the ages that this has not always been the case.

The detail of Jesus being in a manger is how the shepherds will know they have found the right baby (verse 12).

Manger Danger[1]

Please note:

the contents of this manger
constitute a danger,
they are not fit
for animal consumption.

You are also advised:

teachings emanating
from the occupant of this trough
will be hard to swallow
and are not recommended
for humans of a comfortable disposition.

May cause:

personal upheaval,
temporary distress,
and radical reappraisal
of priorities, ambitions and direction.

---

1. Paul Canon Harris, Advent 2012. (In Paul Canon Harris, *Overturning Tables – Subversive poems for Christian Worship*, Kevin Mayhew, 2016.)

In the event of accidental ingestion:

immerse in water
and seek immediate advice
from a member
of the clerical profession.

(NB: You may find
a sympathetic friend
more helpful
in the end.)

First Sunday of Christmas

(except when Christmas falls on a Sunday)

Naming and Circumcision of Christ

LUKE 2:15-21

Isaiah 61:10–62:3; Galatians 4:4-7

Introduction

Shepherds in the Christmas narrative represent ordinary hard-working people from humble origins without much education. They were often figures of fun in Jesus' time and since. They stand in contrast to the wise men. It is typical of the gospel that it is these people who are the first witnesses of the birth of the Messiah. Also, it is no accident that Jesus, born in the city of David, the Shepherd King, would later announce himself as the Good Shepherd.

Traditionally throughout Europe shepherds were buried with a twist of wool in one hand so that St Peter would know their work and understand why they were often absent from church! The Bethlehem shepherds needed no such excuse. Recovering from the stunning appearance of the angels, they felt compelled to hurry away from their flocks to see what had happened (verse 15).

They were not disappointed – everything was just as they had been told (verse 16). Instinctively, they realised that the role of messengers of good news had passed to them. Imagine them going almost house to house, despite the early hour, sharing their amazing news (verses 17, 18, 20).

Mother's musings (verses 19, 21)

Whenever a baby is expected, all sorts of names are bandied about – people love trying to guess what the parents have chosen. Mary and Joseph had been told they must name the child 'Jesus' because he would save his people. No wonder that Mary treasured the words of the shepherds and pondered them in her heart. They took Jesus to be circumcised, marked out as God's, and named as instructed.

Reflection

Shepherds had a legitimate excuse for sometimes being peripheral to church life. What would people hold in their hands today by way of explanation?

Second Sunday of Christmas

MATTHEW 2:13-END
Isaiah 63:7-9; Hebrews 2:10-end

Introduction

Sharp-eyed church members will spot that today's Gospel reading is the second half of Matthew chapter 2, the first half of which will be read *next week* on Epiphany Sunday. When worshipping Eternal God, a little bit of time travel comes easily! The Gospel recounts the escape into Egypt and the subsequent return to Nazareth in Galilee. As a child, Jesus was a refugee, a returner and a newcomer.

Great Escape (verses 13-15)

Joseph by this stage in these great events was presumably more comfortable with the idea of God speaking to him in his dreams. God's early warning system was working overtime! The wise men are warned to take another route home due to Herod's anger (see next Sunday) and for the same reason Joseph is instructed to flee to Egypt with his little family. Matthew notes the fulfilment of another Old Testament prophecy (Hosea 11:11). It is an irony that the promised Saviour has to flee to Egypt for safety – the land which his forebears left *en route* for the Promised Land.

Terrible Irony (verses 16-18)

There is further irony of a tragic nature. The birth of the one who had come to save his people and be the Prince of Peace triggers an act of barbaric revenge by Herod. The pain of this atrocity was not softened by the fact that it also had been prophesied (Jeremiah 31:15).

What brought you to Nazareth? (verses 19-23)

People often ask someone they are getting to know what it was that brought them to a particular place. It would have been interesting to hear Joseph, Mary or Jesus as he grew up answer that question. After a long interlude, Joseph and his family settle back in Nazareth in Galilee. Joseph is told that 'those who were trying to take the child's life are dead'. They were indeed no longer a threat, but in time a new group of people would want Jesus dead. The reading ends with the fulfilment of another prophecy.

Epiphany

MATTHEW 2:1-12
Isaiah 60:1-6; Ephesians 3:1-12

Introduction

The Epistle, from Ephesians 3, spells out clearly the significance and place of the Gentiles in God's plan. The Apostle Paul wrote (verse 6), 'This mystery is that through the gospel the Gentiles are heirs together with Israel, members together of one body, and sharers together in the promise in Christ Jesus.'

Illustrations

Even today people sometimes speak of having 'something of an epiphany'. They mean a revelation, usually a significant one. There is often an element of surprise attached to it. The significance and surprise of Jesus being visited by and revealed to travellers from beyond Israel was that it set out God's stall(!) from the outset. His gift of Christ would be to the whole world, not simply to his chosen people the Jews.

Whenever an artist has an exhibition of his/her work, they usually arrange a private viewing for invited guests and friends. This is partly to thank them for their support but also in the hope that they will be advocates and spread news of the show.

Wise Men seek a King (verses 1, 2)

By mysterious means, a small group of educated and spiritually open men arrived in Jerusalem, looking for a king. They were clearly significant for Herod to bother to engage with them.

Disturbing news (verses 3-6)

News of the arrival of the wise men and their probable entourage spread throughout the city. It soon became common knowledge that they were looking for a new king. Herod was a vassal ruler and of no real royal line – hence the effect of the visitors' question. The religious leaders were well aware of messianic prophecy, such as Micah 5:2. It is tempting to wonder what sort of notes in official circles were made of these strange events. The words in Micah speak of a shepherd king.

Herod's Subterfuge (verses 7, 8)

Herod is only one of many leaders throughout history to have feigned an interest in worshipping God for their own political ends. Recent history shows political candidates courting religious leaders to gain votes.

Stellar Directions (verses 9, 10)

Having been delayed and distracted by Herod, the seekers were understandably thrilled when they resumed their journey, guided again by the star.

Gifts of Worship (verses 11, 12)

The scene described by Matthew is a familiar one. There is a simple and beautiful clarity to it. They see the child and his mother and instinctively they express their worship through their posture (bowed down) and their gifts. Many, possibly unwarranted, assumptions have been made based on these verses. Three gifts are mentioned, though there may have been more than three wise men. The only true king mentioned in this passage is the baby Jesus. The gifts have been interpreted as being prophetically significant, signalling Jesus' kingship and death. They are valuable commodities, fit for a king but essentially an expression of the magi's worship.

Genuine worship is usually costly and spontaneous, something that is offered by way of a gift, not as a transaction to gain blessing.

First Sunday of Epiphany/ Baptism of Christ

MATTHEW 3:13-END
Isaiah 42:1-9; Acts 10:34-43

Introduction

It is natural to concentrate on the Baptism of Jesus today. However, the Isaiah reading includes wonderfully encouraging words of compassion which may find a place somewhere, not least in the intercessions: 'A bruised reed he will not break, and a smouldering wick he will not snuff out' (Isaiah 42:3).

The reading from Acts includes Peter referring to Jesus' baptism in his sermon in Cornelius' house: 'God anointed Jesus of Nazareth with the Holy Spirit and power' (Acts 10:38).

Role reversal? (Matthew 3:13,14)

Jesus went from Galilee to John the Baptist in the Judaean desert and, as it were, joined the queue to be baptised. John was taken aback by the request and aghast that he should baptise the one whom he knew was his Lord. 'I need to be baptised by you' (verse 14). It is possible even in this brief account to feel his extreme discomfort. At some point or another, most people have offered their seat on a train to someone more deserving or more worthy of honour. If the offer is declined, however graciously, the person sitting down feels uncomfortable for the rest of the journey.

Not jumping through a hoop! (verse 15)

In submitting to baptism, Jesus was not simply ticking a box or making an empty gesture. He was identifying fully with ordinary people, including those who had come to John to repent and be baptised. There was a sense of rightness about this, not because of any need or deficiency on his part but as an expression of the righteousness and plan of the Father.

That's my Boy! (verses 16, 17)

This was an event of enormous personal significance for Jesus first and foremost. God was affirming him, reassuring him of his love and effectively anointing him for his public ministry and all that lay ahead. Occasionally, people can get the idea that it was at this point that Jesus became different, super-charged. Of course, he was fully divine throughout his life.

Illustration

The moment a royal prince or princess is born, they become heir to the throne (if first-born), while at some later date they may be prepared, submit to various investitures and so on, prior to their accession and coronation. The point is that they are heir from day one, purely by token of who they are.

Second Sunday of Epiphany

JOHN 1:29-42
Isaiah 49:1-7; 1 Corinthians 1:1-9

Introduction

The way in which the calling of the first disciples is sometimes presented can make their response seem impetuous to the point of implausibility. John's account shows clearly that several of them were already active in something akin to a revival movement within Judaism. They were disciples of John the Baptist and, as such, showed they were spiritually minded and committed.

Worth noting

Isaiah 49:6 – 'I will also make you a light for the Gentiles' – are words that some or many will recognise from the Song of Simeon or the Nunc Dimittis canticle.

I am not – He is! (John 1:29-31)

Earlier in John chapter 1, people had come to John the Baptist at Bethany near the Jordan and asked him if he was the Christ. He stated categorically that he was not. In today's reading, he points to Jesus as soon as the latter appears. He describes him in clear theological terms: 'the Lamb of God, who takes away the sin of the world!' John's raison d'être was related to Jesus being revealed. The same could be said of all Christians to a greater or lesser degree.

I saw, I knew (verses 32-34)

It seems from this account that the baptism of Jesus had already taken place. John the Baptist recounted what he had seen. He described the two signs he had received that Jesus was the expected Messiah. He saw what seemed like a dove descend on Jesus. He knew this was the Holy Spirit of God. He also said that he had heard (audibly or within his mind/spirit) God tell him that Jesus was the expected one. 'I have seen and I testify that this is God's Chosen One.' If John, the Gospel writer, was a writer for stage or screen he should have issued a 'spoiler alert'.

Disciples follow (verses 35-39)

These five verses shed light on the recruitment of some of the first disciples. John the Baptist was not in any way possessive about his followers. He pointed them to Jesus in the full knowledge that he would lose them. The two disciples attached themselves to Jesus by following him (verse 37). The conversation must have had an almost comic element – 'Are you two following me? What do you want?' (verse 38). They addressed him as a teacher and asked him where he was staying. Jesus invited them to accompany him and told them they would see.

Family and Friends (verses 40-42)

The call to discipleship is always invitational rather than directional. This should characterise approaches to mission. Similarly, the invitation most commonly comes through a family member or a friend, as opposed to coming from a stranger. Andrew immediately sought out his brother Simon and took him to Jesus (verse 42). It is not clear whether Jesus is exercising supernatural knowledge in his greeting of Simon, or whether he knew him by repute. Becoming a disciple of Jesus resulted in Simon being renamed. Followers of Jesus receive a new identity even if their name remains unchanged.

Third Sunday of Epiphany

MATTHEW 4:12-23

Isaiah 9:1-4; 1 Corinthians 1:10-18

Introduction

In the dark gloomy days of winter, promises of light and warmth are welcome. Darkness in people's personal circumstances is no respecter of seasons. Words from Isaiah chapter 9 will ring Christmas bells with people. The opening line may be particularly welcome: 'there will be no more gloom for those who were in distress' (verse 1).

The Gospel reading helps congregations to continue to consider Jesus' call of his first disciples and, by extension, their own call to follow him. Preachers may want to comment on how the account today from Matthew harmonises with last week's Gospel reading from John. They illuminate each other.

John's imprisonment the trigger (Matthew 4:12-17)

The destinies of Jesus and John the Baptist were entwined. News of John's imprisonment by Herod (for having denounced the latter's marriage to his sister-in-law) seemed to act as a trigger or indicator for Jesus (verse 12). People sometimes overlook the fact that his centre of ministry was not Nazareth. He based himself in Capernaum on the lakeside (verse 13). Strategically, this made travel by boat for that stage of his ministry a possibility. Typically, Matthew quotes the Old Testament prophecy which this move fulfilled (verse 14). Initially, Jesus' message took up John's call to repentance (verse 17) and related it to the coming of the Kingdom.

Family ties (verses 18-22)

Jesus began recruiting a close group of disciples. Although there would be many more in time, he concentrated initially on an inner circle of twelve. Within that group, he had a few who were even closer confidants. Two pairs of brothers brought the closeness of family, even though they had to leave their wider family and work (verses 19, 20).

It is unlikely that Andrew, Simon, James and John would have understood at that stage the significance of Jesus' comment about making them 'fishers of men'.

Verse 23 summarises the ministry in the region. It was Jesus' habit to go to the synagogue as his first port of call.

Fourth Sunday of Epiphany

JOHN 2:1-11

1 Kings 17:8-16; 1 Corinthians 1:18-end
(See also Year B Epiphany 3 and Year C Epiphany 2)

Everybody loves a wedding! Or do they?

The first of Jesus's Kingdom signs and wonders is done at a wedding. Compared with later miracles of raising the dead, healing the sick and even walking on water, it can seem like a gentle warm-up, his starter for ten! There is a real almost comic element in the account, though this should not distract from the wonder of the miracle. At weddings, there are certain elements that one can almost guarantee will be present. Cana was no exception. Anxiety over whether enough food and drink has been ordered, a proud but fussy mother finding it hard not to interfere, a single guest who brings friends.

Anonymous wedding couple! (verses 1, 2)

This is one of the most famous weddings in history and yet the happy couple were never named. They remain anonymous to this day. Jesus was there with his disciples. Never mind a single person asking if they can bring a 'plus one'. Jesus is there mob-handed!

Mother knows best! (verses 3-5)

On this occasion, Mary, the mother of Jesus, sounds like a Jewish mother from a Woody Allen film. She noticed the wine had run out, mentioned it pointedly to her son and ignored his observation that his 'time had not yet come'. If Jesus heard Mary addressing the servants (verse 5) he might well have exclaimed: 'Mother!'

That should do the trick! (verses 6-11)

Fortunately, there just happened to be six jars holding about 180 gallons of water (verse 6). Older listeners/readers might remember buying a Party Seven which seemed a lot of beer at the time. Jesus was going to meet the pressing need in a remarkable way. There would be no half-measures. It is possible to infer great theological significance from the facts that jars associated with the traditional ritual cleansing were used and that the new wine was superior to the first serving (verses 7, 10). Sometimes this can sound a little like special pleading. Jesus' actions certainly flew in the face of any nascent asceticism. The most important thing is that this was the very first of Jesus' miraculous signs (verse 11). It did not seem to be a pre-planned intervention. In time, he would be identified as the bridegroom and the Church as his bride. On that day, a wedding couple and their families were spared the shame of failing to provide a good time for their guests. Jesus' disciples were not only impressed, they were inspired (verse 11).

Presentation of Christ in the Temple

LUKE 2:22-40

Malachi 3:1-5; Hebrews 2:14-end

Introduction

Occasionally Christians speak of Jewish traditions in a way that is at best dismissive and at worst offensive. Certainly, Jesus did not shrink from confronting the Jewish leaders of his day but this was because of their hypocrisy and spiritual dullness. When John the Baptist was hesitant to baptise him, Jesus said they 'should fulfil all righteousness' (Matthew 3:15). His upbringing was a devout Jewish one. Today's reading shows his parents doing what was expected of them as Jewish parents. It may be helpful to point out that the previous verse (Luke 2:21) tells of Jesus being circumcised and named on the eighth day. The presentation in the Temple is a separate occasion. At the end of his life the Temple assumed an even greater symbolic importance. Early in his account, Luke included two visits to the Temple from Jesus' childhood and youth.

To the letter of the law (verses 22-24)

Jesus' parents fulfilled the requirements of the law. The position of being first-born had a special significance in Jewish culture.

Simeon (verses 25-35)

Simeon was a truly spiritual man. He was one of those, a minority, who were looking for God to act to rescue Israel (verse 25). He was holding on to a personal prophetic promise that he would see the Lord's Christ with his own eyes – a true Messianic Jew (verse 26). He was very sensitive to the promptings of the Holy Spirit (verses 27, 28). His beautiful words of praise as he held Jesus bridged the Old Testament and the New Covenant for the whole world. These famous words are known and loved by many as the canticle the Nunc Dimittis (verses 29-32). Notwithstanding the remarkable circumstances of Jesus' birth, Joseph and Mary still marvelled at what was said over and about their son (verse 33). Simeon blessed them as parents and spoke solemn words of warning to Mary (verses 34, 35).

Prophetess Anna (verses 36-38)

The words of Simeon were echoed and reinforced by Anna, a godly old woman who was also a prophetess. Simeon had been described as 'waiting for the consolation of Israel' (verse 25). Anna gave thanks to God for Jesus and immediately started telling people who were 'looking forward to the redemption of Jerusalem' all about the child.

A settled home and a growing boy (verses 39, 40)

In these two verses Luke tells how the family were finally able to settle down to life back in Nazareth. Jesus thrived physically and spiritually. He was strong, wise and full of grace.

Proper 1

MATTHEW 5:13-20

Isaiah 58:1-9a; 1 Corinthians 2:1-12

The number of 'Sundays before Lent' varies each year depending on the date of Easter. The readings allocated for the 5th, 4th or 3rd Sunday before Lent are known as 'Propers'. Preachers should check which Proper is allocated to which Sunday in any given year.

Introduction

The Old Testament reading from Isaiah 58 describes the nature of true fasting. It is timely as we prepare for the season of Lent. The Gospel reading is obviously a segment of the Sermon on the Mount. It is sometimes good to remind people that Jesus travelled for the best part of three years, preaching as he went. On occasions, a recent event, the local context or a questioner would trigger a response, but the basic message of his Kingdom must have been one he repeated many times.

Illustration

Contemporary health advice encourages people to keep their salt intake low. The younger generation are denied the pleasure of releasing the little blue bag and salt 'n' shaking their packets of crisps. Salt historically was a preservative, an antiseptic and of course something to use in cooking – used to bring out, rather than to mask, the taste. Hypertension fears apart, society still needs the metaphorical salt of God's Kingdom.

The verses about salt and light refer to the importance of living out the teaching of Jesus.

Salt of the earth! (verse 13)

So-and-so is the 'salt of the earth'. Not such a common expression these days, but still used occasionally. It means that someone is straightforward, down-to-earth and good. When Jesus coined the phrase, he was encouraging his followers to add savour to their society.

He wanted them to exercise a long-lasting influence for good. This was central to their task. A follower that loses their saltiness, their edge, is no good to anyone! He was putting some pepper on it!

Light show (verses 14-16)

Similarly, Jesus wanted his followers to know that they were to shine and be proactive in combatting the natural darkness that spoils life. His listeners would all have been familiar with the sight of hilltop towns shining as beacons at night. In other settings and for different reasons, he warned against showing off or making an exhibition of their piety. Here, however, Jesus wanted to stress that his followers should live lives that were noticed by others, lives that inspired others to praise God.

Live out the Law by living righteously (verses 17-20)

Jesus and his disciples were sometimes accused of having a cavalier attitude to the Jewish laws. Here, he set out his own attitude to the law in unequivocal terms. He had not come to replace it, but rather to fulfil it. Breaking the law, and trying to get others to break the law, was reprehensible. The point was that most of the scribes and Pharisees of his day focused on the minutiae of countless regulations and missed the greater purpose of the law: to love God and one's fellow human beings. Keeping the law gave people a sense of merit; Jesus had come to preach and exhibit grace. This would liberate people. It was as though they lived in fear of tripping over traps laid for them in the law – it was like tiptoeing through a minefield. God wants people to be able to lift their heads and not be living in fear of making mistakes and falling foul of the law.

Proper 2

MATTHEW 5:21-37

Deuteronomy 30:15-end; 1 Corinthians 3:1-9

Introduction: Preachers proceed with extreme caution.

Today is one of those Sundays on which it is all too easy to cause distress or trigger unhelpful guilt. The Gospel (good news!) reading from Matthew covers murder, adultery, divorce and oaths. They are all important topics and should not be dodged. However, it is probably well-nigh impossible to do justice to one of them, let alone the whole set, in the time available for the typical Sunday sermon! Small groups or a one-off discussion group may be a helpful follow-up. Commentaries suggest that the sermon may be structured so as to illustrate the principle(s) Jesus was espousing (i.e. emphasising contrast). Jesus uses the teaching technique of using extreme and absurd statements to ram home the seriousness of the subject.

Context

It may be useful to recall that this segment of the Sermon on the Mount was preceded by Jesus talking about being salt and light and fulfilling the law by living righteous lives.

Murder (verses 21-26)

The introduction, 'You have heard . . . but I tell you . . .' was an almost formulaic saying. It emphasises the new, radical nature of Jesus' teaching. The Kingdom of God was to be about motives, inner radical change, rather than keeping external regulations. Jesus takes murder as his jumping-off point. The wrongness of murder was not up for discussion. Jesus shifts the focus on to anger (verse 22) and to angry speech (verse 22). Bearing a grudge against a neighbour disqualifies a person from bearing a gift to God. God is not bought off. Jesus wanted people to seek reconciliation (verses 23, 24). Idealism and pragmatism underpinned his teaching in equal measure. 'Do the right thing because it is the right thing and because it is good for you' (verses 25, 26).

Adultery (verses 27-30)

People knew the teaching then, as they do now. Through the ages when people have sought clarification, they have often not been asking 'How can I be holy?' – what they have really wanted to know is how much they can get away with! Jesus was raising the bar. He did this by shifting the talk to the cause of adultery – namely, lust (verses 27, 28). Jesus was not promoting self-harm and mutilation. He was emphasising that destructive patterns of behaviour need decisive action and radical responses.

Illustration

'We will be tough on crime and on the causes of crime!' has been a repeated and vote-winning political slogan. Most people agree it is important to talk about the underlying cause of crime. When it comes to their personal lives, people are usually less eager to discuss their underlying attitudes. Often it is underlying lying!

Divorce (verses 31, 32)

There is evidence that men in Jesus' day were abusing the concession of divorce to cover their unfaithful behaviour. The law allowed a man to write a bill of divorce to an unfaithful wife. Things were skewed in favour of men. It seems that, if a man was attracted to another woman, he would divorce his wife so that he could not be accused of adultery. Then, when it suited him, he might attempt to remarry his wife.

Oaths (verses 33-37)

Jesus taught that ideally there should be no need for people to take an oath. Their word should be true. It is always strange if people preface a comment in a meeting with 'to be honest' – as though it was not the norm!

Proper 3

MATTHEW 5:38-48
Leviticus 19:1-2, 9-18; 1 Corinthians 3:10-11, 16-23

Introduction

Today's Gospel reading is another segment of teaching from the Sermon on the Mount. It includes one-line instructions that Jesus gave. Over and above the specific teaching, Jesus was wanting his listeners to realise that the more important thing was their underlying attitude. Generosity and gentleness of spirit lead to change actions.

You have heard it said, but I say to you (verses 38-42)

This was the way Jesus introduced teaching throughout the sermon and whenever he taught. It emphasised that his teaching was fresh and a radical development of the traditional teaching that people knew. The difference was in the application. It appeared that many of the scribes and Pharisees of Jesus' day were locked into a strange mixture of legalism while trying to find ways of minimising the cost of obedience. Jesus referred to teaching from the Mosaic law about revenge. Although originally intended as a way of making sure retaliation was proportionate to the injury done, this law was being applied in a vengeful 'I'll have my pound of flesh' way.

Then, as now, applying this teaching may sound as though it is a recipe for becoming a door mat. Jesus' intention was that his followers should be generous and conciliatory, going above and beyond.

Application

Allowing this teaching to shape the way people respond to requests from the homeless is a useful practical exercise. Combining a generous heart with common sense is not always easy.

Love your enemies (verses 43-47)

In western culture, 'love' tends to be associated with romantic love, or love for family members. Perversely, it is also used in way that strips it of any real meaning, as in when someone says, 'I love cupcakes'. In the New Testament, the word love is expressed in terms of acts of care done for someone else that don't spring from warm fuzzy feelings. The practical actions of loaning a tunic or money, not retaliating and so on (see above) could all be expressions of love. Jesus took the old teaching of loving neighbours and hating enemies and added to it. Jesus linked this to an understanding of what it meant to be sons/daughters of God (verse 45a). In other words, the children should resemble the Father, and in so doing reveal him to the world. God does not show favouritism – he blesses good and bad alike (verse 45b).

The sayings 'charity begins at home' and 'we have to look after our own' are all too prevalent in modern society. Jesus taught that loving and caring in such a restricted way was no virtue (verses 46, 47).

Be perfect (verse 48)

This sounds like an impossible instruction. True perfection is only to be found in God. Perfect here means in the sense that a screwdriver is perfectly suited to the task.

Second Sunday before Lent

MATTHEW 6:25-END

Genesis1:1–2:3; 1 Corinthians 3:1-9

Introduction

It may be pastorally sensitive of preachers to acknowledge that telling a born worrier not to worry is no more helpful than telling a depressed person to cheer up. Jesus' teaching about worry is down-to-earth and helpful, but should not be presented as simplistic. This section on worry comes immediately after a section of the Sermon on the Mount about not being beguiled by earthly treasures.

Jesus challenged everyday worries

Jesus knew what ordinary people living ordinary lives worried about: clothing, food and drink, health. He names these worries and challenges them in three places (verses 25, 28, 31). He was realistic about life. 'Each day has enough trouble of its own' (verse 34).

Jesus knew the effect of worry

He knew that worrying was futile (verse 27), harmful and a distraction. Worry about material matters was a characteristic of the pagans (verse 32). It is worth recalling that he was speaking in a culture that was not wedded to consumerism in the way the modern world is!

Jesus offered an antidote to worry

He taught through contrasts. If God provided for the birds and clothed the plants, how much more ready must he be to provide for his people who are far more valuable (verses 26, 30). He reiterated his earlier teaching about serving God rather than money. The secret was to seek God's righteousness for its own sake and trust that God would provide what was necessary (verse 33).

Illustrative song

Churches that use digital projection and/or a PA system may want to play some or all of the song: *Don't worry, Be happy*. It was first recorded in 1988 by jazz vocalist, Bobby McFerrin, and won song of the year at the Grammy awards in 1989. Bob Marley's *Three Little Birds* is an alternative – they are often confused.

Sunday next before Lent

MATTHEW 17:1-9

Exodus 24:12-end; 2 Peter 1:16-end

Introduction

The Gospel and the Epistle today focus on the Transfiguration. Immediately before Lent, this is an opportunity to reflect on Christ's glory. Of course, Jesus sometimes spoke about his impending death and resurrection in terms of the Son of Man being *glorified*. The events recounted in the Gospel happened a week (verse 1) after Jesus had predicted his death in plain terms (Matthew 16:21-28). Peter had been rebuked for his refusal to accept the outcome Jesus predicted.

Holy Mountain – Holy Moses (verses 1-4)

In his second Epistle, Peter described what he and the others heard and saw on the 'sacred mountain'– Mount Tabor by tradition, but possibly Mount Hermon. Whichever it was, this is a true mountain-top experience. They saw Jesus shining with the glory of God (verse 2). The appearance of Elijah and Moses would have confirmed to them that this was a genuine messianic experience (verse 3). They must have felt overwhelmed. This was supernatural double plus! The parallel account in Mark 9:6 makes it clear that the disciples were frightened. This was not something one simply took in one's stride. Peter's response was to do something practical. His suggestion that he make three shelters seems bizarre to the modern mind. For him as a Jew there would be a sense that there should be some special accommodation for holy people and holy things (e.g. Tabernacle, Temple, etc.).

Voice from the cloud (verses 5-8)

Many fell-walkers and mountaineers know the experience of being suddenly enveloped in cloud. Visibility is affected and clothing is soaked. For Peter, James and John, lost vision was replaced by an audible voice from within the mysterious bright cloud (verse 5). The wording was very like the Father's words heard at Jesus' baptism. The Father's affirmation of Jesus was followed by an instruction to listen to him. This may relate back to Peter and the others not wishing to hear Jesus talk about his death and future glory. They had coped with seeing Jesus shining, and with Moses and Elijah appearing, but the voice frightened them to such an extent that they threw themselves to the ground (verse 6). The description of what Jesus did next is very tender. He went to each of them, touched them and told them not to be afraid (verse 7). When Christians today are frightened, they need a similar sense of his presence and reassurance. 'When they looked up, they saw no one except Jesus' (verse 8). This sounds rather like when a patient comes round after anaesthetic and focuses on the loved one sitting by their bed.

A time to speak and a time to stay silent (verse 9)

Coming back down the mountain they must have been talking about everything that had happened. Jesus told them they were to keep this remarkable event under wraps until after he had been raised from the dead.

Ash Wednesday

MATTHEW 6:1-6, 16-21
Isaiah 58:1-12; 2 Corinthians 5:20b–6:10

Introduction

As Lent begins, the three set Scripture readings combine by way of preparation for practising spiritual disciplines. The Isaiah passage addresses the nature of true fasting, tying it inseparably to social justice. The verses from 2 Corinthians cover reconciliation, suffering and sacrifice for the sake of the gospel. The Gospel reading (see below) is about charitable giving and prayer. An approach might be to take three or four of these disciplines and make one single point in turn from each of the readings.

Heavenly rewards, NOT earthly Brownie points

Jesus taught that God responds favourably to things done 'in secret' (Matthew 6: 4, 6, 18): 'your Father, who sees what is done in secret, will reward you'. One of the criticisms of the religious hierarchy of Jesus' day was that they made a great show of their outward religious observances. In most cases, there was no internal spiritual reality underpinning their actions. Jesus taught frequently that God looks on the heart, that motives matter and that real inner change is expected.

Acts of kindness (verses 1-4)

There is a website called www.randomactsofkindness. Anne Herbert is credited with inventing the phrase, having written 'Practice random acts of kindness and senseless acts of beauty' on a place mat in a restaurant in Sausalito, California, in the early 1980s. Whatever her motives, it is safe to say that Jesus would have approved. He taught that acts of kindness should neither be done for show nor accompanied by any sort of fanfare. He did not shrink from criticising those who were hypocritical in their giving. They would receive only a limited return on their gift.

Private Prayer (verses 5, 6)

Similarly prayer, which in the Jewish tradition happened at particular times in the day, was not meant to be practised in public with a flourish. Retreating to a private place was the ideal.

Fresh clean fast-acting! (verse 16-18)

Again, Jesus seemed to have a group of religious leaders in his sights when he condemned hypocritical behaviour. Fasting was expected; making a show of it was not!

Note

There is an apparent contradiction here with Matthew 5:16: 'In the same way, let your light shine before others, that they may see your good deeds and glorify your Father in heaven.' The resolution, if one is needed, is in the fact that the effect of being salt and light in the world should be visible/felt and should result in people thanking God. Financial giving and acts of kindness should be done out of a desire to serve others, not out of show or to enhance personal reputation.

Conclusion: Lent Challenge

In recent years, encouragement by social media and a preoccupation with losing weight have resulted in many non-churchgoers embracing a Lenten fast. This can be a positive thing. However, church members might like to see if they can add to the benefit of any Lenten abstinence by keeping it secret throughout the season.

First Sunday of Lent

MATTHEW 4:1-11

Genesis 2:15-17, 3:1-7; Romans 5:12-19

Introduction

Different congregations will have differing levels of understanding on aspects of today's readings, particularly on issues such as original sin, the nature of evil and the Devil, and substitutionary atonement. The readings from Genesis and Romans give a theological context to the Gospel account of Jesus' temptation in the wilderness. It is a tall order to expect to unpack them in the time available within a typical service! Preachers should decide 'at what level they wish to play'!

Conflict (verse 1)

'Then Jesus was led' – this extended time of testing, alone in hostile terrain, followed on directly from the high spot of Jesus' baptism and affirmation by his heavenly Father. Life is like that, and most people will recognise that. What church members may feel less comfortable about is that Jesus 'was led by the Spirit to be tempted by the Devil'. They may well pray the line of the Lord's Prayer – 'Lead us not into temptation' – with greater fervour today. A high view of the sovereignty of God helps in understanding this verse. God, being God, can 'use' any agent, spiritual or temporal, to fulfil his purpose. On a pastoral note, however, it may not be the healthiest thing if people begin to explain every little temptation as a diabolical attack! C.S. Lewis's observation in *The Screwtape Letters* about equal and opposite errors is apposite in this regard.

Hunger (verse 2-4)

The wives of many a grumpy husband over the years have detected hunger at 40 paces! Fasting can heighten one's spiritual senses but tiredness and hunger can leave people vulnerable. At the end of Jesus' fast he is tempted about food, or at least he appears to be! 'Turn these stones into bread' is the temptation. Jesus rejects the suggestion by referring to Scripture. Even in his vulnerability he recognised that the issue was about what really mattered and where he should look for sustenance. Insofar as this was preparation for his public ministry, it was important that he did not use his divine power frivolously. The signs and wonders he subsequently performed were neither mere conjuring tricks nor acts of self-indulgence.

Security (verses 5-7)

Knowing where our personal sense of security and safety is vested is an important part of human identity. Again, Jesus countered the temptation with reference to Scripture. He knew that this was an inappropriate and unnecessary test of his Father. The day would come, in the garden and on the hill, when he would have to entrust himself in the deepest sense to God.

Loyalty and power (verses 8-10)

At various points during the next three years people would encourage Jesus to make a play for earthly, political power. He was not beguiled by the appeal of power, nor by any shortcuts to achieve his rule. Here, on the threshold of his ministry, his allegiance and motivation were tested. Nothing would shift him from fulfilling his heavenly Father's mission and purpose. 'Get away from me, Satan' (in older translations 'Get thee hence') has been used as a mantra by Christians through the ages when they have found themselves tempted.

Second Sunday of Lent

JOHN 3:1-17

Genesis 12:1-4a; Romans 4:1-5, 13-17
See also Trinity Sunday

Context of other readings

Genesis 12:1-4a recounts the call of Abram to trust and to follow. Abram(Abraham) stepped into the unknown to know the One True God. The Romans 4 excerpts emphasise that Abraham believed and that resulted in him receiving the gift of righteousness. 'The promise comes by faith' (Romans 4:16) is crucial to understanding the nature and working of God's grace. This sheds an important light on the encounter and exchange between Jesus and Nicodemus. It is reiterated in Hebrews 11:8-40.

Open-minded and inquisitive Pharisee (verses 1, 2)

The Pharisees were the group who most often came in for cutting criticism from Jesus, yet Nicodemus was evidence that they were not all closed spiritually. Note how he used the 'we' form in his opening comments (verse 2). His opening statement was not flattery. He may have been saying: 'I come in peace.' It has the sound of someone prefacing a tricky question in a Q&A session. The implied question was probably along the lines of 'Exactly who and what are you?' Later Nicodemus asked two questions. The setting of him coming by night seeking enlightenment is significant.

Jesus' opening gambit (verse 3)

John described this as Jesus' reply, even though a question had not been explicitly asked. This is one of many times when a stage direction indicating the correct inflexion would have helped! Jesus could have been reflecting on the fact that Nicodemus had displayed a measure of spiritual insight by what he had said in verse 2. Or it could be that Jesus was raising the bar and setting the terms of the discussion –

e.g. spiritual birth and insight. The phrase 'born again' has in recent years been associated with specific forms of churchmanship and evangelism. It may be worth noting that it was coined by Jesus and not by a twentieth-century evangelist.

Question 1 (verses 4-8)

How can a man be born when he is old? This and his secondary comment are a little surprising. Nicodemus was no fool and yet he took an entirely literal approach to understanding Jesus. His reference to childbirth led Jesus to respond by using terms of natural conception and birth to describe the spiritual experience/event that he had in mind. Jesus stressed that he was talking about the spiritual dimension, not a material, earthly one. The work of God is unpredictable, cannot be pinned down or contained. Although he told Nicodemus he should not be surprised (verse 7), his description made it sound surprising and 'other'. Spiritual birth was essential, mandatory even!

Question 2 (verses 9-15)

How can this be? (verse 9). Jesus and Nicodemus are not engaged in the sort of point-scoring debate that characterised many of Jesus' encounters with the Pharisees. Nicodemus was an honest seeker. Jesus seemed genuinely taken aback by Nicodemus' apparent ignorance of spiritual matters (verse 10). Although John has placed this episode near the beginning of his Gospel, it seems likely that there had already been a fair amount of engagement with, and opposition from, the Pharisees. 'We testify to what we have seen, but still you people do not accept our testimony' (verse 11). Jesus then focused on himself as the Son of Man, his impending death (being lifted up, verse 14) and gift of eternal life (verse 15). This was the answer to Nicodemus' question.

Gospel encapsulated (verses 16, 17)

Scholars differ over whether these verses are a continuation of the conversation with Nicodemus. That is not a primary issue. They read as a couplet; the first part is expressed positively – 'For God so loved . . .' – and the second, although hugely positive, begins with a negative phrase: 'For God did not . . .'. God loves the world, wants to give life to all and any who believe. He does not want to condemn, but to save it. These are the reasons he sent his Son. No one knows how much of this Nicodemus grasped at the time but it may be good to remind people that he spoke up for Jesus (John 7:50-52) and helped Joseph of Arimathea prepare Jesus for burial (John 19:38-42) – all of which suggests an inner change took place in him at some point.

Third Sunday of Lent

JOHN 4:5-42

Exodus 17:1-7; Romans 5:1-11

Introduction

In this age of social media, celebrities and chat shows, it can sometimes seem that no one is bothered who knows about their past relationships and sexual history. However, in most if not all churches, there will be people who regret past choices and who may have been hurt and/or caused pain in previous relationships. Jesus' encounter with the Samaritan woman at the well is helpful in this penitential season. It is important that people go away having heard these words knowing that they do not need to carry a burden of guilt with them.

Geographical context

Jacob's Well in Samaria. Samaria was hostile territory for Jews. They looked down on the Samaritans, viewing them as second rate, not *kosher* as it were. The Old Testament reading from Exodus 17 is about Moses providing water for the people. In fact, Genesis 29 provides another background parallel with the Gospel. Jacob met Rachel, his cousin and wife-to-be, at a well. He kissed her there before going to meet her father. This adds significance to Jesus' encounter with the woman. The well at Sychar was probably on land that Jacob had bought (see Genesis 33).

Noon-day heat (verses 4-6)

The scene could have been set for a film. The sixth hour means about noon. Jesus was alone (verse 8), tired and hungry (verse 6).

Taboo or not to taboo! (verses 7-9)

They were in Samaria, so a Samaritan woman was no big surprise – but the woman herself knew that it was extraordinary for Jesus, a Jewish man, to engage with her. For reasons that become plain, she was not collecting water at the time other women would have done.

Living water (verses 10-15)

Jesus parries her question with leading comments designed to move the conversation on to his identity and the gift of living water. There is an innocent irony about her question: 'Are you greater than our father Jacob?' (verse 12). Like most people, the woman found it hard to see beyond the practical advantages of everyday life. Save me a journey! (verse 15).

Personal revelations (verses 16-26)

Jesus had insight into this woman's personal relationships. Far from fazing her, this knowledge convinced her that Jesus was, at the very least, a prophet. Jesus told her that distinctions between Samaritans and Jews would in his Kingdom disappear. People who worshipped God in spirit and truth would be united. The woman then, somewhat surprisingly, revealed her own knowledge and belief in the coming Messiah (verse 25). This elicits from Jesus a clear declaration of his identity (verse 26).

Enter disciples stage right (verses 27-34)

At this point the disciples returned and, though surprised to see Jesus talking with her, they did not hassle the woman (verse 27). 'Leaving her water jar, [she] went back to the town' (verse 28) was a nice ironic detail. Her testimony was remarkable; the fact that Jesus knew about her troubled past and untidy present was no disincentive to her inviting people to go with her to see Jesus.

His disciples were keen that he should eat. Jesus used food in much the same way as he used the topic of water with the woman. He likened his food to obeying and completing the work he had been given (verses 34-38).

Many believe (verses 39-42)

Because of the woman's spontaneous and honest testimony, many others listened to Jesus over the next couple of days. Someone else's second-hand account became their first-hand personal experience (verse 42).

Fourth Sunday of Lent

JOHN 9

1 Samuel 16:1-13; Ephesians 5:8-14

Don't eat it all at once!

The Gospel reading is a long passage but does cover one episode, the fall-out from it and the teaching point Jesus made from it. One way of presenting the material is to divide it into three parts, as though they were a sequence of TV programmes. The illustration of a TV advert (see below) sits naturally with this approach.

Alternatively, the Old Testament reading from 1 Samuel 16:1-13, the account of Samuel anointing David, can be fruitfully addressed as a stand-alone episode.

The Healing – Medical Drama and Neighbours (verses 1-12)

Jesus and his disciples passed a man blind from birth (verse 1). The disciples, like second-year undergraduates, were getting into theological theory. Their first thought was not 'How can we help this man?' They wanted to explore issues of cause and effect, sin, blame and suffering (verse 2). The prevailing traditional view at the time was that health and wealth were a sign of God's blessing, while misfortune, illness and death were the result of sin. Jesus stated categorically that neither the blind man nor his parents had sinned (verse 3). He made it an opportunity to declare and demonstrate that he was the light of the world (verse 4).

On this occasion, Jesus' method of healing appeared more like conventional medicine. Not many faith healers today are big on mud and spit followed by an eye bath (verses 6-7). In passing, it may be worth pointing out that there is no single technique when it comes to praying for healing. The man was healed but, having been sent to the pool of Siloam, he does not know Jesus' whereabouts when questioned by his neighbours (verses 8-12).

The Legal Drama (verses 13-34)

The fall-out from Jesus' act of kindness had various elements. The religious leaders demanded an inquiry (verse 13). They focused first on the legitimacy and authority of Jesus' ministry. They established the facts (verse 15). They considered the Sabbath law-breaking and what this meant about Jesus (verse 16). Opinion was divided. They asked the ex-blind man what he thought – a prophet, he replied (verses 17, 18). Then they questioned the man's parents to determine whether he was a fraud (verses 18-23). The man was questioned a second time, by which time he was losing patience. His question 'Do you want to be disciples too?' wound them up (verses 24-29)! By now the man was astonished at their wilful refusal to accept his testimony and Jesus' authority and power (verses 30-34).

Epilogue – Thought for the Day (verses 35-41)

On hearing what had happened, Jesus met with the man. He questioned him so that he could come to his own personal confession of faith – 'Lord, I believe' (verses 35-38). Jesus said he had come to judge the wilfully blind and took a parting shot at the Pharisees (verses 39-41).

Illustrations

'There's none so blind as those who will not see!' – a sixteenth-century proverb reflecting Jeremiah 5:21, used by eighteenth-century writer and Dean of St Patrick's Cathedral, Dublin, Jonathan Swift.

The series of Specsavers adverts (e.g. the couple appearing to sit on a park bench but accidentally getting onto a big dipper, the moon rocket team landing at Luton Airport by mistake) are illustrations to use in passing about the danger of faulty vision.

Fifth Sunday of Lent

JOHN 11:1-45
Ezekiel 37:1-14; Romans 8:6-11

Introduction

At this time of year, the Gospel readings are not 'bite-sized'! There are similarities with last week's Gospel. It is a drama in three acts. Jesus performs a remarkable miracle, uses the event to teach about an important subject (resurrection) and, finally, is reported to the Pharisees. Again, the Old Testament reading is a 'purple passage' which merits a sermon in its own right!

Act 1 – Late for Lazarus (verses 1-16)

At first sight Jesus appears to lack compassion and pastoral insight. Most clergy over the course of their ministry look back with regret to occasions when they did not respond quickly enough to a pastoral request. It happens despite people's best intentions. Jesus, on hearing of his friend's illness from the sisters, deliberately delayed setting off for Bethany (verses 1-6). When he eventually suggested going, some of the disciples tried to dissuade him on the basis that it would be too dangerous (verses 7, 8). This is an occasion when Thomas can be seen in a very positive light (verse 16). One of the key themes of this whole episode is Jesus' sense of timing and of being in control (verses 9-15).

Act 2 – Blame and Comfort (verses 17-37)

Whenever anyone dies, there is usually a point in the experience and cycle of grief when people say: 'If only . . .'. Martha and Mary both greet Jesus with such a comment (verses 21, 32). Even in their remonstrating with Jesus, it is possible to see the faith they had in him (verses 24, 26). The exchange with Martha includes one of Jesus' most famous and hope-filled sayings: 'I am the resurrection and the life. The one who believes in me will live, even though they die; and whoever lives by believing in me will never die' (verses 25, 26). Jesus asked Martha directly, 'Do you believe this?' The question echoes down the centuries to people today. Jesus was not using this tragic scenario callously, nor was he lacking in care as some onlookers believed (verse 37). He shared the household's sadness (verse 33). Jesus wept – the shortest sentence in the Bible (verse 35). He was moved.

Act 3 – Resurrection preview (verses 38-44)

Then he demonstrated his authority even over death by ordering them to roll the stone away from the tomb (verse 38). Later, after Jesus' resurrection, people must have looked back and made all the connections between these two graveside incidents. It is important to remind people that, strictly speaking, this was a resuscitation. Lazarus was raised, only to die at a subsequent date (verse 43). He did not have a resurrection body first time around!

Palm Sunday

MATTHEW 21:1-11
Isaiah 50:4-9a; Philippians 2:5-11

Introduction

If (as is common) the church distributes palm crosses today, it may be helpful to reflect on the most common ways people use or display their cross. Young children usually cannot resist the temptation to use them as a sword – the way of the sword was not Christ's way. Some people use them as bookmarkers in their Bible – God's Word is a lamp to our feet. Others pin them on the wall or on a noticeboard – it's good to keep the cross in view as a reminder. It is also common for people to have them in their car, often by the rear-view mirror – while not encouraging superstition, the Cross of Christ offers protection.

The other readings

Isaiah 50:4-9a describes the Servant of the Lord as obedient and not shrinking from his enemies, even at the cost of physical pain and suffering. Philippians 2:5-11 is Paul's classic description of Christ's humility in taking the form of a servant, and his obedience in being prepared to go to the Cross. Jesus entering Jerusalem without regal trappings was a powerful expression of servant leadership.

Triumphal entry (Matthew 21:1-11)

Matthew, as ever, was at pains to make sure that his predominantly Jewish readership understood the extent to which Jesus fulfilled prophecies (verses 4, 5).

Practicalities (verses 1-3)

Jesus knew the donkey and colt would be there, either because they belonged to friends and he had made prior arrangements or because he knew supernaturally. How the arrangement was made is not central to Palm Sunday – riding a donkey was. The willingness of the owner to loan the donkey was commendable either way. In passing, it may be worth asking people how available their possessions are to God!

Crowd reaction (verses 6-9)

Probably some of the crowd understood the significance of what was being played out before them. Human nature being what it is, others simply got caught up in the moment. The excitement and gestures were akin to those of a royal visit.

Stirred – not yet shaken (verses 10, 11)

The city was stirred, and people asked the key question: 'Who is this?' Issues about Jesus' identity and authority were central to the events in Jerusalem. The Easter narratives will include Pilate asking Jesus who he was and the detail of the sign above him on the Cross. The Kingship of Christ remains a central challenge to people today.

Maundy Thursday

JOHN 13:1-17, 31B-35
Exodus 12:1-4, 11-14; 1 Corinthians 11:23-26

Introduction and context

When this reading is used in the context of a service/gathering in which the washing of feet is re-enacted, it requires little by way of explanation. Actions speak louder than words! This Gospel reading is the beginning of the Upper Room discourse (chapters 13–16): Jesus' 'Famous Last Words'. John does not include the actual institution of the Eucharist/Lord's Supper, although the words and actions of Jesus and the others harmonise with the accounts in the other Gospels. It is also helpful to remind people that the words at the heart of the Eucharistic Prayers/Prayers of Consecration are taken directly from Paul's letter to the Corinthians

Love the motive – Love the mission (verse 1)

John introduces the evening in the Upper Room beautifully, in terms of love. Jesus demonstrated the depth and scope of his and his Father's love for his disciples and for his future followers down the years.

Taking the form of a servant (verses 2-5)

Paul's famous words from Philippians 2:5-11 about Jesus taking the form of a servant are clearly illustrated in this account of the menial task of personal care that Jesus undertakes here. In most churches, there are members who are engaged in such work either for loved ones or on a paid basis in hospitals and care homes. While not the main thrust of the passage, this can be hugely affirming for them.

Note that Jesus washes their feet as a consequence of his knowing that 'the Father had put all things under his power' (verse 3).

Jesus and Peter (verses 6-11)

The interaction between Jesus and Peter in the Upper Room looms large. Peter's characteristic eagerness to serve, his slowness to understand

and his insecurity were there for all to see. To his credit, Peter realised the inappropriateness of their leader performing a task that was part of the customs of hospitality and ritual of eating together (verse 6). An honoured guest or the senior member in any gathering should not be expected to serve up or clear the table, let alone wash guests' feet.

Jesus told Peter that he would grasp the significance in due course (verse 7). So many of Jesus' words have a double meaning only understood in retrospect – for example, what it means to be clean (verses 8, 10).

Having remonstrated with Jesus, Peter then asked to be cleansed more fully (verse 9).

It is striking that Jesus washed Judas Iscariot's feet in the full knowledge that he would be betrayed by him. We can only speculate on the thoughts and emotions of the two men at that moment (verse 11).

Do you get it? (verses 12-17)

Jesus was at pains to make his purpose plain. On many occasions during their three years together, he had given the disciples space and time to mull over and understand what he taught. Now that time was short, he spelled it out. His purpose was that they should grasp the importance of true servant leadership and grow in their awareness of their relationship to each other and supremely, of course, to God whom they served.

Good Friday

JOHN 18:1–19:42
Isaiah 52:13–53:12; Hebrews 10:16-25

Introduction

The readings on this solemn holy day are, by tradition and of necessity, long! It is a day for unhurried sober reflection. A good rule of thumb for priests, ministers and other worship leaders is 'less is more' when it comes to their own input. Here are two brief outlines:

The Lord's Servant in Isaiah 52:13-53:12

What he was like (verses 2, 3)

His attractiveness was not based on outstanding looks or physical traits. On that level, he was ordinary. He knew what it was to be rejected, treated as though worthless, familiar with pain and sorrow.

What we are like (verse 6)

Aspects of our human nature make us wilful, prone to straying and behaving in a self-centred manner.

What they did to him (verses 4, 5, 7-9)

Subjected to physical violence, misunderstood (considered stricken by God!) and killed.

What he did (verses 4, 5, 12)

In some real yet mysterious way, he carried our sorrows, our failings and the consequences of them. He won life, light and freedom from guilt for humanity. He shared the spoils of victory and his inheritance.

The Cross and Death of Jesus in John 18:1-19:42

John's narrative of Jesus' arrest, trials and death contains details of fact which are also ironic and symbolic. Reading the account is in some ways like interpreting a medieval painting and reading the clues within the composition (use of light, shade, posture and position).

Light of the World

His captors come to a dark place to carry out a sinister deed, bearing torches and lanterns (John 18:3).

Man for Others

In his darkest hours, Jesus pleads for the freedom and life of his followers. 'If you are looking for me, then let these men go' (John 18:8).

Prince of Peace

Despite the expectations of others, Jesus' Kingdom was never to be gained, nor ever has been, through a resort to violence. 'Put your sword away' (John 18:11, 36).

Peter's denials

Peter was admitted to the courtyard but could not admit to being a disciple (verses 16, 17). He warmed himself by the fire but was chilled by his own failure (verses 18, 27). His denials have been echoed through the years since, at some point or another, in the lives of most followers of Jesus.

Jesus and Pilate

The Roman governor seemed to sense the inappropriateness of him judging Jesus. Truth and kingship loom large in their exchanges (John 18:33, 37, 38; 19:15). Pilate recognised his innocence (John 19:6).

King of the Jews

The sign above Jesus' head was in three languages. He would draw all to himself when lifted up! (verse 20).

Love to the end (19:25-27)

Even at his death Jesus showed his love, bringing together his mother and closest friend in mutual support and interdependence.

Easter Day

MATTHEW 28:1-10
Acts 10:34-43; Colossians 3:1-14

Key phrases

Acts 10:40 – 'but God raised him from the dead on the third day and caused him to be seen'; Colossians 3:1 – 'Since, then, you have been raised with Christ'; Matthew 28:6 – 'He is not here; he has risen.'

Illustration

In an era when making new banners for churches was all the rage, one church that was very keen to attract seekers decided to emblazon words from Matthew 28:6 across two banners. They were beautifully made but, unfortunately, when they were hung only the one bearing the words 'He is not here' caught the eye of people entering the church – somewhat discouraging for anyone coming to church hoping to meet Christ!

Background note: the guards

Of all the Gospel writers, Matthew included significant detail about the guards who were detailed to guard the tomb (see Matthew 27:62-66; 28:11-15). This information is particularly significant when discussing the historicity of the Crucifixion and Resurrection. It shows that Pilate and the authorities had taken steps to prevent Jesus' disciples trying to 'rig' a resurrection disappearance of the body!

Eager mourners (verse 1)

As soon as the Sabbath 'curfew' ended, Mary Magdalene and the other Mary (probably *not* Mary the mother of Jesus) went to the tomb. Remind people that the burial had been hurried.

Resurrection (verses 2, 3)

Matthew was inspired to describe the Resurrection as he did. It is not fully clear whose testimony he drew on – quite possibly one of the guards who spilled the beans later, notwithstanding the hush money that had been paid! As when Christ died on the Cross, this event's cosmic significance was reflected by upheaval in the natural world. No wonder the guards were scared to death (verse 4).

He is not here; he has risen (verses 5-9)

Supernatural events, including appearances of angels, are terrifying. The angel told them there was no need to be afraid (verse 5). The women were invited to see his former, now vacant, resting place (verse 6). They were instructed to tell the disciples that Jesus would meet them in Galilee (verse 7). In the light of this information, they must have been doubly surprised, if that were possible, to be met by Jesus himself almost immediately. They were already at one and the same time frightened and joyful (verse 8). Jesus greeted them, in this account did allow them limited physical contact, and reiterated the instruction for them to tell the disciples (verses 9, 10).

Conclusion

There is significance in the first witnesses to the resurrection being women. The mix of fear and overwhelming joy felt by the women has often been mirrored in the experience of Christians over the years when the penny has dropped and they have encountered the Risen Christ by faith.

Second Sunday of Easter

JOHN 20:19-END
Acts 2:14a, 22-32; 1 Peter 1:3-9

Introduction

The reading from Acts 2 is set to be used as either the first or second reading today. It is placed here in the lectionary despite being a major part of Peter's Pentecostal sermon, because it demonstrates how central the death and resurrection of Christ were to the apostolic teaching from the outset.

The Risen Christ brings peace where there is fear (John 20:19-21a)

Having appeared to Mary Magdalene, Simon Peter and John at the beginning of the day, Jesus appeared to a larger gathering of the disciples at the end of that same day. They were in fear of their lives, aware that the authorities would accuse them of stealing the body and be bent on silencing them. Jesus suddenly materialised among them in the locked room. He showed them his wounds and twice spoke a greeting/prayer of peace over them. Their fear turned to joy.

The Risen Christ sends and equips (verses 21b-23)

Having bade them peace, Jesus then commissioned them. They were given a message and a mission that could not remain behind locked doors. He breathed on them, signifying that they would receive/were receiving the Holy Spirit. Empowered, they would have spiritual authority, including being able to preach and to give or withhold forgiveness.

The Risen Christ does not condemn doubters! (verses 24-29)

History has not been kind to the apostle Thomas. 'Doubting Thomas' – the name has stuck and yet is palpably unfair. Dead men do not ordinarily come back to life. He had not been there when Jesus appeared (verse 24) and found his friends' testimony hard to believe, expressing his difficulty vehemently (verse 25). Thomas had previously been loyal and determined (John 11:16) as well as honest about his and the other disciples' difficulties (John 14:5). One can only speculate how Thomas felt during the week before Jesus appeared to them again. He may well have felt like an outsider, secretly kicking himself for having missed the previous gathering. Jesus appeared exactly one week later (verse 26), again unrestrained by locked doors and physical obstacles. He was clearly aware of the challenge and condition that Thomas had laid down. He met the request head-on, inviting the sceptic to touch his wounds – not an altogether attractive prospect. After the initial invitation, Jesus' tone became more authoritative. The same voice that had stilled the storm and summoned Lazarus from the tomb commanded Thomas, 'Stop doubting and believe' (verse 27).

To his eternal credit, Thomas immediately uttered a personal profound creed: 'My Lord and my God!' (verse 28). Jesus responded by pronouncing a blessing on the multitudes who would subsequently believe without the physical evidence Thomas and the others had been given (verse 29).

So much more one could say (verses 30, 31)

These two summary verses set out the scope and the purpose of John's account. He was inspired so that his readers would believe and have life.

Third Sunday of Easter

LUKE 24:13-35

Acts 2:14a, 36-41; 1 Peter 1:17-23

Introduction

Luke gives a full account of Jesus appearing to a pair of his followers (possibly a couple?) on the road to Emmaus. Mark referred to the same incident but only briefly (see Mark 16:12, 13). Having considered the experience of Thomas last week, it is interesting to note that Mark records that the pair were not immediately believed by the other disciples. This has an authentic ring to it and mirrors well the experience of many Christians whose journey to faith and grasp of the Resurrection has been slow and incremental.

Stranger on the road (verses 13-16)

The risen Jesus fell into step with Cleopas and his companion (note in verse 33 they report to the Eleven) who were rehearsing and wrestling with all that had happened. The fact that they were 'kept from recognising him' begs various questions but suggests that God's purpose was that Jesus would identify himself in a particularly significant way.

Leading Questions (verses 17-24)

Just as he had done in his earthly ministry, Jesus employed leading questions to tease out faith from the disciples (verses 17, 19). The two gave a clear account of what had happened and expressed their disappointment and sadness (verses 17, 21). It was significant that they described Jesus as a prophet (verse 19), thereby echoing the many discussions there had been surrounding Jesus' identity.

Putting them right (verses 25, 26)

Jesus scolded them for their slowness of mind and spirit (verse 25). He countered their use of the word 'prophet' by saying that they should have known that the Christ had to suffer and die (verse 26). He then treated them to an extensive Scripture lesson, showing that the Christ was the interpretative key to understanding what we know as Old Testament passages (verse 27).

He made himself known to them in the breaking of the bread (verses 28-32)

This has become a famous and memorable phrase. Having accepted their invitation of hospitality (verses 28, 29), Jesus took a lead in the meal-time ritual of giving thanks for the food (verse 30). In so doing, he became recognisable to them. As soon as he was known to them he disappeared, leaving them once again with much to discuss (verse 31). Unlike their conversation on the road, they now had new, exciting and personal certainties to share. The events of the evening fell into place (verse 32).

'It is true! The Lord has risen!' (verses 33-35)

They wasted no time in walking back to Jerusalem. They were no doubt bursting to share their experience but were met by the Eleven, equally full of having seen Jesus themselves. It is almost comic.

Fourth Sunday of Easter

JOHN 10:1-10
Acts 2:42-end; 1 Peter 2:19-end

Other readings: short but significant

The end of Acts 2 includes a summary description of the life of the early Church in Jerusalem. It is not a highly developed template for churches but is worth re-visiting when reflecting on the health of a local church. The qualities and values described in these summary verses can be expressed in various ways in different settings.

The reading from chapter 2 of the First Letter of Peter is the second part of a difficult section in which Peter addressed the topic of submission to rulers and employers (owners, in the case of slaves). It is an appropriate springboard from which to pray for the persecuted Church throughout the world. It sheds light on the 'path of pain being hallowed'. The last verse about the straying sheep returning to the Shepherd and Overseer is the link to the Gospel reading.

The Shepherd and his flock (John 10:1-10)

It is important to note that in the verses immediately before this reading the Pharisees were accused by Jesus of spiritual blindness. These men were meant to be tending the flock of Israel.

Illustration: Stranger Danger.

Sadly, these days people know they should be on guard against people on the doorstep, on the phone and online who are not who they claim to be. Similarly, the threat of identity theft is one with which people have had to become familiar.

True Shepherd (verses 1-6)

Jesus contrasted himself with false, dangerous shepherds who had to resort to 'breaking and entering' (verse 1) and whose voices the sheep would not recognise (verse 5), whereas he was known, recognised by watchman and flock, and personally acquainted with his sheep (verses 3, 4). His listeners did not grasp the comparison he was making between himself and the Pharisees (verse 6).

Changed metaphor: the Gate (verses 7-9)

Gates are a means of containment for reasons of protection and the preferred route leading out to pasture (verse 9). By comparing himself to a gate, Jesus was demonstrating two aspects of his role as Messiah. He spelled out his assessment of those who came before him claiming to be prophets or messiahs. There had been plenty of those in the immediately preceding years.

I came that they may have life (verse 10)

This is a well-known and much-loved verse. Jesus' intention was the diametrical opposite of those he was warning against. He had come to bring life to his people, life in as full an expression as possible of that term.

Fifth Sunday of Easter

JOHN 14:1-14

Acts 7:55-end; 1 Peter 2:2-10

Context

Today's Gospel passage is part of the Upper Room discourse, or Famous Last Words as they have more colloquially been called. John 13:1 is where this section begins. Jesus prepared his disciples in action (foot washing) and word (teaching) for what lay ahead in terms of his Passion, Death and Resurrection. The ground is also laid for the coming of the Holy Spirit/Pentecost.

Comfort and the promise of reunion (verses 1-4)

Jesus' words of comfort, 'Do not let your hearts be troubled', sound like words spoken by angels at his birth and at his tomb and by himself on his Resurrection appearances. God knows how frightening and disturbing it is to engage with his purpose and witness him at work. Jesus promised that they would be reunited (verses 2, 3) and that they knew the way to go (verse 4). Jesus seemed more confident in their levels of understanding than they were!

Thank you, Thomas! (verses 5-7)

Despite Thomas being remembered as the arch-doubter, his honesty led to one of the most famous and best-loved of Jesus' sayings. (The way, the truth, the life, verse 6). Honest expression of difficulties in belief and understanding is often a precursor to growth and new insight.

Thank you, Philip! (verses 8-11)

Jesus was spelling out his divinity to them – throughout chapter 14 the message is 'like Father, like Son'. There was a note of exasperation or disappointment in Jesus' response to Philip. He referred Philip to the evidence of his inspired words and his miraculous deeds.

Inspiring exhortation, with scope for misunderstanding (verses 12-14)

As Jesus reflected the Father, so he expected his followers to 'imitate' him in the way they lived their lives. Faith in Jesus has enabled ordinary people to live remarkable lives. His followers cannot emulate him – only he could die for their sins on the Cross. The words 'greater things than these' (verse 12) have been the subject of much speculation and debate over the years. The key point here may well be that Jesus 'was going to the Father' – thereby opening a whole new era in the purposes of God. Similarly, a simplistic understanding of 'ask me for anything, and I will do it' (verse 14) has been the cause of disappointment to some Christians over the years. Taken at face value, everyone would be pulling up to church in their dream car and none of their loved ones would ever die! 'In my name' is sometimes seen as the determining caveat. Finding the right balance is, as ever, a hard thing to do. Some ask in a self-seeking undiscerning way and others rarely, if ever, ask for anything.

Sixth Sunday of Easter

JOHN 14:15-21

Acts 17:22-31; 1 Peter 3:13-end

Other readings

Today the Gospel reading spells out Jesus' promise of the Counsellor, the Holy Spirit. The other two readings include a significant example and wise advice for sharing faith. The Acts 17 passage is the famous account of Paul in Athens. On seeing an altar 'to an unknown God' he declared his belief in the 'knowable God'. This was culturally relevant evangelism. In the section from 1 Peter 3, the apostle who had learned the hard way from his denial of Christ advised people: 'Always be prepared to give an answer to everyone who asks you to give the reason for the hope that you have. But do this with gentleness and respect' (verse 15). Such culturally relevant and sensitive evangelism is made possible by the guidance of the Counsellor.

Pentecost is getting nearer (John 14:15-21)

In these verses Jesus continued his pattern of teaching the disciples by spelling out the expected/logical consequences of believing in him, loving him, obeying him – 'If ... then you will ...'. If A, then B. Jesus spelled out the promise of the Holy Spirit (verse 16). He called him the Counsellor (source of wisdom, direction) who was the Spirit of truth (true precepts, authentic integrity) (verse 17). This is an opportunity to remind people that the Holy Spirit is not a thing or an impersonal force. He is God the Holy Spirit. Always 'he', never 'it'! This is also a clear Trinitarian passage (see verse 16).

Illustration

Remind people of the game of Consequences in which they write a line, turn it over and hand it on. These verses have a series of consequences that form a cycle of discipleship.

If his followers loved him > they would obey him > they would receive the Holy Spirit > they will know him > they will live for ever > they will love him > they will be loved for ever.

Ascension Day

LUKE 24:44-END
Acts 1:1-11; Ephesians 1:15-end

Poor Relation?

Of all the great milestones of Jesus' life and ministry, Ascension Day often feels like the least celebrated. It marks the logical conclusion to Christ's physical and post-Resurrection time on earth. Luke is recognised as the most forensic historian among the four Gospel writers. He is inspired and chooses to end his Gospel and begin his sequel Acts with descriptions of Christ returning to heaven. For modern-day readers, it can sound too much like science fiction – 'Beam me up, Father!' Unsurprisingly, some understand these events figuratively. It must by definition be mysterious. In the account in today's readings, the event is plainly linked to the promise of the Holy Spirit to empower Christ's followers.

Fulfilment (verse 44)

There is a symmetry and sense of completeness to the conclusion of Jesus' earthly ministry. Details of his birth as well as subsequent baptism are recorded explicitly as fulfilling Old Testament prophecies – part of the long-awaited Divine Plan. Jewish tradition held that Moses had been taken back into heaven (see Deuteronomy 34:6) and so the same was expected of the Messiah.

Enlightenment (verses 45-47)

The teaching element of Jesus' Resurrection appearances is often overlooked. These verses are a further example of the extent to which, after his death, Jesus helped his shocked, joyful followers to piece together events from both before and after the Crucifixion and Resurrection.

Empowerment (verses 48, 49)

The promise of being 'clothed with power' and the commandment to wait in the city until this happened are restated. The disciples would be enabled to testify to what they had seen.

Final Blessing (verses 50-53)

For Jesus, there must have been a sense of 'mission accomplished' and yet the era of the Church's mission was only about to begin. We can only speculate about how he felt on the human level, leaving his beloved disciples. His final act was to bless them and it was while doing so that he was taken back into heaven.

The joy of the disciples and their decision to return to Jerusalem and to worship at the Temple contrasts starkly with the fear they had felt immediately after Jesus' death and first appearance (verses 52, 53). Transformation had begun!

Seventh Sunday of Easter

JOHN 17:1-11

Acts 1:6-14; 1 Peter 4:12-14, 5:6-11

Sunday after Ascension

More, or less, is made of Ascension according to local tradition and people's personal circumstances. Some may have missed it during the preceding week. The reading from Acts provides an account of the ascension of Jesus which was glorious and mysterious in equal measure. Read in tandem with Jesus' high-priestly prayer in John 17 it shows that, despite the popular saying about being 'so heavenly minded as to be no earthly good', Jesus was clearly focused on heaven.

Eavesdropping on Jesus (John 17:1-11)

Overhearing another praying can feel intrusive and instructive in equal measure. The way in which Jesus prayed at the end of his life was inspiring and revealing.

Our Father, who art in heaven (verses 1, 5)

When asked by his disciples early in their time together to teach them how to pray, Jesus gave them what became known as the Lord's Prayer. He looks to heaven, addresses his Father and asks him to glorify himself. Father in heaven, hallowed be your name, your will be done on earth as it is in heaven. All the key elements that Jesus included in that prayer were also part of this prayer. He taught from his actual experience.

Eternal life (verses 2-4)

As his death drew ever closer, Jesus prayed about eternal life for his followers. People often think of eternal life as something that goes on for ever and ever, that happens after they die. These verses give the clear definition of eternal life – 'Now this is eternal life: that they know you, the only true God, and Jesus Christ, whom you have sent.' This knowledge, this relationship, begins in the here and now.

Jesus prayed for his followers (verses 6-11)

It is clear from how he prayed for them that the disciples of Jesus were a gift from the Father to the Son (verses 6, 9). Jesus had nurtured them, taught them and guarded them. They, for their part, had grown in their knowledge and love of Jesus and of his Father (verses 6-8). Remarkably, the disciples, with all their flaws and failings, had brought glory to Jesus (verse 10). More was to follow in the ensuing era of the Church. Just as parents anxiously deposit their children at university or watch them make their way into adult life, so Jesus feels the impending pain of parting. He prayed that the Father would protect them (verse 11).

Pentecost

JOHN 20:19-23
Acts 2:1-21; 1 Corinthians 12:3b-13

Introduction

Today, the so-called birthday of the Church, it makes good sense for preachers to draw from the Acts 2 reading *and* from the Gospel from John 20. For some, who may labour under misapprehensions about the Holy Spirit, combining the two readings gives the opportunity to show that: a) the Holy Spirit was pre-existent, b) the Holy Spirit was not the ghost of Jesus, c) God keeps his promises, d) the Holy Spirit equips Christians.

Risen Christ – Given Spirit (John 20:19-23)

Congregations will be used to having heard and reflected on these verses in the context of Easter. Today they will be heard through a Pentecostal filter.

- The giving of the Holy Spirit is a consequence of the Resurrection.

- People are sometimes scared about the Holy Spirit – the context here is one of focusing on the risen Jesus, on joy and on peace.

- The Spirit is associated here with breath because Jesus breathes on them.

- The giving of the Spirit is central to the commissioning of all who are sent.

- The gift of the Spirit equips and enables Christ's followers for ministry (here the ministry of absolution, reconciliation and restoration (forgiveness)).

Illustration

Most people know what it is at some time or another to feel breathless. Those who suffer from asthma are grateful for the use of an inhaler. At times the Church and individual Christians seem spiritually asthmatic. In the words of the old hymn: 'O Breath of God come sweeping through us, revive your church with life and power.'

Trinity Sunday

MATTHEW 28:16-END
Isaiah 40:12-17, 27-end; 2 Corinthians 13:11-end

So-called 'Ordinary Time' resumes on the Monday following the Day of Pentecost. The readings set for each Sunday after Trinity Sunday are known as 'Propers'. They are numbered 4–25. Because the number of Sundays after Trinity varies each year depending on the date of Easter, preachers should check which Proper is allocated to which Sunday in any given year.

The Grace (2 Corinthians 13:14)

Most Christians are familiar with the Grace – often spoken aloud at the end of services and other gatherings. Not all of them will know or remember that the words are from the end of Paul's Epistle. Today is a great day for reminding people what a great Trinitarian greeting it is.

The Great Commission (Matthew 28:16-end)

The first eleven (verses 16, 17)

The remaining eleven disciples obeyed the instruction Jesus had given them via the women on Easter morning. They needed to regroup and to process the remarkable events they had witnessed so it was natural to go back to familiar country. Throughout the Old Testament, mountains and/or wilderness were the natural setting in which to encounter God. As has been noted on other occasions in the year, Thomas was not the only disciple to hold and express doubts. 'When they saw him, they worshipped him; but some doubted.' There is and always will be an element of mystery in the workings of Almighty God. When Christians today wrestle with theological truth (as they may well do on Trinity Sunday!), they are in good company. Doubt and questions usually lead to new understanding.

'In the name of the Father, the Son and the Holy Spirit' (verses 18-20)

Jesus commissioned the disciples with authority, to go into all the world to teach and baptise people in the name of God – Father, Son and Holy Spirit. Although Church Councils would formulate theology, expressed in creeds later, it was plain that Jesus was revealing God who is One in Three and Three in One.

Apocryphal story

An anxious curate struggled desperately with nerves in his first sermon. He asked his vicar for advice. The older man advised him to relax next time by praying and drinking a small glass of whisky. The curate was due to preach on Trinity Sunday. He took a little too much whisky and was *very* relaxed. Discussing his sermon the following day, the vicar said, 'Well, you were certainly more relaxed but I'm not sure that referring to the Holy and Indivisible Trinity as 'Big Daddy, Junior and the Spook' went down very well!'

Proper 4

MATTHEW 7:21-29

Deuteronomy 11:18-21, 26-28; Romans 1:16, 17; 3:22b-28[29-31]

Context

Today's Gospel reading follows on immediately from Jesus speaking about good trees bearing good fruit and bad trees bearing bad fruit. Towards the end of the Sermon on the Mount, he emphasised the importance of putting faith into action. Jesus had also spoken about the importance of entering God's Kingdom through the narrow gate (Matthew 7:13, 14).

Actions speak louder than words! (verses 21-23)

These words of Jesus probably shocked his hearers. Saying 'Lord, Lord' was not an open-sesame to the Kingdom. The implication here is that people claimed to have done all sorts of things in his name – but they were hollow claims. The things mentioned, such as casting out demons and performing miracles, could be authentic signs of the Kingdom. Doing the will of God is what mattered.

Parable of the wise and foolish builders (verses 24-27)

This parable, much loved by children, is the memorable way Jesus concluded this body of teaching. Many had heard the Sermon on the Mount and various sections were doubtless repeated on other occasions. People admired Jesus as a teacher and preacher. Such admiration counted for little if the teaching was not applied. Putting Christ's teaching into practice lays good foundations and leads to resilience when things get tough. Hearing but not applying the teaching is akin to building a house with weak foundations. People in Jesus' time will have been familiar with badly constructed buildings collapsing. On another occasion, Jesus referred to the disastrous collapse of a tower.

Illustration

These days people are more careful about exposure to the sun. Parents are advised to use high protection sun creams on their children. Having sun screen in one's bag is useless. It must be applied. So it is with Christ's teaching.

Amazing authority (verses 28, 29)

Matthew concludes this section with these summary verses. People found Jesus' teaching amazing because it had an edge and he had an authority which was lacking in their teachers of the law.

Final thought

Live service, not lip service, is what God wants.

Proper 5

MATTHEW 9:9-13, 18-26
Hosea 5:15–6:6; Romans 4:13-25

Matthew called, a woman healed, a girl raised

In his own words (verses 9-13)

Matthew took the opportunity to recall his own call to discipleship. Jesus had healed a paralysed man in his home town (see Matthew 9:1). His encounter with Matthew occurred as he left that place (verse 9). It was highly likely therefore that he knew Matthew already. He was known as Levi at that point. In the same way that the call of the fishermen disciples may have been less impetuous than it seems, it is safe to assume that Matthew had seen and heard what Jesus had done up to that point. Matthew's actual call to follow Jesus came when he was at his place of work (verse 9). As a tax collector he would have been despised for collaborating with the occupying Roman regime. Matthew followed Jesus and immediately they went to his house (verse 10). The account has parallels with Jesus going to the home of Zacchaeus. Matthew's erstwhile colleagues and other friends joined him at his house. Jesus was at ease in this company but the Pharisees were outraged. They knew Jesus was a gifted teacher and so they struggled to square this with his desire to spend time and to contaminate himself by spending time and sharing food with such people (verse 11). Jesus heard them question his disciples and answered with a clever one-liner that took the Pharisees' assessment of the assembled company as its starting point. Healthy people did not need a doctor. Sick people did. He had come to be the great Physician (verse 12). He then pointedly told his critics to go away and learn a lesson. He prescribed mercy not sacrifice (verse 13). He concluded by telling them that he had come to call sinners – not those who were righteous in their own eyes.

Emergency house call (verses 18-19)

It is interesting that having criticised and interacted with some Pharisees Jesus' next miracle involved one of the ruling elite. Jesus was in full flow, teaching, when a ruler desperate with grief for his young daughter came and knelt before him. Showing remarkable faith, he pleaded with Jesus to go to his house and lay his hands on her so that she would live again (verse 18). Jesus always responded to people showing faith. Coupled with deep compassion, it moved him to action (verse 19).

Multi-tasking – healing *en route* (verses 20-22)

Matthew records briefly how a woman who had suffered for 12 years with a gynaecological condition approached Jesus surreptitiously for healing. Her reticence was as understandable as her desperation. Women with such a condition were viewed as ritually unclean under the Old Testament 'holiness code'. Like the girl's father, she had remarkable faith in Jesus' ability to heal her (verse 21). Jesus sensed something when she reached out to him. He spoke a word of encouragement and healing to her (verse 22).

Grief turned into joy (verses 23-26)

When Jesus arrived at the ruler's house, the customary mourning rituals were in full swing. There was a cacophony of grief (verse 23). Jesus told them to go away. They were not required because from his perspective she was not dead, only sleeping. The people ridiculed him but he would have the last laugh (verse 24). The account of what happened next is striking in its simplicity. Jesus went into her room, took her by the hand and she got up (verse 25). Simple! It followed that news of this remarkable miracle spread throughout the region (verse 26).

Proper 6

MATTHEW 9:35–10:8

Exodus 19:2-8a; Romans 5:1-8

Context

Today's Gospel reading, following on as it does from Pentecost and Trinity Sunday, rams home the message that God's people are called, equipped and sent into the world. Additionally, the related Old Testament reading recounts how at Mount Sinai God told Israel that they would be 'a kingdom of priests and a holy nation' for him (Exodus 19:6). The Romans 5 reading reiterates the two great truths that: a) God has poured his love into our hearts by the Holy Spirit (verse 5) and b) while were still sinners, Christ died for us (verse 8). For congregations that appreciate sequential teaching it is worth noting that today's New Testament reading from Romans is the first of a sequence that runs over the next few months.

It is as though, having celebrated the great festivals and as churches continue into the weeks after Trinity, the question 'How should we then live?' is posed and answered.

Recruitment drive/staff shortages? (Matthew 9:35-38)

Matthew summarises Jesus' ministry throughout the region. He was truly an itinerant preacher. It was natural for Jesus to start at the synagogues but he never allowed himself to be limited by buildings (verse 35). The ministry combined teaching and healing. This was an expression of compassion and a practical demonstration of his message (verse 36). Jesus' comment to his disciples about there being a lack of workers was more an expression of the size of the task than a strategic observation at this point in his ministry (verse 37). His intention was to work with his close inner circle of disciples and then with a wider, but still limited, group of followers. After the Resurrection and Pentecost, the numbers would grow enormously (verse 38).

Teaching practice/training exercise (10:1-8)

In most professions and walks of life there must be the first time someone takes a lesson, flies solo, sees a patient, and so on. Everyone who can drive can probably recall the first time they drove alone without L-plates. Jesus sent out the Twelve. They had been given the chance to observe Jesus in action – now it was their turn. He assured them that he had given them real spiritual authority (verse 1).

The apostles are named and of course there is the irony that Judas Iscariot was an integral part of the group (verses 2-4).

Scope and style of mission (verses 5-8)

At this stage, the Twelve were to restrict themselves to Jewish territory and communities. This was not primarily because of their inexperience but rather that, at this stage of his ministry, Jesus knew he was to go first to the lost house of Israel (verses 5-7). The extent of their spiritual authority was reiterated to them. They were not exactly given an easy starter for ten: heal the sick, raise the dead, cleanse lepers and exorcise the possessed. As a first foray into ministry it was hardly a walk in the park or Sunday school picnic.

Ministry was to be offered freely, as an expression of the fact that they had freely received power and authority from God (verse 8). As Peter wrote late in his life, ministers should not minister for their own benefit and reward (1 Peter 5:1-3). The next couple of verses from Matthew 10 (not included in the lectionary reading) place an emphasis on the disciples travelling light and with a simplicity of lifestyle – always a challenge to western Christians!

Proper 7

MATTHEW 10:24-39
Jeremiah 20:7-13; Romans 6:1b-11

More from the Initial Training Manual (Matthew 10:24-39)

Today's Gospel reading is a continuation from last week of Jesus' instructions when he sent the disciples out on their first ministry expedition. The segment begins half way through an extended warning with advice about rejection and persecution. Jesus made it clear that these things would be inevitable. The Old Testament reading from Jeremiah is a section of the prophet complaining about persecution but concluding with an assurance of God's care.

Students reflect their teacher, staff their bosses! (verses 21-23)

Jesus had earlier made the point repeatedly that his followers should reflect him and their heavenly Father. Here he used the same logic to warn his disciples that they should not be surprised by their opponents' behaviour. They are reflecting their master, the Evil One.

What's the worst that can happen? (verses 26-31)

Jesus reassured his disciples by telling them not to be afraid (verse 26). Easier said than done, they might have muttered! Knowing that fear can cause people to lose confidence and become frozen in inactivity, Jesus encouraged them to be open and bold in proclaiming the message because one day everything would be revealed anyway (verses 26, 27). The worst thing that could happen was that they might get killed! Much worse would be to disobey or disappoint God who has ultimate authority (verse 28b). This teaching may sit uncomfortably with people's understanding of God. This is one of the rare occasions when Jesus sounds rather like an archetypal sergeant major 'encouraging' new recruits. Fortunately for them and for listeners today, he quickly 'regains' his compassionate pastoral side. He reassured them by reminding them that they were far more valuable than sparrows (verses 29, 31).

The verse about God numbering the hairs on our head (verse 30), such is the level of his care, normally produces an exchange of rueful looks between bald members of a congregation!

Disturbing words (verses 32-39)

Taken at face value without explanation, these verses can seem harsh, to say the least, laden with threat and promise (verses 32, 33) and with malevolent intent (verses 34-36). Jesus neither minced his words nor sugar-coated the truth. His followers then and now cannot complain that they were caught out by not reading the small print. Verses 34-36 are a classic example of *Jesus expressing effect as though it were purpose.* It was a recognised and common feature of Jewish teaching. Division and opposition, even from relatives, would be an inevitable outcome of Jesus' ministry and of people's choice to follow him. This did not mean he wanted it to happen.

This may be a good opportunity to remind people that 'allowing scripture to interpret scripture' is an important principle of biblical interpretation. Jesus set the bar high. He wanted his followers to recognise the supremacy of God's claim on their lives, putting it even before family ties (verse 37). However, elsewhere he commanded that people should honour their father and mother. He demonstrated this in his own life, committing his mother Mary into John's care (and vice versa) even when dying on the Cross. To follow Christ is to walk the way of the Cross (verse 38) and in the other-worldly economics of God's upside-down Kingdom, to lose one's life is to gain it (verse 39).

Proper 8

MATTHEW 10:40-END
Jeremiah 28:5-9; Romans 6:12-end

Short and sweet (Matthew 10:40-end)

Today's reading is the last brief portion of Jesus' instructions to his disciples as they prepared to embark upon their first mission expedition. After some forthright advice and warnings of opposition, these last three verses fall into the category of KISS advice (Keep It Simple Stupid!). Essentially, Jesus was saying to his disciples, 'Do not worry, in the greater scheme of things you and those who welcome you will not be short-changed.' He assured them that they were going on the highest authority and would be received as such, by some. They were ambassadors of Jesus and of God the Father (verse 40). There was a long-standing tradition within Judaism of offering hospitality to strangers and to receiving 'servants' of God appropriately (verse 41). It was a point of honour to do so. Finally, Jesus said that, if someone were to offer as little as a cup of water to a child because they were a disciple of Jesus, they would be rewarded. To summarise, having warned the disciples about hostility, he encouraged them by promising hospitality. Throughout the New Testament, the offering of hospitality features in any list of qualities that leaders should exhibit. The contemporary Church does well to remember this. In Hebrews 13:2 people are reminded that, in offering hospitality, they might be entertaining angels unawares.

Proper 9

MATTHEW 11:16-19, 25-END
Zechariah 9:9-12; Romans 7:15-25a

Talking about this generation (Matthew 11:16-19)

Jesus sounds like a cross between a sociologist and everyone's grumpy aunt! 'To what can I compare this generation?' (verse 16). Over the last few decades, marketing experts and missiologists have spoken about Generations X, Y and Z, Millennials and so forth. Older people still use phrases like 'Young people today, I don't know what the world is coming to!' Perhaps, it was ever thus!

At this stage in his ministry, Jesus was beginning to receive criticism from different groups. He was ruffling the feathers of the Establishment. Also, John the Baptist had been imprisoned. Jesus pointed out the contrariness of his critics by quoting a song or saying (verse 17). They disapproved of John's asceticism (verse 18) and of Jesus' apparent liberal approach to hospitality and enjoyment of life in very mixed company (verse 19). Time would tell, truth would out!

It may be worth noting that the missing verses (i.e. not included in the reading) are ones in which Jesus denounced in the strongest possible terms the cities that had not responded to the miracles he had performed in them.

Showing his softer side! (verses 25-30)

There was no inauthenticity in Jesus, no contradiction. He reflected the love of God by speaking truthfully, by confronting wrong and injustice and by showing compassion in action. Having speculated and expressed frustration about the responses of people, Jesus then reflected that it was often the young and the 'simple' in the eyes of the world who were the first to grasp and embrace his message of the Kingdom (verses 25, 26). It was God's will and an expression of the mysterious unity of the Father and the Son that such revelation was given and received (verse 27). The chapter and section ends with Jesus' wonderful invitation and promise to the weary and burdened (verses 28-30). Some people receive more invitation than others in life. Everyone feels weary sooner or later. This invitation still stands. The weary are also often wary. When people feel fragile in life, they do not wish to be overwhelmed by the energetic and enthusiastic. They crave gentleness and rest. Jesus was gentle and humble in heart (verse 29). Ironically, he offers the weary a yoke. This is not the straw to break the camel's back. Rather, it means being taken into his care and set to his purpose. His yoke fits (see below).

Illustration

Nearly everyone buys shoes at some time or another. Various comedians have developed routines around what is in principle a simple activity – the measuring, the silly, self-conscious walk up and down the shop, the choice of style over comfort or vice versa! When Jesus described his yoke as being 'light' he was not minimizing the cost of being a disciple. He meant that it was perfectly fitted.

Proper 10

MATTHEW 13:1-9, 18-23
Isaiah 55:10-13; Romans 8:1-11

Other readings

Today the lectionary offers three purple passages. Sitting down to prepare, a preacher might be forgiven for thinking they are like the editor of the football programme *Match of the Day* on a day when so many goals have been scored it is almost impossible to choose highlights. Here are two, one from each of the other readings. The first links specifically to the Gospel reading – Isaiah 55:10, 11: 'As the rain and the snow come down from heaven, and do not return to it without watering the earth . . . so is my word that goes out from my mouth: It will not return to me empty, but will accomplish what I desire and achieve the purpose for which I sent it.' The second is at the heart of the Gospel and of the Communion service – Romans 8:1: 'Therefore, there is now no condemnation for those who are in Christ Jesus'.

Parable of the Sower (Matthew 13:1-9)

There is the risk of 'familiarity breeding contempt'. It is all too easy for people to miss the importance of this parable. It may be worth giving a brief background to the parables, reminding people that they were riddles intended to tease and to provoke further reflection more than they were memorable stories to aid understanding! The omitted segment (verses 10-13) sets this out plainly. The context of Jesus teaching from a 'floating pulpit' (verses 1, 2) added to the charm and memorability of this parable. The setting might have lent itself more readily to a nautical parable – of which there are a few. Jesus' listeners would have recognised the effects of the sower's *broadcast* – to use that word in its older sense! There is an argument for saying that this parable should more accurately be described as the 'parable of the soils'. Same seed, different locations, different results.

The meaning of the parable (verses 18-23)

This is one of those rare occasions when the meaning of the parable is spelled out by Jesus himself. The text suggests that it was only the disciples that were privy to this explanation. The path, the rocky ground, the thorns and the good ground each represented a different response to Jesus' message. These reflected levels of understanding (verse 19), responses to trouble (verse 21), levels of worry and materialism (verse 22) and spiritual receptiveness (verse 23) respectively. Preachers may want to point out that, although in this parable each element stands for something (God, the message, hearers, etc.), not all parables can be 'decoded' in this way.

Application

Although the parable seems to describe and explain the responses of first-time hearers it also stands as a helpful challenge to all Christ's followers at every stage of their pilgrimage. Anxiety, the allure of wealth, and other distractions can all creep in. The parable may also help people to understand the varying responses of their friends and family towards faith.

Proper 11

MATTHEW 13:24-30, 36-43
Isaiah 44:6-8; Romans 8:12-25

Context

Matthew chapter 13 is a cluster of Jesus' parables. The parable of the sower and Jesus' subsequent explanation shapes the way the rest of the chapter, including today's reading, is received.

The parable of the weeds (Matthew 13:24-30)

Older church members may recall words from the old harvest hymn: 'wheat and tares together sown, unto joy or sorrow grown'. The parable is like a piece of flash fiction, a short story of agricultural rivalry and subterfuge. As in the parable of the sower (see above, Matthew 13:1-9) the seed was good. The man's servants were surprised to find weeds growing as well. Jesus' listeners might even have detected an element of the staff covering their own backs in their comments. Living as they did in an age before selective pesticides, they will also have recognised the wisdom and established practice of waiting until harvest-time to separate wheat and weeds. The story will have had an authentic ring to it.

The meaning of the parable of the weeds (Matthew 13:36-43)

The disciples' request for an explanation from Jesus is, of course, an admission that they did not get it yet (verse 36). Jesus explained what each element represented (verses 37-39). Again, people may need reminding that not every parable has so many metaphors or representational elements in it. Right and wrong co-exist in life. Some people have a more positive and generous approach to life than others. The parable envisages a decisive day of reckoning. There is no place for evil and wrong-doing in God's Kingdom (verses 40, 41). To modern minds such a stark statement of judgement (including fires) may sound almost medieval (verse 42). It may be worth pointing out that in life sometimes the bad guys seem to prosper and get away with exploitation and violence. Belief in a day of reckoning, of judgement in some form, stands against a sense of eternal injustice. Jesus ended his explanation on a positive note – 'the righteous will shine like the sun' and with a call for those with ears to hear (verse 43)!

Proper 12

MATTHEW 13:31-33, 44-52
1 Kings 3:5-12; Romans 8:26-end

The parables keep on coming – mustard seed and yeast (verses 31-33)

Jesus' parables came in different forms and sizes. Some were fully developed stories and others little more than one-line riddles or observations. Those of a botanical bent may want to research what type of plant Jesus had in mind when he spoke about what is translated as mustard seed/plant. It sounds as though he was speaking about cedars of Lebanon! Biblical commentators over the years have offered a range of suggestions. Too much concern over the plant will lead to people missing the point – something Jesus warned was always a danger. The parables of the mustard seed and the yeast both illustrate a Kingdom principle of cause and effect. In God's economy, there is a principle of working from small to large. God, in his wisdom, chooses to use the weak, the smallest and the least to achieve his purposes. From inauspicious beginnings (e.g. Bethlehem, Calvary, 12 disciples, etc.), great and momentous things developed. These two parables spoke of the need to wait and to see how things turned out. God's Kingdom was to be all-pervasive – like yeast in dough – with obvious effects.

Four rapid-fire parables (Matthew 13:44-52)

Hidden treasures (verses 44-46)

Most people will be familiar with seeing metal detectorists scouring beaches or fields looking for lost valuables or buried treasure. Similarly, vintage goods are all the rage. People love rummaging through piles of tat in the hope of finding something of great worth. 'Finders keepers' is an old saying and custom. Jesus' hearers would have understood and related to the idea of someone finding a treasure and then taking all necessary steps to secure it. These two short parables express the idea of God's Kingdom being something that had to be looked for. When found, it was worth giving up everything for.

The parable of the net (verses 47-50)

This parable reprised exactly the teaching of the longer parable of the weeds (Matthew 13:24-30). The wicked and righteous live cheek by jowl, and may even overlap. Eventually, in God's purposes, everything will be revealed and exposed for what it is.

Got it? (verse 51)

Jesus put his disciples on the spot by asking them if they had understood what he had told them. They were adamant that they had. At this stage, it was unlikely that they did. One can only guess at the hours they must have chewed over Jesus' teaching in the months and years after his death, resurrection and subsequently Pentecost. If ever the sound of pennies dropping was deafening, it would have been later. Preachers might be advised not to apply verse 51 too often unless they are ready to back-track if necessary!

Old and new (verse 52)

Jesus ended this section with another one-liner in which he made it clear that the teaching they were receiving was both new and a development of teaching they had grown up with.

Proper 13

MATTHEW 14:13-21
Isaiah 55:1-5; Romans 9:1-5

From the other readings

A wonderful invitation (Isaiah 55:1-5) – 'Come, all you who are thirsty, come to the waters; and you who have no money, come, buy and eat! . . . ' Most people like to receive an invitation. This is a particularly welcome one for those who are struggling, especially in settings where food banks need to operate. It relates directly to the Gospel reading in which Jesus fed the five thousand. The short segment from Romans (chapter 9) is a part of Paul's argument in which he speaks of the divine glory of being adopted as God's children.

Feeding of the five thousand (Matthew 14:13-21)

Having presented a range of Jesus' parables, Matthew now focuses on some of the miracles of Jesus. They were described as signs and nearly always stood as enacted parables and demonstrations of Jesus' power. As such, they were also clues as to his full identity, as Messiah, the Son of God.

Jesus' distress (verse 13)

This miracle followed on immediately from a significant and sad event in Jesus' life. In the first 12 verses of this chapter, Matthew recorded the death of John the Baptist at the hands of Herod. He was beheaded because he had publicly denounced Herod's immoral marriage (14:1-12). Jesus was undoubtedly affected by this news. John was his kinsman and, in the purposes of God, his herald. He sought privacy by sailing to a solitary place (verse 13a). Such was his popularity and appeal by then that the crowds made their way around the lake (verse 13b).

Jesus' compassion (verse 14)

It would have been understandable if Jesus' heart had sunk when he landed and saw the crowd waiting for him. His plan for some personal space disappeared. There is always a danger of members of the caring professions neglecting their own physical and emotional needs to serve others. By the opposite token, in life there are also some who avoid putting themselves out for others on the flimsiest of excuses. Many of the crowd had followed Jesus because they were needy and desperate for help. Sad as he was, Jesus did not succumb to compassion fatigue. He healed their sick (verse 14).

Jesus' challenge (verses 15-17)

The disciples were clearly concerned for Jesus, maybe even a little impatient. They suggested that it was time for Jesus to send the people away so they could buy food before the day ended (verse 15). Many preachers know what it is like to see either a husband or wife or a churchwarden standing at the back of church pointing at their watch in the hope of bringing proceedings to a close! Jesus responded that they did not need to go away. He challenged the disciples to feed them (verse 16). Surprised at this, they spelled out how limited their resources were (verse 17).

Jesus' provision (verses 18-21)

Jesus told them to bring the fish and bread to him and the rest is history. Jesus met the crowd's need. He demonstrated his power. He gave an example of the Kingdom multiplication – the principle of something small having a great effect. Perhaps for a few then, and for many more with hindsight, he re-enacted God's act of providing manna for Israel when they were hungry in the wilderness. Jesus' food satisfied and was more than enough (verse 20).

Proper 14

MATTHEW 14:22-33
1 Kings 19:9-18; Romans 10:5-15

Bringing it all together

In two places in the Epistle from Romans 10 it states that anyone who throws themselves on God and trusts him will be saved (verses 9, 13). The Old Testament reading from 1 Kings 19 is the account of the prophet Elijah feeling burned out and in despair encountering God: he is given rest (verse 5) and refreshment (verse 6); he is renewed and recommissioned and reinforced (verses 11-18). In the Gospel (see below), Peter starts to sink on the water and calls for help. Gatherings of God's people are made up of those who have called out to God in one way or another.

Jesus walks on water (verses 22-27)

Having fed the five thousand (plus women and children), Jesus finally managed to get the personal space he had been craving since hearing news of the death of John the Baptist. He sent the disciples on in their boat back across the lake while he went up into the hills (verses 22, 23). The boat was a long way from shore (it was not within walking/paddling distance!) and was struggling to make progress due to a headwind (verse 24). Sailors throughout the world are known for being superstitious and prone to spectral sightings. Jesus walking on water scared them witless. They were sure it was a ghost (verses 25, 26). Jesus reassured them with words that would take on a greater resonance later when he appeared to them after his resurrection (verse 27).

Peter walks on water . . . nearly (verses 28-31)

Many people relate readily to Peter. He seemed full of good intentions, eager to please Jesus and yet so often falling short of the mark because of his wavering faith and personal insecurity. This was another of his famous near-misses. It was a remarkable mark of faith, as yet only partially developed, to say that he would walk to Jesus on the water: 'Lord, if it's you, tell me to come...' (verse 28). Jesus always responded positively to even the slightest demonstrations of faith. So, Peter clambered over the side and headed towards Jesus (verse 29). When he realised how rough it was, he lost his nerve and began to sink. Immediately he prayed a version of the sincerest prayer known to humankind: 'Help!' It was a personal SOS or Mayday (verse 30). Jesus caught hold of him, rescued him and asked him why he had doubted (verse 31). Preachers may like to give people a moment of quiet reflection in which they can consider what their own answers might have been! There is no stage direction in the margin indicating what tone Jesus took with him.

A revelation (verses 32, 33)

All's well that ends well. They climbed back into the boat, the wind died down and the disciples quickly processed what they had witnessed. Their wonder turned to worship as they took a giant step forward in their faith. 'Truly you are the Son of God.'

Proper 15

MATTHEW 15: [10-20], 21-28
Isaiah 56:1, 6-8; Romans 11:1-2a, 29-32

Splintered readings – Mind the Gap

The set readings today all feature segments of readings. Although the missing parts may not be read or even referred to in the sermon, it is always a good idea for preachers to check the joining passages, if only to be ahead of any church member who cannot resist checking for themselves! More seriously and obviously, they form part of the context. Today's Gospel reading addresses issues of ritual cleanness – a particularly important subject for Matthew's predominantly Jewish readers.

Clean and unclean (Matthew 15:10-20)

Jesus' message of the Good News of the Kingdom sounded like dangerous liberalising teaching to staunch traditionalists (verse 12). Jesus was trying to get them to see beyond ritual obedience to understand the underlying purpose of the law. Outward observance should reflect inner reality. Then, as now, outward behaviour should in that sense be sacramental – an outward visible sign of an inner spiritual reality. The disciples experienced some of this same difficulty, and by this stage Jesus seemed on occasions disappointed at their slowness to grasp his message (verses 15, 16). Jesus used a brief parable of planting to tell his followers not to be unduly concerned by the complaints of the Pharisees. In essence, time will tell, truth will out (verses 13, 14). Jesus spelled out the fact that observing the 'holiness code' was done by living in a holy way, not by washing one's hands. He resorted to a rather basic example to do so (verses 17-20)! If Jesus' words challenged a traditional, albeit flawed, understanding of the law, then his next actions were an even greater challenge.

Jesus rewards the faith of a Canaanite woman (Matthew 15:21-28)

NB. The short reading from Isaiah 56 is an assertion that non-Jews who 'bind themselves' to the Lord will not miss out on his blessing. Jesus moved on deeper into Gentile territory (verse 21). He was approached by a woman who was desperate for help for her disturbed daughter. She used a messianic term in addressing him (verse 22). In the light of what followed, this was significant. The impatience of the disciples was not altogether surprising (verse 23) but Jesus' initial apparent reticence does seem strange. On some occasions, he hesitated in order to give space for people to demonstrate (or not) the extent and nature of their faith. This seemed to be one such occasion. The woman was determined not to be put off. Kneeling before him, she addressed him as Lord (verses 24, 25). Jesus' initial response sounds terribly politically incorrect. In those days, Jews did refer to their Gentile neighbours as dogs. He was engaging in word play with the woman (verse 26). She was feisty, desperate and faithful. Jesus was impressed by her persistence and belief. Her daughter, who was apparently at a distance, was healed immediately (verses 27, 28).

Application

The UK's Brexit vote and the American election of 2016 showed that people still struggle with attitudes towards outsiders. There seems to be in many a natural wariness (at best) towards people from other backgrounds and places. Today's readings challenge this. They also show the importance of persistence in faith.

Proper 16

MATTHEW 16:13-20
Isaiah 51:1-6; Romans 12:1-8

Pivotal passage (Matthew 16:13-20)

In the Gospel accounts and in the life of Peter, today's reading is presented as a critical point in the flow of Jesus' ministry. Over the preceding few weeks, the Gospel readings have included examples of Jesus' frustration at the slowness of his disciples to grasp his teaching.

Who do people say I am? (verses 13, 14)

Finally, it all comes down to the central question about the identity of Jesus. Note that it is Jesus who initiates the exchange (verse 13). Jesus used his favourite title for himself – Son of Man. By this stage of his ministry there was much speculation as to his status and identity. Was he a prophet, an Old Testament figure reappearing (verse 14), a deluded individual, a fraud or, as some were beginning to hope, the Messiah?

Who do you say I am? (verses 15, 16)

Jesus made it personal (verse 15). Then, as now, the important thing is what each person thinks about Jesus for themselves. Second-hand opinions and second-hand expressions of faith only go so far. People must decide for themselves. This can be particularly hard for Christian parents or those whose partners do not share their faith to accept. This was Peter's moment to shine. Eager as ever, he responded to Jesus' question instantly and unequivocally. 'You are the Messiah, the Son of the living God' (verse 16).

Rewarded and renamed (verses 17-19)

If Peter had been a faithful Golden Retriever, he would have looked like the proverbial dog with two tails! Jesus congratulated him effusively. In the light of Jesus' earlier frustration, Peter's light-bulb moment must have seemed like a breakthrough. Peter had received divine revelation (verse 17). Peter – the word play in his name was deliberate – was going to be a foundational character in the subsequent establishing of the Church (verse 18). Jesus promised that Peter would be given great spiritual authority. Such authority (given not only to Peter but to subsequent believers) is critical to the part of the Lord's Prayer 'Your Kingdom come, on earth as it is in heaven' becoming a reality (verse 19).

A time to speak and a time to keep silent (verse 20)

This was an occasion when the latter applied. Jesus had a keen sense of the Father's timing in his ministry. From here onwards, Jesus' thoughts and actions turned towards Jerusalem.

Proper 17

MATTHEW 16:21-END
Jeremiah 15:15-21; Romans 12:9-end

Comfort from Jeremiah! (Jeremiah 15:15-21)

The Jeremiah passage is a lament in which the prophet complains about the unfairness of his situation. This is followed by a promise of restoration in due course. Consequently, it complements the Gospel reading in which Jesus predicted his ill-treatment and death.

Predictions, instructions and warnings (Matthew 16:21-end)

Peter's confession of Christ appeared to trigger a new phase in Jesus' ministry and in his thinking. The focus began to be on the events that would unfold in Jerusalem. Verse 21 is a summary verse that makes the change in Jesus' words and actions clear.

Peter – hero to zero (verses 22, 23)

So soon after his moment of glory at Caesarea Philippi and perhaps emboldened by it, Peter makes the mistake of remonstrating with Jesus (verse 22). Having demonstrated insight previously, he cannot grasp why Jesus is speaking of his death. For Peter, and to Jewish minds generally, the notion of a crucified Messiah was nonsensical. He was put in his place in no uncertain terms. It must have stung him enormously (verse 23).

Take up your Cross – losing, finding, gaining (verses 24-26)

To follow Jesus is to walk the way of the Cross. In plain terms this always involves self-denial and having a spiritual or heavenly perspective on life. This is another example of the upside-down economy of the Kingdom which stands in contradistinction to the ways of the world.

Final reckoning (verses 27, 28)

Jesus repeatedly taught that there would one day be a day of reckoning in life and for the world. Although this is often unfashionable and unpopular in contemporary western culture, it is a clear expression of accountability. The way people treat their neighbours and the environment matters. This is not an expression of 'salvation by works' but it is a clear warning that people cannot live with no regard for others and think it does not matter. Ultimately, God knows how people live (verse 27). Exactly what Jesus meant in verse 28 has been the subject of much debate and speculation. If people assume these words relate to the end of time and the so-called second coming of Christ, they are particularly problematic. If 'the Son of Man coming in his kingdom' is taken to refer to his death and resurrection, they are readily understandable (verse 28). The immediate context provides the most compelling clue: Jesus was talking to his disciples about his imminent death.

Proper 18

MATTHEW 18:15-20
Ezekiel 33:7-11; Romans 13:8-end

Sort it out! (Matthew 18:15-20)

Today's Gospel reading shows how intensely practical the Bible is. Jesus knew that the disciples he had chosen would need to know how to resolve disputes in the years to come as they oversaw the foundation and growth of the early Church. The teaching here clearly shaped the practical advice that the apostles Peter, Paul and James gave to the Church in their epistles. Among any group of people, there are bound to be moments of tension and disagreement. The Church has been no exception. The way disputes are resolved is what can enhance or detract from its distinctiveness. Jesus' advice reads like a three-step plan that would not be out of place in a management manual.

Amicably (verse 15)

Address the issue at source, face to face without involving others. The sooner it is addressed and sorted the better. Drawing others in escalates the issue and runs the risk of people gossiping and taking sides.

Accountability 1 (verse 16a)

If it cannot be sorted out amicably, then there is the need to involve others. This was not meant by way of ganging up and intimidating the other person. It was to provide a degree of accountability and an establishing of the facts.

Accountability 2 (verse 17)

The third step that Jesus recommended was to present the issue to the whole assembly. Some translations use the word 'church' here but at the point at which Jesus was speaking 'assembly' would be a better rendering. If it is established that the person is in the wrong and they still will not recognise their mistake, there are sanctions to be taken.

This involves temporary exclusion from the assembly. Throughout church history there have unfortunately been times when churches were too quick to bar people who were perceived to have stepped out of line. This often led to a lack of grace and stifled honest debate. Unity, not uniformity, has been a common cry.

Authority (verse 18)

At this stage of his time with the disciples, Jesus repeatedly reminded them that they were being given spiritual authority. They were to use this in combatting evil, in their ministry of healing and reconciliation.

Agreeability (verses 19-20)

This segment ends on a positive note. When Christians agree on issues and share a common mind, blessing results. Verse 20 and the promise of Christ's presence even in the smallest of gatherings have encouraged believers over the years, especially those in beleaguered circumstances.

Proper 19

MATTHEW 18:21-35
Genesis 50:15-21; Romans 14:1-12

Context

Last week's Gospel (Matthew 18:15-20) was Jesus' teaching on reconciliation between believers. Today's reading follows on immediately and is about forgiveness.

Other readings

The reading from the end of Genesis (chapter 50) is about reconciliation and forgiveness between Joseph and his brothers. It is a moving passage and a great example of forgiveness in a dysfunctional family. The Epistle from Romans marks the last in the series that has spanned Paul's letter. It so happens that the set passage (Romans 14:1-12) addresses the issue of accommodating fellow believers who hold different views and follow different practices. The verse after the reading (Romans 14:13) warns against judging one another.

The parable of the unforgiving servant (Matthew 18:21-35)

See above regarding the way this follows on from the previous segment. Eager Peter wanted to apply the teaching about forgiveness and so asked for advice. He may have thought that his opening bid of forgiving seven times over was impressive (verse 21). Readers can guess at the look on Peter's face when he heard Jesus' reply (verse 22). Suffice to say that Jesus felt moved to tell a detailed story by way of a parable. It is not altogether impossible that some of Jesus' parables were allusions to actual events that his listeners may have recognised. In any case, a story about people showing mercy would resonate with most people.

Reckoning and mercy (verses 23-27)

Older church members may remember using a 'ready reckoner' in the days before calculators and computers. The beginning of the parable reinforces another of Jesus' themes – namely, that everyone will be held accountable on the day of reckoning. The handling of money (talents) features in some of the parables. In an age when defaulting on mortgages and the repossession of property has been common, this parable has a contemporary ring. The servant who could not pay pleaded for mercy. Such a person would have asked for more time or easier terms. The complete cancellation of the debt would have been a remarkable feature of the story (verse 27).

'Forgive us our debts as we forgive our debtors' (verses 28-31)

Having received such grace and kindness, it was reasonable to expect the servant to show kindness to others. He did not need the relatively small amount owed to him by a colleague. Jesus included the detail about him grabbing his fellow servant and throttling him. His listeners might have been on the point of booing the baddie! In the light of his earlier teaching about members of the wider assembly becoming involved to resolve a dispute, it is noteworthy that other servants reported the matter to the master. This does not come over as mean-spirited informing. It was shared accountability and their sense of natural justice being offended.

Mercy rescinded (verses 32-34)

In the story the master acted swiftly and decisively when he heard what his servant had done to his colleague.

Clear warning – God prizes and expects forgiveness (verse 35)

Jesus could not have been clearer in his warning. His followers must practise true forgiveness 'from your heart'.

Quote

'The person who refuses to forgive destroys a bridge they will one day have to cross themselves.' (Corrie Ten Boom – concentration camp survivor.)

Proper 20

MATTHEW 20:1-16
Jonah 3:10–4:11; Philippians 1:21-end

Note

The set New Testament reading is the start of a new series of sequential readings from Paul's letter to the Philippians. The letter has sometimes been dubbed 'Ode to Joy'.

The passage from Jonah shows him grumbling about the mercy God showed to the city and people of Nineveh. It echoes the complaints of the workers in the vineyard from Jesus' parable.

The parable of the workers in the vineyard (Matthew 20:1-16)

In recent years in the UK there has been much talk and legislation around levels of pay. There is the minimum wage and the living wage. There have also been various scandals around levels of remuneration for seasonal migrant workers. All of which gives this parable a contemporary feel. The key point in Jesus' story is that there was an *agreed* wage which was more than fair.

Hiring fair (verses 1-7)

The parable begins as so many others with the phrase 'The kingdom of heaven is like . . .' (verse 1). The owner of the vineyard (a well-known metaphor for Israel) hired workers early in the day and promised them a fair day's wage (verse 2). He went out on four subsequent occasions (3rd, 6th, 9th and 11th hours) and offered people work and promised to pay them what was 'right' (verse 4). The term 'at the eleventh hour' is still used, especially when describing labour disputes.

That's not fair! (verses 8-12)

Come reckoning time at the end of the day the different groups had varying expectations. Those who were hired last were paid first – not something calculated to go down well (verses 8, 9) but reflecting an aspect of God's Kingdom. Normal rules do not apply: the first shall be last and the last first (verse 16). The last group to be taken on had given up hope of being included in the Master's plans. The group who had been picked first and given a whole day's work grumbled because they had expected to receive more (verse 10). There is a key phrase in their complaint. 'You have made them equal to us . . .' (verses 11, 12).

What's your issue? (verses 13-15)

The owner of the vineyard answered one of those who complained. The use of the word 'friend' is not insignificant. The owner pointed out that he was not being unfair. He had kept his word. He had a right to do whatever he wanted with his money. He had chosen to be generous and recognised that this was why the workers were envious. In the years that followed, Jewish followers of Jesus would have to find it in their hearts to welcome Gentile believers into the Church. It was not easy, but it happened.

Proper 21

MATTHEW 21:23-32

Ezekiel 18:1-4, 25-end; Philippians 2:1-13

Context

The exchange and following parable in today's Gospel reading are from a point in Matthew's account after Jesus had entered Jerusalem triumphantly on a donkey (Matthew 21:1-11).

I have it on good authority . . . (Matthew 21:23-27)

Jesus had made a bee-line for the Temple complex and was teaching in the very courts from which he had driven out traders. Most English cathedrals have CCTV and the staff have smart identity cards on coloured lanyards – if Jesus was on earth today he would undoubtedly have been on their watch list! As it was, the religious leaders wasted no time in challenging him. They wanted to know what his authority was and who had given it to him (verse 23). This was one of many occasions when Jesus responded to a question with another question (verse 24a). It was a smart move and a feature of rabbinical debate. He said he would answer but only if they were prepared to answer a question about the legitimacy and authority of John the Baptist's ministry (verses 24b, 25). It must have been infuriating for men who were not used to being challenged, not least because it put them in a difficult position (verse 25b). They knew they were on the horns of a dilemma (verse 26), caught between appearing resistant to God and/or out of step with popular opinion. They refused to answer – which sounds as lame now as it must have done then (verse 27a). Having outwitted them, Jesus similarly refused to answer their question. However, his point was made. He drove it home with a parable aimed directly at them.

A parable of two sons (verses 28-32)

The parable could fairly be called the Tale of Two Responses. The son who initially refused to do what his father wanted had a change of heart and eventually obeyed him. He represents people like prostitutes, tax collectors and assorted sinners who had lived disobediently before looking for God's grace. The second son gave his father the desired response but failed to act on it. Jesus challenged his erstwhile inquisitors with another question. There was only one answer they could give. The first son was the one who obeyed (verse 31). Jesus then applied the parable in the most pointed fashion. The prostitutes and tax collectors responded to John the Baptist, whose ministry these leaders would not endorse. By having made that response they were entering the Kingdom of God ahead of the leaders who could not bring themselves to repent and change their lives.

Proper 22

MATTHEW 21:33-END
Isaiah 5:1-7; Philippians 3:4b-14

From the other readings

Isaiah 5:1-7 is known as the Song of the Vineyard. It is a clear example of the way in which Israel was historically depicted as the Lord's Vineyard. This is important for people to remember when they read the many New Testament references to vineyards. This week's segment from Philippians might be described as a purple passage, not because it talks about bishops, but because it is packed with so many striking verses. Paul explained the new covenant and the Kingdom almost as though a new accounting system or currency were being introduced.

The parable of the vineyard tenants (Matthew 21:33-end)

Spoiler alert! Jesus had the chief priests well and truly in his sights when he told this detailed parable. They were enraged, but hamstrung by Jesus' popularity ratings with the crowds (verses 45, 46).

Introductory Illustration

Most people know the difference between being a freeholder of a property and being a tenant. Of course, there are good and bad landlords and tenants. A good landlord takes care to present their property in good order and expects a reasonable and fair return from it. Bad tenants tend not to care for a property as well as they should and in extreme cases default on what they owe.

The landowner and his vineyard (verses 33, 34)

The landowner planted the vineyard and tended it, and built a winepress in expectation of fruitfulness and a watchtower so it could be protected. In due season, he sent his servants to collect his fruit.

The tenants and the servants (verses 35, 36)

The tenants treated the servants shamefully. They did this brazenly and repeatedly. This represented the way Israel in times of rebellion and apostasy had treated God's messengers, the prophets.

The tenants and the heir (verses 37-39)

Finally, the landowner sent his son to the tenants in the belief that he would be respected. On the contrary, the tenants sensed and seized their opportunity and threw the son out of the vineyard and killed him. In applying this parable, it is important to stress that God was not taken by surprise when Jesus was rejected and killed.

Judgement and justice (verses 40, 41)

The story reaches its resolution with the arrival of the landlord himself. The tenants are dealt with and their tenancy offered to others who would be prepared to give the landowner what was rightfully his.

Capstones and stumbling blocks (verses 42, 43)

Jesus immediately put pepper on it in his application of the parable. 'Have you never read in the Scriptures?' is a rhetorical question, effectively removing any grounds for excuse from the chief priests and Pharisees. The passage from Psalm 118 was also quoted by Peter (1 Peter 2:6-8). Peter no doubt had strong memories of this encounter.

Proper 23

MATTHEW 22:1-14
Isaiah 25:1-9; Philippians 4:1-9

The parable of the wedding feast

Following hard on the heels of the parable of the vineyard and tenants, this is another parable of rejection (verse 1). It follows a similar structure. A king makes provision to celebrate his wedding and offers an invitation to which he expects a response. The invitation is rejected and the messengers killed. Punishment and alternative invitations are issued to the unexpected and undeserving.

Illustration

Receiving an invitation is a common experience. It should be a source of pleasure. For practical reasons and as a matter of courtesy a reply is expected – RSVP. These days it is becoming increasingly common for couples to send out Hold the Date cards or emails well in advance. People have less excuse for missing the big day!

First refusal (verses 2, 3)

Preparations were made and servants sent out to those who were invited to make acceptance easier, but rejection ensued.

Second time of asking (verse 4)

The king sent out servants a second time with more details about his preparations.

Mixed response (verses 5, 6)

Instead of licking their lips and nodding their heads, the invited guests turned their backs. Responses ranged from mild rejection due to other priorities through to extremely violent rejection.

Rage and retribution (verse 7)

In the story the king fights fire with fire and destroys all trace of those who refused his invitation and killed his servants.

Let the people come. The good, the bad and the ugly! (verses 8-10)

The king does not cancel the wedding banquet. He sends his servants out to invite the B-listers. In fact, they invite the least, the last and the lost, good and bad alike.

Tricky supplementary (verses 11-14)

On some occasions, Jesus added to the original parable, sometimes to emphasise his teaching and occasionally to make an additional point. This is one such example. It seems harsh.

Dress code (verses 11-13)

Formal invitations often still indicate if there is a dress code – e.g. Black tie, Smart Casual, etc. When it comes to weddings, there are various customs ladies are aware of. Never upstage the bride or her mother. Observe a colour theme if there is one. Take a spare dress to avoid the embarrassment of wearing the same outfit as another guest! In the parable, the king spotted someone inappropriately dressed and had them expelled. The man in the story was speechless as Jesus' hearers would have been. How can a last-minute guest be blamed for not having the right clothes? Jesus was never afraid to shock. Seeing this as a supplementary, almost separate, parable resolves an apparent difficulty. Elsewhere in the New Testament, much is made of putting off old clothes and putting on robes of righteousness provided by God.

The chosen few (verse 14)

The notion of people being chosen becomes a strong one as the gospel unfolds and the Church developed. In isolation, this seems a restrictive hard teaching. The purpose is to stress the importance of responding and the blessing of being invited. Elsewhere it is revealed that God not only invites but also by his grace enables people to respond.

Proper 24

MATTHEW 22:15-22

Isaiah 45:1-7; 1 Thessalonians 1:1-10

Note

The Epistle today marks the beginning of a sequential series from 1 Thessalonians. The Gospel reading from Matthew 22 shows Jesus neatly evading a trick question. It raises issues of divided loyalties and civil obedience. Contemporary listeners need to be reminded that Jesus and his hearers were living under an occupying force. That was rather more demanding than people today simply submitting their annual tax return.

Tax return (Matthew 22:15-22)

Angered and stung by Jesus' attacks on them through his parables, the chief priests and Pharisees went on the offensive. They set out to trap him in his words. This was a deal more sinister in intent than trying to outdo him in debate. They wanted to lure him into saying things that could be taken as an incitement to resistance against the Romans or against the vassal ruler Herod (verses 15, 16). They would waste no time informing on him if successful. It is a dynamic all too familiar to people who have lived under an oppressive occupying force.

Is it right to pay taxes to Caesar? (verse 17)

Jesus was not fooled by their obsequious flattery (verses 16-18). The question was one which was probably discussed by many Jewish people. The paying of taxes was an unpopular issue. No one ever likes parting with money and getting nothing to show for it. It was humiliating from a nationalist point of view. Tax collectors were money-grabbing collaborators. Caesar's head depicted on the coins was also part of his claim to be worthy of worship and therefore idolatry for the Jews. In other words, there were many compelling reasons to refuse to pay tax.

Heads I win – tails you lose! (verses 19-22)

Jesus told them to bring one of the coins used to pay the tax. Other coinage would have been in circulation – tokens for temple tax, etc. Jesus' simple question lured them in. 'Render to Caesar that which is Caesar's' still has currency(!) in everyday speech. His opponents knew they had been outmanoeuvred and withdrew.

Application

Christians live under a higher authority and yet as far as possible they should live in obedience to their earthly rulers. Throughout history there have been times when Christians have led the way in civil disobedience but this is in the face of serious issues (e.g. apartheid, resisting the Nazis, etc.).

Proper 25/Last Sunday after Trinity

MATTHEW 22:34-END

Leviticus 19:1-2, 15-18; 1 Thessalonians 2:1-8

Context

The segment from Matthew 22 between last week's Gospel reading and this week's is the section in which Jesus responded to a trick question from the Sadducees. The Pharisees had tried to outwit him over paying taxes to Caesar. The Sadducees, who did not believe in a resurrection after death, had come up with a question about whose wife in heaven a woman, who had been married on earth to each of seven brothers, would be. Jesus had seen them off with as much ease as previously with the Pharisees. The first verse of today's Gospel reading refers to that exchange. Undeterred, the Pharisees came back for more.

Illustration

In this section of his Gospel, Matthew shows Jesus sparring with various groups amongst his opponents. The late great heavyweight boxer Muhammad Ali boasted early in his career: 'I am the greatest.' His subsequent achievements backed up his claim and he is widely considered the greatest boxer ever. The two parts of this Gospel reading cover two questions of greatness: Which is the greatest commandment? Who is the greatest?

Round 1: Which is the greatest commandment? (Matthew 22:34-40)

In a culture obsessed with law, its observance and avoidance, the question the Pharisees put to Jesus was probably a hot topic of the day. By greatest they meant the most important. That suggests the law was being treated as a multiple-choice exam paper – 'Attempt 4 from 10!' Jesus' questioner was an expert in the law. Jesus answered by quoting two parts of the law, combining them to emphasise that obedience springs from and expresses itself in a love for God (Deuteronomy 6:5) and a love for fellow human beings (Leviticus 19:18b). It has always been God's intention that our worship and living should be rooted in his love. It is a travesty of the faith when it is reduced to dry, legalistic obedience. Jesus summed up by saying that these two verses encapsulated and provided the foundation for the whole law (verse 40).

Round 2: Who is the greatest? (Matthew 22:41-end)

The Pharisees had erroneously thought they would get Jesus on the back foot. Having answered their question with a straight answer, unlike those occasions when he responded with a question of his own, he now goes on the front foot and asks them a question (verse 41). Although they could not and would not recognise Jesus as the Messiah, they did share a belief in a Messiah who would one day come and save Israel. He asked about the parentage, and therefore effectively the status, of the Messiah (verse 42). The lens that coloured their view of the Messiah was a Davidic one. They answered 'the Son of David'. In itself this was not altogether wrong, but Jesus' supplementary rhetorical question and observation show that they had drawn the wrong conclusion from it. The clincher in this exchange was when Jesus asked: 'Why did a divinely inspired David call the Christ Lord?' Before long and in the ensuing Christian era the Lordship of Christ would be central to emerging Christian theology. It is also central to contemporary Christian discipleship.

All Saints' Day

MATTHEW 5:1-12
Revelation 7:9-end; 1 John 3:1-3

Note

The approach to these readings and the sermon may vary according to whether a church is observing All Saints on 1 November or on the following Sunday.

Introduction

The word that describes declaring someone a saint in the Roman Catholic Church is 'beatification'. It is generally recognised that candidates for sainthood should exhibit godliness in the way they lived. There is also the more technical, and in some quarters more contentious, issue of their having performed well-attested miracles. Most ordinary Christians would think it a miracle ever to be considered for sainthood! In the New Testament, the word 'saints' is used to describe fellow believers. All Saints' Day is an opportunity to give thanks for the examples of the great and the good, celebrated and unnoticed, who have gone before on the journey of life. Their example is valued and noted on this day.

The Beatitudes (Matthew 5:1-12)

Fittingly, the Gospel reading set for today features the Beatitudes from the Sermon on the Mount. These are guidelines to living a godly life that demonstrates the values of the Kingdom of God. These days, recruitment specialists talk about candidates for some roles needing to demonstrate 'soft skills'. What they mean by this is normally the ability to make good relationships and to help other people work and get on together. They stand in contradistinction to brash, thrusting, go-getting characteristics sometimes associated with success. Jesus in his living modelled power through gentleness and love. His teaching here majors on characteristics and behaviours such as gentleness, compassion, forgiveness, mercy, a desire for righteousness, justice and purity (verses 5-8). Peacemakers, those who mourn and those who endure persecution are praised (verses 4, 9-12). He set this out at the beginning of his ministry. Throughout the subsequent centuries, these words have remained a template for anybody who wants to grow in saintliness.

Reflection

It is customary to allow extended time for quiet reflection on this day. People naturally recall those for whom they are grateful. In many cases, they may still mourn their parting. They may like to recall the qualities featured in the reading in the lives of those they are commemorating.

Fourth Sunday before Advent

(Unless All Saints' Day kept instead)

MATTHEW 24:1-14

Micah 3:5-end; 1 Thessalonians 2:9-13

Note

This is the countdown to the countdown season of Advent! It is also the countdown to the end of the liturgical year.

Signs of the end of the age (Matthew 24:1-14)

Despite the apparent and much-reported decline in Christian belief, people remain fascinated with stories, films and computer games associated with apocalyptic visions of the end times. Political developments and environmental concerns also trigger apocalyptic anxieties. People seem to be aware that life will not go on forever and ever as it is. Maybe it was ever thus? It is important when reading Jesus' teaching about the end of the age to remember that much of what he said was probably focused on the impending doom in the form of the Fall of Jerusalem in AD 70. Apocalyptic writing, in common with other prophetic material, usually has two or three foci – the immediate, a longer-term intermediate application and a final, end of the world as we know it, view.

Temporary temporal Temple (verses 1, 2)

Today's reading follows on immediately from a series of woes Jesus had pronounced. The setting is Jerusalem. The new, partially incomplete Temple loomed large in people's view and in their thinking. It was an important metaphor in Jesus' teaching. Jesus told his disciples, 'This great edifice will not last.'

Significant location! (verse 3)

The 'stage direction' that has Jesus sitting on the Mount of Olives when he responds to the disciples is of greater significance than appears at first glance. Traditional Jewish belief about cataclysmic events at the end of time included prophecy concerning the Messiah and the mountain: 'On that day his feet will stand on the Mount of Olives, east of Jerusalem, and the Mount of Olives will be split in two . . .' (Zechariah 14:4). The disciples had grown in their understanding and belief by now. They asked Jesus, 'What will be the sign of *your* coming?'

Previously Jesus had taught in parables, but by now he was speaking plainly. He spelled out the following:

- There would be impostors and people would be deceived (verses 4, 5, 11).

- Inevitably there would be wars, rumours of wars, earthquakes and famines – these would be early signs (verses 6-8).

- Persecution and execution would be a feature. His followers would be unpopular, hated and betrayed (verses 9, 10).

- There would be widespread loss of faith and wickedness (verses 10-12).

- Those who held on to the faith would be saved (verse 13).

- The good news of the Kingdom of God would be preached throughout the world. Traditionally this has been understood to be the mission era of the Church (verse 14).

As the disciples sat and listened to Jesus spell out this scenario, they might have been forgiven for finding it hard to hold on to a sense of the Good News of the Kingdom. Christians today may feel the same as they look at the world and hear the news. People say: 'I don't know what the world is coming to!' They cannot say they were not warned!

Third Sunday before Advent

(Sometimes Remembrance Sunday)

MATTHEW 25:1-13

Amos 5:18-24; 1 Thessalonians 4:13-end

Context

After Jesus' explicit teaching about the end of the age, Matthew includes four parables that Jesus told to illustrate the importance of being ready and prepared for such a time. The parable of the ten virgins is the second of these. It has proved over the years to be a memorable and popular parable. The story tells of ten bridesmaids, traditionally young girls whose role in a wedding at that time was to greet the bridegroom and his companions when they arrived at the bride's house.

Preparation (verses 1-5)

The bridesmaids shared the same task and set of expectations. Five wise ones were prepared, five foolish ones were not. They all tired of waiting because the groom was longer in arriving than expected. They all fell asleep. It is easily done, as anyone who has sat up waiting for an event late into the night can confirm.

Consternation (verses 6-9)

Word went up that the bridegroom was getting near. They all woke up and lit their lamps in readiness, only for the foolish ones to discover that their lamps were going out. This is not a parable about the virtue of sharing or of responding positively to requests for help. Hence, the wise virgins were hard-nosed about making sure they had enough for their own lamps and refused to share. This forced the foolish bridesmaids to go on a late-night shopping expedition to buy oil. No 24-hour supermarkets in their day. Their plight is probably intended to be almost comic.

Celebration and exclusion (verses 10-12)

Inevitably, the groom arrived while the foolish ones were away hunting for oil. The wise ones fulfilled their duty of welcoming and began to enjoy the banquet which got under way. The foolish ones arrived later; whether they had been successful in their quest was not stated, but they were refused entrance in no uncertain terms.

Application (verse 13)

Jesus had two points he wanted to make. The precise timing of the Day of the Lord/end of the age is unknown. People should remain alert. This teaching is repeated and reinforced during the approaching season of Advent.

Second Sunday before Advent

MATTHEW 25:14-30
Zephaniah 1:7, 12-18; 1 Thessalonians 5:1-11

Introduction

The Gospel reading relates the third of four parables told by Jesus to reiterate the importance of being prepared for the end of the age that Matthew included at this point. It follows on directly from the parable of the wise and foolish virgins (last week's Gospel passage). The readings from Zephaniah and 1 Thessalonians 5:1-11 also address the theme. Neither of them are for the faint-hearted, although the latter passage finishes with the words: 'encourage one another and build each other up'.

The parable of the talents (Matthew 25:14-30)

This parable is frequently misapplied, primarily because of the translation of the word 'talents'. It features frequently when churches are reviewing their financial giving and the contribution of church members to the wider effort. Both those things can clearly be taught from this passage but they can obscure the fact that this is first and foremost an apocalyptic parable about the importance of being ready to give account to a returning master! Commentators and others have probably spent too much time speculating over the significance of the different amounts entrusted to people. Jesus' use of the word 'again' (verse 14) to introduce this parable showed he was continuing in a similar vein.

The set-up (verses 14-18)

A man going on a journey entrusts the care of his wealth and property to his servants. They share in the same task but the amount entrusted to them varies. They are all subject to the same expectation. In the previous parable, the split of wise and foolish virgins was 50/50. Here in the case of the servants it is two thirds/one third. Two of them make the money work, in an unspecified way, and one digs a hole. He was keeping it safe but not expecting to make any gain.

The settling (verses 19-30)

The fact that a long time elapsed before the Master's return is noteworthy. As in the case of the delayed bridegroom, there was plenty of scope for those entrusted with the Master's business to lose focus and become unprepared. The two servants who had made a profit were commended by the Master, given increased responsibility and shared in his happiness (verses 21, 23). The third servant who had opted for the low-risk, no-interest investment plan said he was afraid of his Master (verse 25). NB. People who insist on decoding every element in a parable have the challenge of explaining why the Master (God) is harsh and unfair (verse 26)! Remember it is a story with one main point – not a detailed allegory! Following the world recession and financial crisis and the role of the banks in that, the advice in verse 27 may not appear to be quite as wise as when originally given. Preachers will do well not to get distracted at this point.

In the parable, the third servant is deemed more culpable because, despite knowing what his Master was like, he was still lazy (verse 26). The consequences of his failure to meet his Master's expectations are inevitable and terrible and the cause of great regret. The faithful servants gain at his expense. Again, this is for effect in the story and not intended as a theological or sociological revelation.

Christ the King/
Sunday next before Advent

MATTHEW 25:31-END
Ezekiel 34:11-16, 20-24; Ephesians 1:15-end

Introduction

The Church's year ends with a powerful parable. It is part of the extended countdown to Advent and Christmas. Fittingly, it distinguishes between those who serve their king in a way that makes a difference to others and those who do not.

Sheep and Goats (verses 31-33)

People who have visited the Middle East or Mediterranean countries will know from experience that in those places sheep and goats are more alike than those seen on British farms. At the end of the age the Son of Man will be like a farmer sorting the one from the other. In the light of how the story develops, it is clearly preferable to be a sheep rather than a goat. Discussing the relative merits of being found on the left or right politically is a temptation that preachers should resist!

Doers, the kind and compassionate (verses 34-40)

The four parables that Matthew records are all ones in which Jesus uses contrast between two groups to make his point (servants working/not working, bridesmaids prepared/unprepared, proactive/lazy servants). This parable begins as a pastoral story in a rural setting and morphs into an extended story about acts of kindness and care. The contrast here is between those whose lives included acts of kindness and compassion extended to people they did not know and those whose lives included no such things. There is no suggestion here about 'salvation through works' – that is not what this passage is about. However, it is reasonable to assert that the lives of Jesus' followers should be marked by acts of care generously and indiscriminately given.

Although it is a subsidiary point, it is significant that the acts of kindness done by the righteous were done unselfconsciously. They were not pious do-gooders. They had to ask the king, 'When was it we did these things for you?' (verse 40).

Illustration

People are aware of examples of people serving royalty unawares. One of the best is the true story of Tsar Peter the Great of Russia working as a labourer in Dutch and English shipbuilding yards in 1697.

Nothing goes unnoticed (verses 37-40)

This is great news for the unseen, unsung, unappreciated women and men who offer care in a wide range of settings. Such people can feel taken for granted; many of them care for loved ones week in and week out with no reward. Every act of compassion and care counts. They count because of the value God places on every human life. Although this parable is the final one in Matthew's Gospel about the end of the age, these additional teaching points are important.

Wasters – the reluctant and mean-spirited (verses 41-45)

As in the preceding parables, there comes a point of reckoning. The unrighteous who have not cared for others are roundly condemned and in the story are punished accordingly.

Reward and punishment, pleasure and pain (verse 46)

The parable ends with a stark statement of the separation of the two groups and their respective fates. Such statements are uncomfortable and hard to hear. They stand as a challenge to all, but should not be allowed to stand apart from the balancing promises of God's mercy and forgiveness.

YEAR B

First Sunday of Advent

MARK 13:24-END

Isaiah 64:1-9, 1 Corinthians 1:3-9

It is the first Sunday of Advent, the beginning of a new Church year and the Gospel reading provides a reality check, an encouragement and a warning. The last verse of the reading is a gift to preachers. 'And what I say to you I say to all: Keep awake!' (verse 37, New Revised Standard Version).

Context

Jesus was sitting with his inner circle, Peter, James, John and Andrew, on the Mount of Olives. They were looking across at the beautiful and yet incomplete Temple. The disciples pressed Jesus about his prediction of the destruction of that great building. Jesus warned them about impending doom and the inevitability of false alarms and gave the assurance of the Holy Spirit's assistance.

Key Question

What is the focal point? Prophecies and apocalyptic passages are usually assumed to have two or sometimes even three focal points: the situation at the time, the time of Jesus and the end of time. The focus of this reading is on the destruction of the Temple in AD 70 during the Jewish-Roman war.

Signs of the times (verses 26-31)

These days, shops start stocking Christmas goods frighteningly early. The first glimpse of 'Book now for Christmas' outside a pub or hotel does not mean Christmas is nearly on us. By contrast, fig trees coming into leaf were reliable, a sure sign of summer. Jesus told the disciples they could be certain that these awful things would happen. Everything would change but his words would last forever.

Keep alert – don't nod off (verses 32-37)

Nodding off can be costly. Many weary commuters have woken at the end of the line, having fallen asleep and missed their station. Most people have dozed off during a film or TV programme only to discover they have missed a key twist in the plot. Jesus warns the disciples that they should not be like a sleepy watchman or dozy servant. Some things do not change. Premises may have CCTV cameras on every corner, but if the person watching the monitors in a control room has a nap, the technology is a waste of time and money.

Jesus wanted his disciples to remain alert and not be surprised by the dangers of the day. The message to his twenty-first-century disciples remains the same. 'Keep awake!'

Second Sunday of Advent

MARK 1:1-8

Isaiah 40:1-11; 2 Peter 3:8-15a

Mark's Gospel is the Gospel for people who like their books and their films to be fast-moving. It is an action-packed account of the life of Jesus, incident piled upon incident. Jesus did this and then he went to there and then again, he did this and said that. It leaves the reader almost breathless and all with the purpose of setting out the Good News about Jesus.

What? No Christmas? (verses 1-3)

Mark started out as he meant to go on. He did not include any reference to Jesus' birth or growing up. He set out his stall and hit his readers with the punch line – 'The beginning of the good news of Jesus Christ, the Son of God.' Without any preamble, Mark quoted from the prophet Isaiah. He wanted to show that the momentous things he wrote about were prophesied and anticipated hundreds of years before. There would be a messenger whose purpose was to prepare the way, a herald preceding a king.

Wild but not woolly! (verses 4-8)

John the Baptist headed the cast of this drama in terms of order of appearance. He was striking: wild and unkempt, uncompromising in his message. He was clear that he was not the main act. He was the warm-up man. He is sometimes described as the last of the Old Testament prophets. The Jewish people were used to rituals of washing as an outward sign of cleansing. John attracted village folk and city-dwellers from Jerusalem. Clearly, word spread and large numbers of people were baptised in the River Jordan. Those who went out to John were what might be called a renewal movement; they certainly were unaware of what was about to happen.

John tried to leave them in no doubt. Someone was coming who would be superior in every way, someone more powerful who would drench them in the power of God, the Holy Spirit.

Key point

Very few, if any, of John's listeners would be able to grasp what he meant. By contrast, John was clear about his role. His whole purpose was to point people to Jesus Christ. The season of Advent is a preparation season for us; preparing not simply to have enough food to feed an army of locusts but to get ready spiritually to celebrate the coming of Christ.

Third Sunday of Advent

JOHN 1:6-8, 19-28

Isaiah 61:1-4, 8-end; 1 Thessalonians 5:16-24

Dipping into the first chapter of John's Gospel today feels reminiscent of children hunting for Christmas presents in their parents' bedroom before the big day. On this 3rd Sunday in Advent, the focus is on John the Baptist.

Messenger not Messiah (verses 6-8)

John, like Mark, starts as he means to go on. He presents Jesus as the Word, the Messiah. The one who will be revealed as King of Kings and Light of the World has a herald. John does not want his readers to be under any illusion. This messenger comes on the highest authority – 'he is sent from God'. John the Baptist has a clear purpose. He will speak about Jesus the light and point people to him. John spells it out: 'He himself was not the light', removing any risk of mistaken identity.

The Inquisition (verses 19-28)

A perennial ice-breaker at Christmas parties is the game in which people have a sticker with the name of a celebrity put on their forehead. They have to discover who they are by asking questions of the other guests.

John the Baptist was clear about his identity and his mission. The Jewish leaders in Jerusalem, intrigued and possibly alarmed by his appearance and appeal, sent a delegation across the River Jordan to Bethany to investigate. Other wild and wacky people had claimed to be prophets and messianic messengers. 'Who are you?' was the investigators' direct question. It drew a direct response: 'I am not the Messiah.'

The group began a process of elimination. First they asked John whether he was the Old Testament prophet Elijah reincarnated – an expected precursor among the Jews of the Messiah's appearance. 'Categorically not!' said John. He also denied being the Prophet –

another name for Moses. They needed an answer to take back, so John told them he was a 'voice in the wilderness', quoting the prophet Isaiah. He is preparing the way of the Lord. His inquisitors were confused – if he was not any of their suggestions, why was he baptising people?

John knew his limits. His baptism was for a season and only with water. There was 'one among them' whom they did not know but who was about to be revealed – John was not worthy even to untie this person's sandals.

Conclusion

A young woman who is now approaching her thirties and has a strategic ministry among young people at a national level was asked when she was 17 what she thought her purpose in life was. 'I exist to make God famous,' she replied. John the Baptist would have approved of such an answer. We do well to follow suit.

Fourth Sunday of Advent

LUKE 1:26-38
2 Samuel 7:1-11, 16; Romans 16:25-end

Birth announcement

St Luke was a physician with an eye for detail and a love of history. His personality and background colour and shape his account of the life of Jesus.

Family ties

The Gospel readings so far in Advent have highlighted the relationship between Jesus and John the Baptist at the point Jesus was beginning his public ministry. Luke shows that their destinies were entwined from the outset in God's greater scheme of things. As doctor and historian, he dates the moment when God sends an angel to Mary according to how far John's mother Elizabeth is advanced in her pregnancy. Part of God's provision for a shocked young Mary was to give her the support of a kinship relationship. Mary's understandable initial incredulity at the news that she will become pregnant is addressed by the angel telling her that the previously barren Elizabeth is pregnant (verse 36).

Servant Mother of the Servant King

There is nothing to suggest that Mary was specially qualified through background or education to take on this unique opportunity and responsibility. She was a young girl from an ordinary rural background. She was engaged to a godly older man and was still a virgin. Leaving aside the appearance of an angel, enough in itself to freak out most people, there is a lot to take in. Apparently, she is going to become pregnant through an encounter with God's Holy Spirit. Again, that is mind-boggling news to take on board. The Messenger does not hold back. Her child is going to be special and holy and must be named Jesus (a variant on Joshua, meaning 'the Lord saves').

A lot to take in

Many people would be tempted to respond by asking for time to process this, to sleep on it. Mary must have been a remarkably faithful and godly young woman. She said she was the Lord's servant or, more colloquially: 'At your service.' We know from later references that she must have spent many hours 'processing' throughout the ensuing years until the remarkable three days at the end of her son's life on earth.

Key point

The key factor in this remarkable exchange was not Mary's faithful obedience, wonderful though that was; it was the fact that God's word is always fulfilled. When God promises – it is as good as done.

Christmas Day

JOHN 1:1-14
Gospel reading from Set 3

Introduction

People have many traditions at this time of year, including what they eat, the games they play and the films they watch. For some, Christmas is not complete without watching *The Sound of Music*. One of the most famous lines from that show is 'Let's start at the very beginning, a very good place to start.' St John agrees. His account of the life of Christ does not begin: 'Once upon a time'. John is at pains to point out that God the Son pre-dates time!

In the beginning was the Word (verses 1-5)

It has always been crucial to be clear that Jesus was and is God in human form. The Son of God was not created (verses 1, 2). He was intimately involved in and integral to creation. This is theology in its purest form. This is *the* biggest miracle: God coming to earth is the most mind-boggling event. In the light of this divine act, everything else miraculous in Jesus' life on earth follows – even the Resurrection.

Carols can be great theological summaries. 'Hark, the Herald angels sing', for example, has the line: 'light and life to all he brings'. It is a travesty of the gospel when people get the impression that Christianity is negative and exclusive. 'In him was life, and the life was the light of all people' (verse 4, NRSV) – life affirming and life illuminating. Darkness presents itself in many forms in life. John does not hold back from what is called a 'spoiler'. He gives the ending away at the start of his unfolding narrative – the light shines in the darkness and cannot be extinguished by it (verse 5).

Jesus was heralded by angels and by John the Baptist (verses 6-9) whose job was to turn people towards the Light.

A note of sadness (verses 10-14)

Although the message of the angels was one of great joy, there is in the prologue of the Gospel a note of sadness. The world that owed its very existence to Jesus did not know him (verse 10). He came to his own people, yet was not welcomed or accepted.

Then follows that tiny word 'But' which, throughout Scripture, so often leads on to great and joyful truths. Here it signposts the good news that all who received him, who believed in his name, received the most wonderful gift. They were given the right and authority to become children of God – something that cannot be earned through human inheritance or design. People often say wistfully, 'Christmas is for the children', because they don't see much in it for themselves. What an irony! It is for the children – for all who accept the greatest gift.

First Sunday of Christmas/
Naming and Circumcision of Christ

See Year A

Second Sunday of Christmas

JOHN 1:[1-9] 10-18
Jeremiah 31:7-14; Ephesians 1:3-14

The Gospel today returns to the familiar territory of John chapter 1. It is an invitation to read these verses through a strong theological lens.

Unrecognised and unwelcomed (verses 10, 11)

Early in his ministry Jesus quoted the saying, 'a prophet is not without honour except in their home town, among their own kin and in their own house'. John makes it clear that this was true of Christ coming into the world, not simply when Jesus had a home-town preaching engagement!

Good News (verses 12, 13)

The Son of God offers the gift of son/daughtership to all who receive and believe. The sense of the word 'power' here is one of authority or the right to be and benefit from becoming children of God. Note that the key decision and action here is that of God.

Like Father, like Son (verse 14)

The greatest miracle expressed in four words: 'The Word became flesh'.
　God the Son came and lived in human form and it was glorious. If people wonder what God is like, they can look at Jesus.

'Full of grace and truth' (verse 14)

Jesus is the embodiment of integrity and authenticity – not primarily propositional truth. He is not first and foremost a walking creed! He is not a statement of the word of God – the Word is God!

Fully God (verses 16, 17)

Jesus lacks nothing. Grace and truth are not commodities to be poured into some receptacle – rather, they are characteristics of God. Jesus being full of grace and truth means he fully bears and represents these elements of God. We all receive expressions of grace and truth because of his fullness.

No one has ever seen God (verse 18)

John reiterates the central truth. Jesus is God. See Jesus, know the Father.

Illustration

One wet afternoon a mother suggested her daughter do some painting to while away the time. Later she went to see how the masterpiece was progressing. The girl had filled the whole page with a smiley face in bright colours. 'Who is it, darling?' 'It's God!' her daughter replied matter-of-factly. 'Well, it's very good, but people don't really know what God looks like.' 'They will now,' remarked the girl, as she put the finishing touches to the Almighty's nose.

Epiphany Sunday

MATTHEW 2:1-12
Isaiah 60:1-6; Ephesians 3:1-12

Introduction

The golden rule for poets, story-tellers and film-makers is *show* not tell! Of course, the Gospels tell in words the life story of Christ but here at the beginning of Matthew's account it is what is shown that stands out. People's reactions and gifts that are given speak volumes. Today is Epiphany Sunday, traditionally the Manifestation (or Showing) of Christ to the Gentiles. Matthew writing primarily for Jewish readers ironically tells of Jesus being worshipped by non-Jewish visitors at the very beginning of his account.

Magi from the East come to worship (verses 1, 2)

People may like singing 'We three kings of Orient are' but it is worth noting that the Bible says nothing about kings and does not number the visitors. The word 'Magi' is used for wise men, priests or magicians. Some scholars say they were most likely Zoroastrian priests from Persia. Three types of gifts, presents fit for a king, were given but there was most likely a group of travellers.

There is an old slogan 'Wise men looked for a king – wise people still do!' It is another irony that the travellers ask in Jerusalem about the birth of the *King of the Jews*, for that would be on the sign over Jesus' head on the Cross. These wise, educated and spiritual men have come to worship the one who has come to be worshipped!

Herod was disturbed (verses 3-6)

From the outset, Jesus is the great disturber. His birth upsets the vassal ruler Herod. The question the Magi ask touches a nerve. Herod has no genealogical claim to be king. He is a puppet with no royal lineage. Matthew, writing primarily for a Jewish readership (in the first instance!), sets out his stall in chapter 1 by showing Jesus' royal heritage

('David's greater son'). He also packs his account with examples of how Jesus fulfilled Old Testament prophecies left, right and centre.

Secret deceit (verses 7, 8)

Herod is utterly spooked and tries to conceive a cunning plan, one that would be confounded but not without cost to innocent families.

Journey of joy (verses 9-12)

The Magi are rewarded for their persistence. Note that the little family have moved up into a house by the time these exotic visitors arrive. Edit memories of Nativity plays accordingly. Encouraged by sighting the star, they arrived and offered worship and gifts full of meaning, portents of what lay ahead for Jesus in due course. Spiritually attuned, they were warned in a dream.

Conclusion

Many people who encounter Jesus at the end of their searching discover that their plans change – they follow an alternative route.

First Sunday of Epiphany/ Baptism of Christ

MARK 1:4-11

Genesis 1:1-5; Acts 19:1-7

Introduction and context

Welcome back, Mark! In the scheme of the Church's readings, St Mark always gets Christmas off! He opens his fast-moving Gospel with the beginning of Jesus' public ministry rather than covering the remarkable events of his birth. Mark's opening sentence does not beat about the bush (verse 1): he declares that this is the Good News about Jesus Christ who is the Son of God. He follows this up with words from Malachi and Isaiah.

John the Baptist (verses 4-8)

Echoing the Church's Advent preparations, this reading describes the wild, Old-Testament-prophet-style herald of Jesus. John the Baptist called people to change their lives and offered baptism as a sign of forgiveness. His baptism was not about belonging to a church or movement. He was calling people to prepare for, and announced the imminent arrival of, the one who would baptise them with the Holy Spirit.

Enter Jesus (verses 9-11)

Mark's readers are introduced to Jesus doing what he came to do – namely, bringing heaven and earth together. He identifies with ordinary broken people by submitting to John's baptism of forgiveness. We know from Matthew's parallel account that John was deeply uncomfortable baptising Jesus. He felt unworthy and knew that Jesus did not need to repent of sin.

It is a serious mistake if people think that this baptism and God's affirmation from heaven represents the moment when Jesus is 'powered up' for ministry. He was always fully divine. In these three verses, we see God – Father, Son and Holy Spirit – acting powerfully.

Illustration

Many older church members may recall that in the popular cartoon series *Tom and Jerry,* the bulldog Spike regularly took his young pup under his arm and, with chest puffed out, declared: 'That's my boy!' Parents these days proudly post their children's milestone achievements on the internet. They are saying, 'Make no mistake, this is our son, our daughter. Look what they're doing!'

Second Sunday of Epiphany

JOHN 1:43-END

1 Samuel 3:1-10; Revelation 5:1-10

The first disciples can appear to be impetuous, unstable types. This is because the Gospel records, here being a case in point, do not often give much by way of background information, the person's spiritual journey being left to our surmise. We are only given the highlight of the conversation – e.g. verse 43, etc. Consequently, hearing and responding to God's call to discipleship can appear to be easy and straightforward. 'Follow me!' 'OK, here I come!' Later in his ministry, Jesus made it clear that following him would be costly and that his followers should count the cost in advance.

Can any good come from Nazareth? (verse 46)

It is typical of God's workings that he chooses unlikely places and people in his salvation purpose. It is a trademark of the Kingdom that he works from the little and insignificant towards the great. Jesus who came 'down from heaven' works in a bottom-up way!

God's knowledge of us (verse 48)

Jesus' foreknowledge of Nathaniel is disconcerting, to say the least. There are other examples throughout the Gospels. Nathaniel asks: 'How do you know me?'

Link to Old Testament reading (1 Samuel 3:1-10)

How God calls. God can call early (when young), when the call is unexpected and may be hard to discern. The role of an older person can help confirm the call. Obedience to God's call always involves listening: 'Speak, for your servant is listening.'

Stairway to Heaven (verses 50, 51)

Many young people who learn the guitar are taught or teach themselves the opening chords to the Led Zeppelin song 'Stairway to Heaven'.

It is almost as though this iconic tune is a compulsory requirement for becoming a guitarist! Nathaniel is taking his first steps as a disciple. He is amazed that Jesus knows him, but Jesus tells him this is just the beginning and that he, with the other disciples, will see much greater things. Jesus seems to refer to the 'iconic' incident from the life of Jacob, the dream in which he sees a stairway to heaven as a sign of the presence of God.

Application

No matter how a person's journey of following Jesus Christ begins, the following statements remain true:

- God knows people better than they know themselves.

- He calls people from even the most unlikely or unpromising settings.

- His intention is always to expand horizons, to give a glimpse of the heavenly in the midst of life.

Third Sunday of Epiphany

JOHN 2:1-11

Genesis 14:17-20; Revelation 19:6-10
(See also Year A Epiphany 4 and Year C Epiphany 2)

Introduction: Everybody loves a wedding? (Or do they?)

Irrespective of time or cultural settings, when it comes to a wedding certain things seem compulsory! There is usually a mother and she is likely to be fussing. The guest list and catering arrangements are central. Something memorable stands out for people. John's account of the wedding at Cana of Galilee does not disappoint; indeed, all the elements are there to the extent that it seems like a Woody Allen or Ben Stiller comedy!

Jesus' mother was there (verse 1)

This is one of the most famous weddings in history and yet the happy couple do not receive so much as a passing name-check! Jesus' mother is there, a proud Jewish mother who believes and knows that her son is special.

Jesus was also invited (verse 2)

Often when a single person is invited to a wedding, they are given the chance of bringing a 'plus one'. Jesus turns up with his disciples. Table plans were almost certainly a good deal more flexible in those days.

Celebratory calamity (verses 3-5)

The wine ran out. This was an embarrassment that would bring lasting shame on the hosts. Mary was aware of the situation and turned to Jesus. From day one in his ministry he had an acute sense of God's timing. His immediate response was that this was not the right time or setting in which to begin his work. Undaunted, Mary instructed the staff: 'Do whatever he tells you.' Good advice then and through the ages!

Nothing by halves! (verses 6-10)

It may be no accident that Jesus used pitchers of water associated with Jewish laws of purification to transform this wedding. He provided over and above what was needed to keep the party going. Similarly, almost certainly John expected his readers to note, in time at least, the significance that the new wine was declared superior by the master of the feast.

The first of his signs (verse 11)

Having performed his first miracle at a wedding and revealed his glory, it is no surprise that Jesus frequently used marriage feasts in his parables.

Application

Wedding couples who choose this reading for their marriage service, often by default, are encouraged to turn to Jesus when their resources run thin. More widely, it teaches not only that Jesus can transform a lack into a rich blessing but, importantly, that the 'wine' of his Kingdom is a new superior vintage compared with people's previous experience of God.

Fourth Sunday of Epiphany

MARK 1:21-28

Deuteronomy 18:15-20; Revelation 12:1-5a

Context

Remember Mark's Gospel moves at full speed. It is full of 'At once' and 'Immediately'. In the preceding verses, Mark recounted the calling of some of the first disciples. They are straight into action; their basic training begins as they watch Jesus.

Capernaum was effectively Jesus' home base for his Galilean ministry.

Stunning debut (verses 21, 22)

Into the synagogue on the Sabbath and Jesus started to teach. People were struck by the fact that there was an authoritative edge to his teaching. (Authority is a key feature throughout this Gospel.) Almost certainly people commented that Jesus was a 'class act' compared with the scribes. This hardly endeared him to the scribes and teachers of the law. Telling visiting preachers they are much better than the normal preacher within the latter's hearing rarely goes down well!

Spiritual conflict (verses 23-26)

There was an individual who was clearly disturbed and distressed, his life marred by evil. Sometimes the Gospels describe people that today would be recognised as mentally ill. It is important to note that Jesus always addressed people with compassion and when, as here, he encountered powers of evil, he was authoritative and firm (verse 25).

There is an irony in the fact that evil spirits recognised Jesus as 'the Holy One of God' who had the power to destroy them. Ordinary people, including the disciples, took much longer to grasp this reality.

This dramatic encounter, a clash of the Kingdoms, concludes with the man set free from what it was that had gripped his life.

Fame spreads (verses 27, 28)

Those who witnessed these events were even more amazed. New teaching with authority. People love the new and the dramatic, so Jesus' fame spread.

Reflection

Historically, Christians have tended to fall into the equal and opposite errors of either under- or over-estimating the existence of the forces of evil. How is it possible to find balance in understanding the role of evil in world events?

Key point

The authority of Jesus brings freedom and peace.

Proper 1

MARK 1:29-39

Isaiah 40:21-31; 1 Corinthians 9:16-23

The number of 'Sundays before Lent' varies each year depending on the date of Easter. The readings allocated for the 5ᵗʰ, 4ᵗʰ or 3ʳᵈ Sundays before Lent are known as 'Propers'. Preachers should check which Proper is allocated to which Sunday in any given year.

Words of encouragement from Isaiah 40

The first part of the Gospel reading is an account of Jesus healing a man. The Old Testament reading includes some much-loved words of encouragement. They apply on the physical and emotional/spiritual level – e.g. strength to the weary, power to the weak, etc., culminating in the promise that 'those who hope in the Lord will renew their strength. They will soar on wings like eagles; they will run and not grow weary, they will walk and not be faint' (verse 31). One idea is to use some of these words as a refrain within the prayers.

Healing (Mark 1:29-34)

Mark's Gospel moves at quite a pace and so it is straight into the action with the briefest of prologues. Within the first chapter Jesus is baptised, calls his first disciples and embarks on his ministry. The Gospel reading today takes up the story with a typical 'as soon as they left the synagogue' (verse 29). Jesus and the two sets of brothers went to Simon Peter's house. Simon's mother-in-law was ill with a fever (verse 30). There are many quips to be made about mothers-in-law, not all of them appreciated. There is an irony that, as soon as Jesus had healed this lady, she got up and started to serve the men (verse 31). News about Jesus was spreading quickly even before this miracle (see verse 28). The headline 'man heals mother-in-law' galvanised the whole town into bringing their sick, distressed and possessed to the door (verse 32). In the cases that involved evil powers, Jesus placed a 'gagging order' on the spirits. Interestingly, this was because they recognised him for who he was and the time was not right for this to be widely known.

Retreating (verses 35-39)

Jesus was divine but not superhuman! He knew he needed to manage and balance his resources. He observed a personal discipline of private prayer, retreating whenever he could to solitary and/or wild places. Having ended the evening giving out in ministry, Jesus got up and went out very early to pray alone and without interruption (verse 35). After a while, Simon and the others found Jesus to share the mixed news that everyone in the town was looking for him (verses 36, 37). Jesus did not want to get bogged down in one place at this early stage of his mission. He suggested they move on to other villages so that he could minister there as well. He was clear in his calling. As with so much in life, timing is of the essence. It is always important to be clear about knowing when to wait and when to move on. Jesus had this clarity.

Question/Suggestion

Preachers may like to raise the possibility of people going on a retreat if they do not already do so. It may be good to start with a local half-day one by way of an introduction to the value of retreats.

Proper 2

MARK 1:40-45

2 Kings 5:1-14; 1 Corinthians 9:24-27

Jesus heals a man with leprosy

(see also the healing of Naaman the leper in 2 Kings 5).

The encounter in today's Gospel reading is particularly poignant. Jesus made the most of his miraculous powers, his miracles being signs of the Kingdom that he often used to illustrate a point of teaching. He responded to even the smallest of signs of faith in the individuals who came to him asking for help. This is one of many occasions where his compassion is mentioned explicitly. The man felt able and compelled to approach Jesus and beg him for healing (verse 40). Given the regulations about lepers having to keep their distance from people, this was a significant move. The phrase 'if you are willing' implied a mix of desperate hope with a note of uncertainty. Jesus responded with compassion, touching the man and telling him that he was willing to cleanse him (verse 41). The man was immediately cured. Jesus always looked beyond the immediate healing of a condition. He saw a person and wanted them to experience wholeness. In the case of this man with leprosy and people like the woman with a gynaecological condition, this meant seeing they were readmitted to society as part of their restoration. To this end, Jesus told the man to waste no time in presenting himself to the priests and making the prescribed sacrifice so he could be given an official clean bill of health (verses 43, 44). Not altogether surprisingly, the man could not restrain his own joy and desire to show and tell people what had happened to him. Consequently, Jesus was so in demand that he had to stay in lonely places. Even this did not stop people flocking to him (verse 45).

Illustration

Middle-aged and older members of congregations will probably remember the significance of Princess Diana's visit to an HIV/AIDS hospital ward. She did not hesitate to touch the men she met, at a time when people generally were ignorant and hesitant in the way they cared for those with this condition.

Concluding question

Who are the 'lepers' in modern society – the unclean or untouchables, those kept at a distance? How can the Church lead the way in overcoming taboos and social barriers?

Proper 3

MARK 2:1-12
Isaiah 43:18-25; 2 Corinthians 1:18-22

Jesus heals a paralytic

This story has been loved by generations of children. The idea of climbing onto a roof, breaking through it and lowering a friend down has the perfect balance of naughtiness, adventure and danger. The fact that it is in the Bible and the friends did not get into trouble only adds to its appeal.

The boys are back in town! (verses 1, 2)

Having escaped the clamour of the crowds for a few days, Jesus and his disciples returned to their home, their ministry base. Word soon got around and before long the house where he was staying was packed, inside and out. Jesus began to preach to them there and then. Have crowd – will preach!

Determined friends – desperate measures (verses 3, 4)

The friends had clearly told their friend that they would take him to Jesus. They were determined to deliver on that promise and would not let the crowd get in the way. It must have been a dramatic scene as they broke through the roof and lowered him down.

Words of forgiveness (verse 5)

Jesus regularly tried to correct the prevailing view of the day that automatically connected illness with sin. On this occasion, his first reaction was to speak words of absolution to the man. Mark does not give any personal background so people can only speculate as to the cause of his paralysis.

Thoughts of disapproval (verses 6, 7)

Religious leaders, teachers of the law, were in the crowd, as they regularly were. Increasingly, they became like a heresy commission or inquisition.

They latched on to the fact that Jesus had pronounced forgiveness to the man. This was tantamount to a claim of divinity.

Words of authority and healing (verses 8-11)

As on many other occasions, Jesus could discern immediately what the teachers of the law were thinking. He challenged them with two questions. The first was designed to get them to look at themselves and to ask why they were critical and sceptical (verse 8). The second got them looking at him and thinking about his words and his authority. This was the set-up for the miracle he was about to perform. He asked which they thought was easier to say – 'You are forgiven' or 'Get up and walk'. In their book, the first question was *impermissible* and the second *impossible* (verse 9). They were caught either way. Jesus' *coup de grâce* in this exchange was telling the man to take up his mat and walk home – which he promptly did (verses 10-12a)! The people were amazed and, more importantly, they praised God (verse 12b).

For reflection

Allow time for people to reflect on whether they are ever sceptical and critical. If they are, what does this spring from?

Conclusion

This story has often encouraged Christians to pray for loved ones and others, including those without apparent faith. The sense of taking people to God in prayer has been strong. Vicarious faith is important in intercessory prayer.

Second Sunday before Lent

JOHN 1:1-14

Proverbs 8:1, 22-31: Colossians 1:15-20

Context

There may have been a sense of déjà-vu as the Gospel was announced today – it is once again the familiar ground of John chapter 1. This is a fundamental passage setting out the mystery and purpose of the Incarnation. In the scheme of the weekly readings, it acts as a bridge between last week's subject of the beginning of Jesus' earthly ministry and next week's marking of the Transfiguration: heaven and earth meet in Jesus.

Key verse (verse 14)

The Word become flesh and dwelt among us, *and we have seen his glory.* Jesus the Word, the Son of God, was central to creation (verses 1, 2). John sets out that Jesus came to bring life (verse 4), to confront darkness (verse 5), to bring light (verses 5, 9) and to give people the right – literally, conferred the authority on people – to become God's children (verse 12). The glory of God was shown as Jesus brought these things into the lives of the people he touched. This is why the miracles are called signs – they signpost or semaphore (to use a word with a similar root) the divinity and glory of Jesus.

Epistle echo (Colossians 1:15-20)

Jesus is the *ikon* of God, his image. The New Testament reading echoes the Gospel message. St Paul had grasped, like John, the importance of knowing and teaching that Jesus was central to the beginning of all things. Jesus is the first-born and has the preeminent place. It follows as a natural consequence that 'in him all things hold together' (verse 17). This is a deep and wonderful theological truth, one which people with broken lives experienced as they met Christ in his earthly ministry. It is the story of countless ordinary people through the ages who have found that all things hold together in Jesus.

Reflection

Struggles and challenges confront most people sooner or later in life. When people are under pressure and finding it hard to cope, they often use the phrase 'I'm struggling to hold it together.' This is where high theology becomes practical down-to-earth help. In Jesus, people can find the strength to hold it together. This often comes through the assistance of others in the Church of which he is the head (Colossians 1:18).

Sunday next before Lent

MARK 9:2-9
2 Kings 2:1-12; 2 Corinthians 4:3-6

Background

In the Old Testament and in Jewish understanding in Jesus' day, there were certain visible actual/symbolic signs of God's presence and of the appearance of the Messiah: dazzling light, a cloud, mountain tops, Elijah (see 2 Kings 2:1-12) and Moses appearing.

Mark chapter 8 ended with Jesus talking to his disciples about some of them seeing the powerful Kingdom of God in their lifetime. They will have struggled (as have theologians since) to understand what Jesus meant on that occasion.

Mountain-top experience

A week later, Jesus takes his inner circle of Peter, James and John with him up a mountain (verse 2). Jesus suddenly appears illuminated and radiant to them. The description seems simultaneously extraordinary and mundane. The whiteness is greater than any launderer could manage (verse 3)!

The disciples saw Jesus talking with people they identified as Elijah and Moses (verse 4), which must have left them astonished and with a fresh perspective on their relationship to Jesus! They were definitely B-listers! Peter typically dived in, feeling he ought to say and do something. Fear has strange effects on us all (verse 6). Intense experiences of the divine are typically frightening and shocking. No surprise that the first words of the angels in the Nativity accounts and of the resurrected Jesus were 'Peace! Do not be afraid!'

Peter's reflex response is to try to capture and contain the experience. God seldom works in this way – whether it is manna in the desert, burning bushes or mountain-top encounters, the pattern is always to move on to fresh things and places.

Clarity in the cloud (verse 7)

Almost everyone who has ever done a spot of hill walking or mountain climbing knows what it is like to be suddenly enveloped in cloud. It is eerie and disconcerting, often causing people to lose their bearings. On this occasion, there was a voice, echoing words heard at Jesus' baptism: 'This is my Son, whom I love. Listen to him!' The words seemed directed to Jesus' closest friends, revealing his divinity, the fact that he is loved and worth listening to!

Conclusions (verses 8, 9)

This remarkable episode ended as suddenly as it had begun; the disciples were alone with Jesus again. They tried to make sense of all they had seen and heard, tried to come to the correct conclusions. One can imagine the conversation as they came back down the mountain. Jesus, knowing that it would be natural for them to share this amazing experience with others, did not want them to go off half-baked. For the time being they were to remain quiet. One day, when he 'had risen from the dead', would be the time to speak. This added to the mystery, though having seen Elijah and Moses might have given them a clue about life after death!

Final word

The Transfiguration was and is *mind-boggling*. The glory of Jesus is *dazzling*. The prospect of reunion with those who have died before us is *encouraging*.

Ash Wednesday

JOHN 8:1-11
Psalm 51:1-18; 2 Corinthians 5:20b–6:10

Introduction

If ever there was a day for combining the Gospel reading and the Psalm, today is the day. John's account of Jesus dealing with the woman caught in the act of adultery and David's great prayer of repentance belong together. However, a word of warning! There has always been a danger of making it seem that sexual sins are worse than things like envy, greed, anger, etc. Congregations vary enormously. In some, pride and attaching undue importance to respectability are the besetting sins. (Decide whether to point out that the authenticity of this passage has sometimes been contested. The choice between mercy and judgement has been timeless!)

Honey trap (verses 1-6)

In spy movies and thrillers based on real life, women are used to trap a target. As Jesus' teaching and miracles made him more popular, so he became a threat to the religious leaders. The woman's actions were not contested. The language of the passage sounds as though she had been arrested and paraded in shame. Strange that her male accomplice somehow avoided being detained! Was this opportunism on the part of the Pharisees or, worse still, a set-up? There certainly was no desire for restorative justice or pastoral care. They wanted to try and catch out Jesus on a point of law. 'In the Law Moses commanded us to stone such women' (verse 5).

Conclusion

The story of the woman taken in adultery raises issues of forgiveness. Central to it is Jesus' challenge to her accusers and the onlookers. No one is without sin. All may choose mercy.

First Sunday of Lent

MARK 1:9-15

Genesis 9:8-17; 1 Peter 3:18-end

Introduction

Lent began on Wednesday, so today is the first milestone or staging post on the journey to Holy Week and Easter. People who have decided to fast or give up something as a Lenten discipline should try and keep that to themselves as far as is possible. The Gospel reading is the second part of Mark's prologue. In the space of a few verses, there is a high point of baptism and divine affirmation followed by wilderness for Jesus and prison for John. It finishes with the proclamation of good news.

Starting as he means to go on (verses 9-11)

Throughout his earthly ministry Jesus lived humbly and identified with ordinary struggling human beings. He began the decisive stage of his life by submitting to baptism by John the Baptist. He was baptised in the Jordan river – an unclean river, one of the banks of which was Gentile territory! It was an intense spiritual moment. At most baptisms, there are proud parents looking on. God the Father encouraged and affirmed his Son with words echoing Psalm 2:7: 'You are my Son, whom I love; with you I am well pleased.' Some earthly fathers struggle to speak positive words which their children are desperate to hear. God is not like that – what he does for his Son, he does for his people.

Retreat to advance (verses 12-14)

There was no celebration, no compulsory cake; Mark characteristically informs his readers that 'at once' Jesus felt led or was driven into the wilderness – a place associated with divine encounters and, of course, with a special significance in the history of the Jews. Mark only gives summary information: Jesus was tempted by Satan. From other accounts, we know that Jesus was tested over issues of his identity, his trust, his physical needs and his ambitions – all of which ring bells for

177

ordinary people. He may have been in the wilderness but he had not been cast adrift. God provided spiritual care through angels.

Make-your-mind-up time! (verses 14, 15)

Again a headline verse moves the action on. John the Baptist was imprisoned for denouncing Herod. In God's plan it was time, all the conditions were right for Jesus to begin his ministry, starting with his home region of Galilee. He declared and demonstrated the Kingdom, calling people to believe and to turn back to a godly way of living.

Conclusion

Among the lessons from this reading is the important one for God's people in every age. The journey of faith is frequently marked by highs and lows, joys and sorrows. God is present throughout.

Second Sunday of Lent

MARK 8:31-END

Genesis 17:1-7, 15, 16; Romans 4:13-end

Introduction and context

Chapter 8, particularly Peter's confession of faith (verse 29 'You are the Messiah') that immediately precedes today's reading, is often considered to be the pivotal point of Mark's Gospel. From here on, the mystery of Jesus' full identity is shown more clearly. Part and parcel of this is that Jesus began to speak about his suffering and death. The notion of a suffering, dying Messiah was as shocking as it was incomprehensible to Jewish minds.

Manifesto of rejection (verse 31)

The message up to now had been the good news of the Kingdom, demonstrated by power and authority. Jesus spoke plainly and specifically about what lay ahead for him, and for his followers.

Peter – hero to zero (verses 32, 33)

The reason so many Christians, when asked to name their favourite biblical character, choose Peter is probably because they can relate to the 'one step forward, two steps back' nature of his discipleship. Having been commended for his insight into Jesus' identity, he was rebuked in the strongest of terms for having remonstrated with Jesus over his predictions of conflict, rejection and death. As ever, human perspective is at odds with God's.

Raising the bar – carrying the cross (verses 34-37)

The prospect of following a popular figure who can heal, calm storms, feed multitudes and be the talk of the town may have been an attractive one. There have never been unpalatable terms and conditions hidden away in the small print of the gospel. Jesus made it clear that following him involved the clear acceptance that the going would be tough, costly and demanding. It involves denying one's own interests, desires and ambitions. This is not sugar-coated truth. The implications of responding to his invitation and call could not be greater. 'For whoever wants to save their life will lose it, but whoever loses their life for me and for the gospel will save it' (verse 35). In an age of martyrs and suicide-bombers, it is important to understand this carefully. This was no call to arms. Jesus was inviting people to share his mission, one which was peaceable and selfless.

The challenge was not only to follow. It set out clearly the choice between wanting the temporary, temporal wealth and acclaim of the world over against choosing eternal spiritual well-being (verse 37).

Sting in the tail (verse 38)

The chapter ends with a stern warning. Jesus was never mealy-mouthed: Be ashamed of me now and I will be ashamed of you then (the day of reckoning). This may not sit well with a comfortable church compromised by consumerism but the cost of discipleship was laid out plainly then – and there are no bargain offers on the table now.

Third Sunday of Lent

JOHN 2:13-22
Exodus 20:1-17; 1 Corinthians 1:18-25

Background

This segment frequently wrong-foots people. Readers and hearers of this passage are surprised to find it so early in John's Gospel. They associate it with the last climactic events of Jesus' life, the last few days in Jerusalem because that is how the other Gospel writers present it. This should not undermine their trust in the truth of the account. The evangelists were inspired to arrange the jig-saw pieces of Jesus' life to help their hearers/readers make sense of the great puzzle Jesus presented.

Similarly, it can be tricky to determine the key point of this reading. It has been linked variously with Sunday trading, commercialism and how to behave in church buildings. All these are understandable but they distract from the essential purpose. Jesus was clearly offended by the commercial practices in the Temple and the lack of true spiritual worship but, most of all, he used the confrontation to speak about his impending death and resurrection.

Note

The combination of the Temple, Jerusalem and Passover is the equivalent of a loud notification alarm on a phone – Important Message arriving (verse 13)!

Gentle Jesus, meek and mild? (verses 14-16)

Any sense that being a follower of Jesus equates to niceness personified is firmly kicked into touch by these verses! Jesus' indignation leads to direct action. It is not commercialism *per se* that offends him. It is the fact that the trappings of the sacrifice and temple tax systems have become an end in themselves. People are distracted and in some cases prevented from drawing near to worship. It is quite possible that this unholy market place was in the Court of the Gentiles – though there is a risk in overstating this!

Commentary verse (verse 17)

John comments that the disciples, helped by the Holy Spirit, later recalled and made the connection with words from the Old Testament (see Psalm 69:9).

Who do you think you are? (verses 18-21)

Unsurprisingly and not unreasonably, people questioned Jesus' authority. They asked him for a sign to which his response was effectively: 'You want a sign? I'll give you a sign.' Jesus spoke cryptically, referring to himself as the temple. ('Destroy this temple and I will raise it again in three days.') Of course, for the Jews, the Temple was the focus and locus of the presence of God. The Temple project was nearing completion after nearly half a century of work. It loomed large in every sense in the consciousness of people in everyday life.

Benefit of hindsight! (verse 22)

John inserts another commentary verse into his account. 'After he was raised from the dead, his disciples recalled what he had said. Then they believed the scripture and the words that Jesus had spoken.' This sheds light on how the disciples must have spent the ensuing years recalling and debating together the significance of Jesus' words and actions. It is also a reminder that faith usually grows and deepens with time and reflection.

Final thought

Jesus' followers are always 'works in progress'.

Fourth Sunday of Lent

JOHN 3:14-21
Numbers 21:4-9; Ephesians 2:1-10

Introduction

From which Christmas carol do the words 'Light and life to all He brings' come? While it may be straining the memory to turn the clocks back to mid-winter – that phrase summarises the message of all three of today's set readings. (The answer, of course, is 'Hark, the herald'.) The Gospel reading includes, arguably, one of the most popular Bible verses. As Easter approaches, a lesson from the wilderness wanderings remind us that the mission of God is one of rescue, salvation and wholeness. It is worth remembering that these verses are taken from the end of Jesus' conversation with Nicodemus, the Jewish leader who came to Jesus by night.

Strange tale – strange allusion (verses 14, 15)

The Gospel reading opens with a reference to an event from the Old Testament which, to the modern mind, may seem strange and smacking of superstition. John likens the impending death of Jesus (being lifted on a cross) to an episode from Jewish history. The people grumbled at Moses complaining that God had deserted them and wished they were back in Egypt. Consequently, they had to endure an infestation of deadly snakes. In life, we try to make sense of bad things that befall us; cause and effect have a certain appeal! Sensing they were being punished, they pleaded with God who provided a strange equivalent of a serum! Moses modelled a snake, and mounted it on a pole so that those who had been bitten could look at it and survive! People may not realise this is why the image of a snake round a stick is still used as a logo by medical organisations!

There has been much fresh speculation and debate in recent years over how the Cross 'works'. A remedy for snake bite may not add much by way of clarification. Perhaps the lesson to underline is the headline one – God wants to give eternal life and wholeness to people.

Love – not condemnation (verses 16-18)

It is a tragedy, and a travesty of the gospel, if people get the idea that God is vengeful and negative. These famous verses emphasise that God's motive was love and his intention was to give eternal life. This is the Divine Imperative; the mission of Jesus is summed up.

Light and darkness (verses 19-21)

It is worth reminding people, who may struggle with references to 'condemnation and rejection', that effect or consequence is sometimes expressed in terms that make it sound like purpose. The thrust of this passage is that God's desire is for people to enjoy living lives that are in the light – open and honest, illuminated by him. Sadly, it has always been the case that some (all of us at times) prefer darkness to light. Lives that seek to live by truth, empowered by love, authenticate and demonstrate the gospel.

Fifth Sunday of Lent

JOHN 12:20-33
Jeremiah 31:31-34; Hebrews 5:5-10

Introduction and context

Today is commonly known as Passion Sunday . . . our attention is turned towards the suffering and death of Christ which are imminent both for us in our calendar and for Jesus in the last stage of his ministry. He was now in Jerusalem. John recounts that Jesus began to speak openly about his death.

Today's reading follows on from Jesus' dramatic entry into the city. Many of the crowd who witnessed him raise Lazarus from the dead were with him. The Pharisees were of the view that they were losing the struggle to suppress and contain Jesus. 'Look how the whole world has gone after him!' (verse 19).

We would like to see Jesus (verses 20-22)

Proof of his universal appeal came in the form of Greeks (presumably Jewish converts) asking to see Jesus. It is a great request with a contemporary appeal – given how often he is obscured by the Church and the unfortunate actions of Christians.

Fruitful dying (verses 23-26)

At first hearing, Jesus' response to being told that people wanted to see him seems slightly left of field – 'The hour has come for the Son of Man to be glorified' – which he followed up with comments about wheat grains falling into the ground. In essence, Jesus was saying: 'They will see me very shortly as I am meant to be seen.' His would be a fruitful death (verse 24). He then moved on to reflect on how difficult it is for people to lay down their life. This was what would be expected of his followers but, in this instance, he seemed to be contemplating his own act of obedient sacrifice. He was convinced that God, his Father, would honour him and subsequent followers, even in the hour of death.

Troubled hearts (verses 27-29)

John records Jesus agonising over the cost of ultimate obedience at this point. This was his Gethsemane moment in brief. He had a clear sense of his destiny and purpose.

Almost in passing there is a lesson for Christians in every age: when our hearts are troubled, we can tell God and others – it is not faithlessness.

At this critical juncture, something supernatural occurred. The disciples and people there heard something. Was it thunder? An angel? Was it God? It is recorded as God responding positively to Jesus' prayer (verse 28a).

The time is here – I will draw all to me (verses 30-33)

Jesus said the voice was for their benefit not his. He reiterated that the decisive time had come. Evil would be defeated through Jesus' death. The cross was a cruel and simple instrument but the 'mechanics' of the Cross are a mystery. Verse 33 is a commentary verse – to show the kind of death he would die. The reading began with a request from Greeks and ends with Jesus declaring that he would draw people from many places and settings to him.

Palm Sunday

MARK 11:1-11
Psalm 118:1-2, 19-end; Philippians 2:5-11

Introduction

The narratives of Palm Sunday are inevitably striking and people are more likely to be familiar with these events than with other incidents in the life of Christ. For this reason, referring to the reading from Philippians chapter 2 in which the humanity and humility of Jesus are emphasised may provide a helpful counterpoint to the Gospel reading.

Are we there yet? (verses 1-6)

Children in the back seats of cars and adults on long plane flights often ask this question. Jesus and his companions will have known the journey to Jerusalem well. At this point they were near. The distance had not been that great but in terms of his ministry they had come a long way. Jesus had left behind him a trail of clues as to his identity, an identity which would be clearly revealed over the next week. He had healed people, raised the dead and taught with authority. Excitement and expectation were mounting among ordinary people.

Jesus delegated the transport arrangements to two disciples. They were sent to borrow a donkey – simply saying who needed it was enough by way of explanation. 'The Lord needs it.'

The crowd's gone wild (verses 7-10)

The events of Palm Sunday were not a second-rate childish enactment of a royal entrance, a pastiche of a victorious king entering his capital – 'We could not afford a white stallion or a red carpet so we used a donkey, our cloaks and palm branches.'

In fact, this was a staged event, worthy of a presidential candidate's PR team! The people's elevated expectations and hopes found expression in words of messianic psalms; prophecy was being fulfilled then and there. They were part of it.

Wait until tomorrow (verse 11)

Jesus entered the city and went straight to the Temple. This was natural for him both as an ordinary pilgrim and as the Messiah aware that the denouement of his mission was about to be revealed. What he saw displeased and disturbed him, but occasionally it is right to put things off until the following day!

Reflection

It may be helpful to give people space to reflect on whether they would have got swept up in the excitement of the crowd. Some people are more expressive and impetuous than others.

Maundy Thursday

JOHN 13:1-17, 31B-35
Exodus 12:1-14; 1 Corinthians 11:23-26
See Year A

Good Friday
See Year A

Easter Day

JOHN 20:1-18
Acts 10:34-43; 1 Corinthians 15:1-11

Evidence that demands a verdict – a claim that requires a response

Introduction

Gatherings of Christians across the world today, even those who usually sit light to any form of liturgy, will share in the Easter shout: 'The Lord is risen – He is risen indeed – Alleluia!' People will be reminded it is a shout – not a whisper or whimper. Jesus is alive, death is defeated. Having begun worship with a response, preachers might use 'Response' as a lens through which to look at the Gospel reading. 'Running' is another lens – some church members enjoy an early morning run – there is no shortage of people running in the Gospel (lovely feet that bring good news?).

Mary Magdalene's first reaction (verses 1, 2)

Mary, a woman with a troubled past, is the first witness to the empty tomb and then to the Risen Christ. Much has been made of the fact that a woman's legal testimony was of little or no standing in that era. Even had she been a man, her evidence would have seemed incredible. The readings from Acts and 1 Corinthians both emphasise the eventual

189

number of witnesses there were to the Resurrection. Mary assumed that unknown people must have opened the tomb and removed the body of Jesus. She ran to Peter and John.

Belief dawns (verses 3-9)

The disciples responded to Mary's news by running to the tomb. John got there first but, perhaps understandably, hesitated to enter the tomb. Peter demonstrated his characteristic impetuosity and went straight in. John records what they both saw in almost forensic detail (verses 5-7). However, it was what they did *not* see that is really important. The body of Jesus was nowhere to be seen.

Not seeing is believing! (verses 8, 9)

John eventually went in and believed. The commentary of verse 9 shows again the gradual nature of faith. The disciples needed time, reflection and the benefit of Pentecost to really grasp the significance of this great miracle.

Gardener's Question Time (verses 10-17)

The disciples went home but Mary Magdalene, in her compounded grief, waited by the tomb. Her reluctance to leave and desire to stay near the 'final resting place' of her Master is a common experience of the recently bereaved. They may find bitter-sweet comfort being near the grave.

Mary was full of questions: 'Why? If only . . .' and so on. She did not recognise Jesus, mistaking him for the gardener until he spoke her name. It was an intimate, shocking and joyous encounter. She naturally wanted to grasp him but he could not let her, for reasons we can only speculate about. He instructed her to tell the brothers and the rest of the followers, many women like herself.

Run, don't walk! (verse 18)

A helpful final reflection might be to ask people whether they think Mary ran or walked to the others (it is not stated). There is a case for either answer! Jesus was alive!

Second Sunday of Easter

JOHN 20:19-END

Acts 4:32-35; 1 John 1:1–2:2

Introduction

The Sunday after Easter has been commonly known as Low Sunday – an ecclesiastical version of 'After the Lord Mayor's Show'. It is a misnomer, as the Gospel readings today and over the next few weeks continue to recount Jesus' resurrection appearances. Let the celebrations continue.

Gifts in place of fear (verses 19-23)

Understandably, the disciples met behind locked doors. They feared the authorities and were disturbed by news that Jesus was alive. A hallmark of Jesus' appearances is that he spoke Peace (Shalom) to them (verses 19, 21, 26). This mirrors the greetings of peace that angels brought to startled people immediately before his birth. Gifts: peace, joy, forgiveness and the Holy Spirit.

Honest Thomas (verses 24-29)

If Low Sunday is a misnomer, so is Doubting Thomas. It was not unreasonable or faithless of Thomas to question the reports he heard from the other disciples, 'We have seen the Lord!' Dead men do not, as a rule, rise from the dead. John had recorded earlier in the Gospel how Thomas was prepared to face death with Jesus (11:16). Thomas had also shown that he was prepared to say if he did not understand things: 'Lord, we do not know where you are going, so how can we know the way?' (14:5). We know that other disciples doubted too. Having laid down his pre-conditions of touch and sight, he was of course confounded to see Jesus appear a week later. Confronted by Jesus, who clearly wanted to meet him at his point of need and disbelief, Thomas was quick to respond: 'My Lord and my God!' (verse 28). Jesus' comment in verse 29 about those who believe without seeing being blessed, links to words in his so-called High Priestly prayer about future disciples (John 17:20).

So that by believing you may have life (verses 30, 31)

These two commentary verses make clear the scope of Jesus' miraculous signs and the purpose of their being recorded.

Conclusion

Most Christians face Thomas moments in their journey of faith, either at the beginning ('Is it true?') or along the way when facing tests and difficulties ('Is it possible that God will help me/be with me?'). As was the case with Thomas, it is encouraging to know that God wants to meet us at our point of doubt and need.

Third Sunday of Easter

LUKE 24:36B-48

Acts 3:12-19; 1 John 3:1-7

Context

Today's Gospel reading follows on directly from Jesus' appearance to two of his followers on the road to Emmaus. They return post-haste to Jerusalem to tell the Eleven and others the news.

The 'Thomas tests' (verses 36-43)

The Gospel reading a week ago focused on Thomas' encounter with the risen Jesus. These few verses confirm that Thomas was not alone in wrestling with disbelief (verse 38). Jesus appeared, they were all frightened, he bade them peace and asked why they were struggling to believe. Newly bereaved people often think they can see their loved one. Claims of sightings of ghosts and other paranormal phenomena are not uncommon. Luke's account shows that Jesus was at pains to demonstrate he was not a ghost, even eating a piece of fish (verses 42, 43). Note that it was not doubt that stopped them fully grasping what was going on – joy and amazement were part of the mix (verse 41)!

Explanation – I told you so (verses 44-47)

Only occasionally during Jesus' earthly ministry prior to the Cross did the penny drop for some of the disciples. Afterwards they began to learn so much. In this encounter, Jesus began to teach them, 'This is what I told you . . .' He made it clear that the events they had been seeing were part of a long-standing Divine plan (verse 44 – NB. Note the prophetic nature of the Psalms). Jesus also speaks about the extent of the Christian mission that would unfold (verse 47). Later, when the apostles were at the heart of the controversies over new Gentile believers, they may well have recalled Jesus' words on this occasion.

Commission and a promise (verses 48, 49)

Jesus spelled out what they were experiencing. They were witnesses to the most remarkable events. His words from the Upper Room discourse and other occasions are reiterated. They would receive the promised Holy Spirit in due course. For the moment, they were to sit tight.

Fourth Sunday of Easter

JOHN 10:11-18

Acts 4:5-12, 1 John 3:16-end

Introduction and context

The image and motif of God as a Shepherd to his people, Israel, was strong and long-established. Even people hearing or reading this passage in an urban or suburban setting will have some concept of what a Good Shepherd is like. The first part of John 10 opens up the contrast between the bona fide shepherd and a robber. Sheep recognise the voice of their own shepherd and will follow him rather than an evil-intentioned robber raider. (NB. The reading also has other important points alongside the nature and character of Jesus.)

Good Shepherd contrasted with the hireling (verses 11-14)

Jesus now contrasts himself not with a robber but with a hired hand. A good shepherd shares a much deeper connection with the sheep – they are his. He will not desert them when danger comes; if necessary, he will lay down his life for them. The hired man runs off because at the end of the day it is just a job and he wants to save his own skin. The good shepherd knows his sheep and is known by them. The bond between the shepherd and his sheep, between Jesus and his flock, mirrors the relationship between the Father and the Son.

Other sheep (verse 16)

In the course of time the Early Church would have to wrestle with the issue of Gentile believers, whether Jewish law and customs such as circumcision applied to them. 'I have other sheep that are not of this sheep pen.' Looking back to teachings of Jesus such as this, the disciples realised that the Kingdom of God was to be so much more extensive and comprehensive than they had realised.

On his authority and by his own volition (verses 17, 18)

Obviously, these words were spoken prior to Jesus' death. Speaking prophetically, he was adamant that his life would not be taken from him. He would give it up willingly because of the authority that was his by right. He knew God the Father had commanded him and that his willing obedience met with God's deepest approval. Although not included in the reading today, it is worth noting that, at the time, his words made some people think he had lost his mind or was demon-possessed!

Fifth Sunday of Easter

JOHN 15:1-8

Acts 8:26-end; 1 John 4:7-end

Which reading to preach on?

Some weeks they almost pick themselves. This week preachers are spoiled for choice. The Acts reading about Philip and the Ethiopian official is a wonderful early example of mission and evangelism – it builds on the teaching from last week about Jesus having 'sheep from a different sheep pen' combined with the image of Jesus being like a sheared and ultimately slaughtered sheep! The Epistle from 1 John 4 gives a worked example of what fruitful lives (as per the Gospel) may look like! The vineyard was another well-established Old Testament metaphor representing God's people, Israel. The Song of the Vineyard in Isaiah 5 stands out.

Gardener – God; vine – Jesus; branches – his people

God is the gardener and will prune his vine (verse 2) and cut away dead wood (verses 2, 6). People should resist the temptation to press this analogy too far. People are shaped and changed by experiences in life. There are lessons to be learned in good times and in bad. The crucial point is that God wants his people to live fruitful lives, expressed positively and bearing love. (See 1 John 4).

Jesus is the vine (verses 1, 5), the root-stock and source of life. A single, disconnected branch cannot bear fruit. Jesus used the word 'remain' no fewer than eight times in the space of four verses. Remain close and connected to be a fruitful follower was his clear message.

His followers are the branches (verses 5, 6). Jesus' words imply that remaining in him is a matter of will and choice. In this context, allowing the life-giving and enlivening 'sap' of his teaching seems to be the key to remaining connected to him (verses 3, 7).

Illustration

If you buy roses, shrubs or young trees from a garden centre, they normally come with a diagram of how you should prune and cut your purchase. Keen gardeners will know that different pruning schemes vary significantly.

Sixth Sunday of Easter

JOHN 15:9-17

Acts 10:44-end; 1 John 5:1-6

Introduction: Love on command? Loving commandments.

In this reading, Jesus continues from his teaching about the vine and the branches. It can sound strange to link love and command. This is not love being forced from anyone. True love is freely given and gives freedom. Love has consequences – sometimes bitter-sweet and costly.

Cascading love (verses 9-12)

Organisations sometimes speak of cascading information – here it is as though love is being cascaded. Imagine a champagne fountain from Hollywood films or posh weddings. The Father loved Jesus, Jesus loved him in return and obeyed him, so now his followers are loved by him, should love him back and love each other (verse 12), and so on. The word 'remain', so evident in last week's Gospel, features again. The way to remain rooted in love is to obey Christ's commands. Jesus said that his motive in saying these things was so that the disciples' love would be complete.

Costly love (verse 13)

Love may be given freely but is always costly. Normally, it is bad manners to say how much a gift cost but here Jesus spells it out so that his followers realise how much they are loved. 'You're worth it!'

Changed status (verses 14, 15)

The flow of Jesus' argument runs somewhat like the old game of consequences: The Father loves me so I have loved you, I laid down my life and the consequence is: you are no longer servants, you are friends!

The first move (verse 16)

In most romances and marriages, the people in the relationship normally have a good idea about who took the initiative and made the first move.

It is important for various reasons that people understand that it is always God who makes the first move, sometimes in almost imperceptible ways. Jesus spelled it out. 'You did not choose me – I chose you.' He appointed them to live fruitful lives. This gave them many benefits by way of knowledge, status and authority. This is Christ's legacy. He underscored his teaching by repeating the command that they should love each other (verse 17).

Ascension Day

LUKE 24:44-END

Acts 1:1-11; Ephesians 1:15-end
See Year A

Seventh Sunday of Easter

JOHN 17:6-19

Acts 1:15-17, 21-end; 1 John 5:9-13

Context

The Gospel reading for Ascension Day ended with Jesus blessing his disciples and leaving. Today's reading goes back in time to Jesus' High Priestly prayer. Hearing Christ's intercession for those he was leaving on earth is reassuring. His people were to be protected even as they were commissioned to go out into the world. This is encouraging for his followers today who at times feel misunderstood and who find it hard to be in the world but not of it.

Jesus' prayer at times reads like a cross between an old-fashioned letter of commendation and an end-of-term report. Jesus' mission was nearly accomplished; in fact, he spoke as though it was as good as done.

Jesus summarises what he has done in nurturing the disciples:

- revealed the Father (verse 6)

- given them the Father's words (verse 8)

- protected them by the name the Father gave (verse 12).

He asks for them:

- unity – reflecting the unity of the Father and the Son (verse 11)

- protection in the world from the Evil One (verses 11, 15)

- deep joy (verse 13)

- sanctification – that is, being set apart for God's purpose (verses 17, 18).

While still on earth, Jesus prayed for his disciples and for those who would follow them over the ensuing years. He still prays for his people, as does the Holy Spirit (prayer not being a divine activity but rather a divine attribute). See Romans 8:26, 27, 34. That prayer does not change.

God's people are not to withdraw from engagement with the world, they are to be his instruments and agents of change.

Conclusion

Jesus knew that his death was imminent. Rather as someone who knows his or her time is nearly up puts affairs in order, Jesus in this prayer was laying out what he wanted to be left for his loved ones. He was making provision for them in every sense.

Pentecost

JOHN 15:26, 27; 16:4B-15
Acts 2:1-21; Romans 8:22-27

Introduction

Pentecost, often called the birthday of the Church, is the beginning of the era of mission. Today the reading from Acts is the account of what happened (the Holy Spirit is given) and the reading from John explains what the Holy Spirit does. Many Christians continue to think of and speak about God the Holy Spirit in impersonal terms. Pentecost is always an opportunity to reinforce this important theological point – He, not It!

Pentecost (Acts 2:1-21)

This was a supernatural event, difficult to describe without divine help and intervention (verses 1-4). People from many different places were enabled to hear and understand the disciples in a way that foreshadowed world-wide mission (verses 5-13). Peter preached an inspired sermon explaining that the outpouring of the Holy Spirit was a fulfilment of long-standing prophecy.

John 15:26, 27; 16:4b-15

Jesus knew that his disciples would struggle to accept and understand why he had to leave them. He acknowledged their mystification and grief (verses 5-7).

The term 'Advocate' or 'Counsellor' (15:26) to describe the Holy Spirit may mislead people whose first thought may be about psychotherapists and an analyst's couch! He comes alongside to teach and to comfort. However, he does more than those gentle things. Although sometimes depicted as a dove, he does more than 'coo' over Christians. He challenges and convinces people about wrongdoing and its consequences. The Holy Spirit's work is Jesus-focused. He will speak about Jesus (15:26), bring glory to Jesus (16:14), take and apply Jesus' teaching (16:14, 15).

Illustration

At times in this passage Jesus sounds rather like a parent who is about to leave children in the care of a grandparent. Or again, he is like a popular teacher reassuring pupils at the end of the academic year that their teacher in the following year will be good for them!

Final thought

Jesus promised his disciples that, although they would be separated for a while – there would be a certain reunion.

Trinity Sunday

JOHN 3:1-17
Isaiah 6:1-8; Romans 8:12-17

Ordinary Time resumes on the Monday following the Day of Pentecost. The readings set for each Sunday after Trinity Sunday are known as 'Propers'. They are numbered 3 to 25. Because the number of Sundays after Trinity varies each year according to the date of Easter, preachers should check which Proper is allocated to which Sunday in any given year.

Comment

Trinity Sunday brings pitfalls for preachers. Out of a desire to explain this mysterious theological truth it is easy to stumble into realms of heresy! Most illustrations that well-intentioned priests and ministers have employed over the years can give the impression of modalism (one God in different modes), subordination or relational hierarchy. E.g. H^2O – water, ice and steam; a person who is a father, a son and a brother, etc. Safer by far to emphasise that the terms Father, Son and Holy Spirit are shorthand for God the Father, God the Son and God the Holy Spirit, all having the same nature and attributes. God in three Persons – the Holy Indivisible Trinity. This last title forms part of the formal name of Gloucester Cathedral, no less!

The Gospel reading (or parts of it) set for today has already featured twice in the lectionary readings (Lent 4, weekday after Easter 2) – preachers may therefore want to major on one of the other set readings.

Awesome God – Isaiah 6:1-8

Awesome is an overused and consequently devalued word these days. 'Baked beans for tea! Awesome!' Isaiah's vision was truly awesome and strangely magnificent. He was overcome with a sense of his unworthiness. He was cleansed and then commissioned.

Declared children by Father, Son and Holy Spirit – Romans 8:12-17

Many Christians sometimes feel under-confident about: a) the doctrine of the Trinity – 'it isn't stated in the Bible'; and b) their own standing in God's eyes and place in his family.

These verses show the three Persons of the Trinity intimately, and equally a part of the assurance of what it is to be children of God.

Night class! – John 3:1-17

Nicodemus the Pharisee came to Jesus by night, seeking enlightenment and wrestling with evidence of Jesus' divine nature. Jesus responded to his honest enquiry by introducing him to the concept of being brought alive by God the Holy Spirit (verses 3, 6, 8). Nicodemus was locked into a system of flesh, works and merit. This was hard for Nicodemus and others to grasp (verse 12). Jesus referred to an Old Testament example of God's deliverance (verse 14).

His words recorded in verses 16 and 17 described the interaction and co-operation (in the strict sense of that term) of God the Father and God the Son in their act of salvation.

Conclusion

The 'pulpit prayer' – In the name (NB. singular) of the Father, the Son and the Holy Spirit – may carry additional weight today!

Proper 4

MARK 2:23–3:6

1 Samuel 3:1-10 [11-20]; 2 Corinthians 4:5-12

Sabbath observance – give me a break!

Made for man, not man-made (verses 23-28)

Jesus and his disciples were kept under scrutiny by the religious leaders. Sabbath observance was a regular point of conflict. It is estimated that there were around 365 regulations relating to Sabbath observance in Jesus' day. On this occasion, Jesus and the disciples were walking through cornfields (verse 23). Any rambler or lover of the countryside will know it is important to resist plucking a few ears of corn in such a setting. The local equivalent of the Spanish Inquisition was straight on to it. They asked Jesus to explain and defend his disciples' actions. As far as the Pharisees were concerned, they had engaged in harvesting work (verse 24)!

Jesus seemed to delight in hoisting his critics by their own petard! Knowing they were so-called experts in the law, he regularly asked them rhetorically whether they had read different parts of the relevant Scriptures: 'Have you never read what David did?' (verse 25). Jesus pointed out that David, in extremis, when he was on the run, broke the law and ate consecrated bread with his companions (verse 26). (Companion – literally means one with whom you break bread.) Jesus applied this in the way a lawyer would apply legal precedent. Sabbath was made for man, not vice versa (verse 27). At this stage of his ministry Jesus was challenged regularly as to whose authority he was acting on. He took the opportunity here to state plainly that he, the Son of Man, was Lord of the Sabbath (verse 28).

Healing on the Sabbath? Hands up all in favour! (Mark 3:1-6)

Another Sabbath, another synagogue, another clash. Jesus was centre of attention in the synagogue. His critics were watching him like hawks. A man with a deformed hand was there. It was a healing waiting to happen (verses 1, 2)! Even all these years later, it is possible to feel the tension. Jesus called the man forward (verse 3). Jesus asked his opponents a question which was a 'no-brainer' (verse 4)! They could not and did not answer. In effect, Jesus equated not healing the man with doing evil, and denying life. This was one of many occasions when Jesus felt a powerful mixture of anger and distress when confronted with people's stubbornness and hard-heartedness (verse 5a). Thinking they were obeying God, they were angering him and working against him. They were sincere – sincerely wrong, a mistake any Christian can make! Jesus promptly healed the man (verse 5b). His opponents went away to form an unholy alliance, determined to kill him (verse 6).

Proper 5

MARK 3:20-END

1 Samuel 8:4-11; 2 Corinthians 4:13–5:1

Introduction

Ask people whether they feel their family understand them. Nearest and dearest can love their sons, daughters, siblings, etc. without really 'getting them'.

Misunderstood by his family (verses 20, 21)

Jesus quickly became a darling of the crowds and common people. However, his family were not so impressed. 'He must be mad!' They were on a mission – to take him in hand! Here is encouragement for all whose families consider faith a sign of weakness or madness.

Misrepresented by the religious establishment (verse 22)

The religious leaders, alerted to Jesus' popularity, questioned his motives and authority. They did not contest his claims of healing and deliverance. They accused him of demon-possession.

Divide and rule (verses 23-27)

Jesus resorted to two linked parables to show those with open minds the nonsensical nature of these accusations. He was neither mad nor bad.

Forgiveness and the unforgivable sin (verses 28, 29)

Many congregations have people in them who are anxious that they may have committed the unforgiveable sin. A pastorally helpful rule of thumb is that if someone is worried they may have committed the unforgiveable sin then almost certainly they have not. Preachers should be ready to offer encouragement and reassurance whenever set readings refer to it! In this context, it appears to relate to people who wilfully and persistently ascribe the works of God to the Evil One.

An obedient son (verses 31-34)

The arrival of Jesus' family provided Jesus, ever the opportunist when it came to teaching, to emphasise that obedience to the Father's will was a family trait. This was not a rejection of his earthly family, as is sometimes stated. It must have been hard for his family to grasp the nature of Jesus and his ministry – notwithstanding the insights given to Mary, his mother.

Proper 6

MARK 4:26-34
1 Samuel 15:34–16:13; 2 Corinthians 5:6-10

Introduction

It may be helpful to offer a reminder about the purpose of parables. They were/are not primarily visual aids or aide-memoires. They were riddles, designed to provoke thought and to tease out faith from the original hearers and subsequent readers. (See Luke 8:10 – 'though seeing, they may not see; though hearing, they may not understand'.) Some biblical parables come with an explanation, some do not.

At this time of year, keen gardeners in the congregation will be seeing the fruits of their earlier labours. Today's reading comprises two parables on a horticultural theme to illustrate the nature of the Kingdom of God.

Mysterious unstoppable growth (verses 26-29)

Farmers plant seed, and in so doing unleash a growth process that continues through various stages independent of further action by the farmer (verse 27). Eventually and inevitably, harvest time arrives and the farmer becomes involved again (verse 29).

Jesus frequently linked parables, using the same subject matter, to develop a theme further or even to make a new point.

Mustard seed's prolific growth (verses 30-32)

The Kingdom of God may have small beginnings but there is an inevitability about its growth. The mustard seed is particularly small yet it produces impressive foliage. (Commentators have debated and some church members may want to waste time speculating on what strand of mustard plant Jesus had in mind. The main thing is to keep the main thing the main thing! Try and avoid getting side-tracked.)

Mixed ability teaching (verses 33, 34)

In these commentary verses, Mark records how Jesus pitched his teaching according to the levels of understanding he detected in his hearers at any time. Parables were central to his teaching method, often linked to miraculous signs. His disciples were given an inside track. He explained things to them while the crowds must have been left pondering and puzzling.

Proper 7

MARK 4:35-END
1 Samuel 17; 2 Corinthians 6:1-13

The Old Testament reading is the account of David and Goliath. Fear on the part of Saul and the Israelites is a strand that runs throughout the reading (1 Samuel 17:11, 24, 33). Preachers may want to link this to the fear of the disciples facing the storm.

Mark states in his typical style that this well-known episode on the lake follows on from Jesus teaching the people (verse 35).

Why did the Messiah cross the lake? To get to the other side! (verses 35, 36)

At the end of a busy day, Jesus suggested that they should cross the lake. He seemed keen to get away from the crowd. The disciples 'took him along, just as he was' – tired and drained at the end of a day. There was a little flotilla of other boats with them.

Sudden storm (verses 37, 38)

Apparently with little warning, as can happen in that area, they found themselves facing a storm, serious enough to put the fear of God into seasoned sailors! The little boat was nearly swamped. Jesus slept through the drama. His frightened followers were indignant. Their indignant question, 'Teacher, don't you care if we drown?', was laden with unconscious irony.

Two rebukes (verses 39, 40)

Jesus got up, and rebuked the elements with instant effect. Clearly, he felt that by then the disciples should have had a better grasp of who he was and what he was about. His rhetorical questions, 'Why are you so full of fear? Do you still have no faith?', probably stung them.

Swapping one fear for another (verse 41)

The reading ends with further irony. They had been frightened by the storm. Now they were terrified by seeing Jesus still the storm and were united in amazement at the extent of his authority.

Application

Most people know what it is to face gigantic challenges (Goliath) or to find themselves in unexpected and challenging circumstances (storm). It may be good to allow space for people to reflect quietly on how the readings apply to them.

Proper 8

MARK 5:21-END

2 Samuel 1:1, 17-end; 2 Corinthians 8:7-end

Context

In last week's Gospel reading, Jesus and his disciples were crossing the lake to Gerasa. While there, he healed and restored a man who was demon-possessed. The people had begged him to leave – he was too hot to handle and had damaged the local pork market! The man himself by contrast had begged to be allowed to accompany Jesus. He was left to spread news about Jesus in his home area (Mark 5:20). Today's reading begins with Jesus back in Galilee.

Illustration about structure of reading

The reading features a young girl and an older woman in differing but dire need. The healing of the older woman is sandwiched between two parts of the account of the raising of Jairus' daughter. Each account affects the other. We open one and find another – rather like a traditional Russian doll! Mark once again contrasts fear and faith.

Jairus comes – Jesus goes (verses 21-24a)

Jesus detected faith in people and connected with them as a result. At a point when many people were making demands on him, his heart went out to this religious leader who pleaded with him to come to his daughter. Clearly Jairus knew about Jesus and laid aside any political considerations out of desperation for his daughter.

A desperate woman (verses 24b-34)

In amongst the crowd was a woman who had suffered from a gynaecological condition for over a decade. She had tried everything, spent much and suffered enormously. Her condition was getting worse and, as if that was not bad enough, under Jewish law she was considered ritually unclean. Like Jairus, she had heard about Jesus. The idea of reaching out anonymously to Jesus for healing appealed to her – she had endured enough humiliation already. It was also an expression of raw, desperate faith (verse 28). Her healing was instant (verse 29); not all recorded healings were!

Jesus knew that there had been a powerful encounter with someone. An older version of the Bible expressed it quaintly like this: Jesus knew 'in himself that virtue had gone out of him' (verse 30, King James Bible).

He was not lacking in pastoral sensitivity in trying to identify the recipient of this gracious gift of healing (verses 30b-32). There is an argument that he should have respected her privacy. However, Jesus wanted her to grow in faith (verse 34). He also wanted to see her restored to her place in society, no longer cowering in the shadows, suffering and ashamed. Healing is good, wholeness is better.

Better late than never (verses 35-43)

We can only speculate how Jairus must have felt while Jesus was attending to this woman. He knew time was short and speed was of the essence. His worst fears were realised when men arrived to tell him his daughter had died. They did seem to lack compassion, whereas Jesus encouraged Jairus to hold on to faith (verses 35, 36).

Jesus ignored the news and opinions of the messengers, as well as the grief and derision of those at the house (verses 37-40). With a minimum of fuss, he took the girl by the hand and she revived, returned to life (verses 40-42). This was resuscitation, not resurrection. All whom Jesus brought back to life would die again subsequently.

Everyone was astonished. Jesus had a keen sense of timing and at this stage in his ministry often told people not to spread the news (contrast with the Gerasene demoniac). It must be said that in this regard Jesus seemed a trifle unrealistic; word spread!

Proper 9

MARK 6:1-13

2 Samuel 5:1-5, 9, 10; 2 Corinthians 2:2-10

Sometimes people forget that Jesus' experience of rejection was not limited to the last dramatic days of his life on earth in Jerusalem. It was a feature throughout the three years of his public ministry.

Beware when all speak well of you! (verses 1-3)

Jesus was the talk of the town and the region. His fame and popularity among those whose lives he touched had grown. However, returning to Nazareth and speaking in the synagogue his ratings plummeted. Attitudes towards 'home-town boys made good' are often shot through with ambivalence. People acknowledged and were amazed at his remarkable powers. They speculated as to where he had got such wisdom and authority. They arrived at the conclusion that this could not be right. 'Hang on, we know his family!'

Unbelief has a negative effect (verses 4-6a)

Jesus found the levels of disbelief in his home town amazing! Consequently, he felt himself limited – though verse 5 has an ironic ring. Most communities would probably be delighted with only 'a few sick people healed miraculously'!

It is important that people do not get the erroneous impression that God's sovereignty is compromised or diminished by human failing. God chooses to invite people to cooperate with his sovereign will for the world.

Authority has a positive effect (verses 6b-13)

The second half of the reading stands in deliberate contrast to the first half. Having been rebuffed and limited in his home town, Jesus sent the twelve disciples out on their maiden mission journey. He gave them directions, instructions and, crucially, authority. Their modus operandi was to be simple: travel light, stay local, respond to welcome, preach repentance and offer healing. Simple! (if only . . .).

Their effectiveness contrasts favourably with Jesus in Nazareth. They were probably shocked.

Key point

At this stage in Mark's Gospel, the importance of faith and the difference it makes is being highlighted.

Proper 10

MARK 6:14-29

2 Samuel 6:1-5, 12b-19; Ephesians 1:3-14

Introduction

Preachers may think twice about preaching on the Gospel reading today if the context for their sermon is an all-age or family gathering. Dancing girls, adultery and a gruesome beheading may not sit easily alongside child-friendly action songs! As ever with the Bible, all of life is here! The Epistle reading from Ephesians focuses on the many blessings of being children of God in Christ – albeit with some tricky theology around predestination. There is a sharp contrast with the debauchery and immorality described in the Mark passage. St Paul writes that Christians were chosen in eternity 'to be holy and blameless in his sight' (Ephesians 1:4).

John the Baptist – a prophet without honour (Mark 6:14-29)

When Jesus was rejected at Nazareth he had used the phrase about 'a prophet without honour'. Mark inserts the account of the death of John the Baptist by way of a flashback. John was often viewed as the last in the line of Old Testament prophets and neither sought nor was afforded honour in his lifetime. Preachers may want to remind congregations that the Herod in this episode is not the same King Herod from the Nativity accounts. This is his son who, in his role of tetrarch of Galilee, maintained the family tradition of brutality and corruption.

Speculation (verses 14-16)

News of the miracles performed by Jesus and his followers reached Herod. People were trying to make sense of what they were seeing and hearing. Among the explanations being advanced was the notion that John the Baptist had come back from the dead. This was in line with a Jewish belief that great prophets might reappear.

Ambivalence (verses 17-21)

John the Baptist had been outspoken in condemning Herod's unlawful marriage to Herodias, his brother's wife. Unsurprisingly, Herodias wanted John killed. Surprisingly, Herod found John an engaging and enigmatic character (verse 20).

Execution (verses 21-28)

Women who sing or dance for kings or presidents on their birthday are usually rewarded one way or another! Mark records the circumstances leading to John's death in remarkable detail. It was a notorious event, undoubtedly witnessed by many attending the banquet. 'Do not promise what you cannot, or may not want to, deliver!' is sound advice. Having offered his niece/step-daughter the reward of her choice, Herod could not lose face in front of his guests. He complied with the gruesome request but not without being greatly distressed.

Conclusion (verse 29)

The last line of this flashback shifts the focus forward. John's disciples collected the body and laid it to rest, just as in due time Jesus' sympathisers and secret followers would do.

Proper 11

MARK 6:30-34, 53-END
2 Samuel 7:1-14a; Ephesians 2:11-end

Context

Today's Gospel reading is a natural continuation of the account from Mark 6:13 (the death of John the Baptist breaks the flow of the narrative).

Many of the messianic clues in Jesus' life were loud echoes of how God had led, protected and provided for his people, Israel, in the past, especially in the exodus out of Egypt. The feeding of the five thousand is a classic example.

In the case of this incident, familiarity may breed contempt. People sometimes miss the true significance, just as some of those present originally must have done. A complimentary lunch – end of! Remind people of the saying: 'there is no such thing as a free lunch'. Everything Jesus did and said demanded a response, either by way of a change of thinking or behaviour, or both.

R & R needed but denied (verses 30-33)

The apostles (NB. Rather than 'disciples' as they have been sent out) return, having earned their first ministry stripes. Jesus, as a good leader, recognised that they needed refreshment and rest. He was demonstrating his own habit of 'engage and retire' – a healthy rhythm. The best laid plans of men and messiahs . . . the crowd run around the lake to where Jesus and the disciples landed.

Compassion rules (verse 34)

This is one of several places in the Gospels where the compassion of Jesus is stated explicitly. Simply the sight of large numbers of people, or of a city, could move him deeply. He was the Good Shepherd. Compassion needs to be central to Christian mission, the divine imperative of love. If it is not, it is no more than a recruitment drive, an expression of self-interest.

Work with what you have (verses 35-38)

Jesus responded to the disciples' concern for the people with a challenge: 'You feed them!' He asked them how much food they had found. Five loaves and two fish was the famous reply. In Jesus' hands this would be sufficient.

And the rest is history . . . (verses 39-44)

Mark includes some interesting detail: the grass is *green,* they sat in groups of fifties and hundreds – there was some serious organisation going on! Jesus' actions clearly prefigured those in the Upper Room and on the road to Emmaus: 'looking up to heaven, he gave thanks and broke the loaves' (verse 41). The people who shared in this remarkable meal were completely satisfied. Five thousand fed, twelve baskets of left-overs. This was a Kingdom sign.

Mission gathering momentum (verses 53-56)

Healing was, unsurprisingly, at the forefront of the popular appeal of Jesus' ministry. Word spread like wildfire. The account reads like descriptions of later Christian revivals. Verse 55 has the detail that people '*ran*' throughout the whole region, carrying the sick!

Proper 12

JOHN 6:1-21
2 Samuel 11:1-15; Ephesians 3:14-end

Feeding of the five thousand – second sitting! (John 6:1-13)

People may have a sense of déjà-vu if they followed last Sunday's Gospel reading (Mark 6). Reassure them that it has not been read by mistake. Newspapers still publish Spot the Difference puzzles – they remain popular. John's account of this famous miracle differs or includes additional detail as follows: on a mountainside (verse 3), near Passover (verse 4), Philip was tested (verses 5-7), a boy donated his packed lunch (verse 9). Preachers may choose to concentrate on the second part of the Gospel reading, the account of Jesus walking on water.

Feeding of the five thousand – the sequel! (John 6:14-15)

After the miracle, people concluded Jesus was the Prophet who was destined to come into the world. Religious and patriotic fervour combined, always a heady and dangerous mix, and the crowd intended to make Jesus king by force. Jesus knew this and knew it was not how his Kingdom would come into being. He withdrew to a mountain.

Walking on water (verses 16-21)

Leaving Jesus on the mountain, the disciples headed off across the lake towards their base in Capernaum. It was dark, the wind was strong and the waters rough – the reality then and a familiar metaphor for how life is for many now! Sailors in most cultures through the ages have tended to be superstitious sorts. On seeing Jesus walking on the water towards them, the disciples were terrified. With obvious and powerful echoes of the time when he slept in the boat during a storm, Jesus told them not to be frightened. They calmed down and took him into the boat. In the classic British comedy series

'Dad's Army', two of the best-known catch-phrases were 'We're doomed!' and 'Don't panic!' Before and after the Resurrection, the disciples were frequently frightened. Jesus almost habitually urged his followers to calm down (another comedy catch-phrase) and spoke the greeting-cum-command 'Peace' over them! His followers in every age since have often found themselves sharing a similar exchange with Christ.

Proper 13

JOHN 6:24-35
2 Samuel 11:26–12:13a; Ephesians 4:1-16

Background
A term associated with some approaches to mission is 'rice Christians'. It was used to describe people who were prepared to say they had been converted in order to receive rations of rice. There always has been, and always will be, an element of people adopting Christianity simply because of the prospect of material benefits. Responsible and mature mission gives people an opportunity to consider the cost of following Christ and the implicit challenge of lifestyle change. The free and gracious offer of life is always held in tension with the expectation of an outworking of faith. The works of faith are different from faith/ salvation by works. This is the challenge that Jesus and his followers since have had to confront – namely, the desire of people to earn a relationship with God based on merit.

Give us daily bread! (verses 24-26)
Jesus knew, and did not shrink from saying, that the people were pursuing him because they liked the free meal they had been given. They had failed to appreciate the significance of the miraculous sign.

Adjust your sights (verses 27-29)
Jesus wanted them to see beyond earning their daily crust. Here, as elsewhere, he encouraged his hearers to raise their sights to spiritual issues that had eternal worth. Death and taxes are not the only certainties! Jesus performed signs and wonders and then explained them to inspire faith in, and draw faith from, people. Believing in God was the work he required.

Never satisfied (verses 30-34)
'Give us another one just like the other one!' is a football chant that sums up the attitude of the crowd. They wanted another miracle from

Jesus, by way of reprising the miracle Moses had performed for their ancient ancestors. Jesus told them that then, as in his own time, people failed to appreciate that it was God who sent the bread (verses 32, 33).

I am the Bread of Life (verse 35)

Jesus declares he is the Bread of Life. 'I am' of course had a double sense – being the way God described himself to Moses. This is the real satisfying 'bread'.

Proper 14

JOHN 6:35, 41-51

2 Samuel 18:5-9, 15, 31-33; Ephesians 4:25–5:2

Introduction

By way of continuation, today's Gospel reading begins with the final verse from last week's passage (John 6:35). The interaction between Jesus and the people is still being conducted in the aftermath of the miraculous feeding of the five thousand.

Declaration (verse 35)

Jesus unequivocally declared that he was the bread of life, provided by God from heaven to bring them spiritual satisfaction. He had been sent to bring life to the world.

Objection (verses 41, 42)

Jesus' listeners took offence at this declaration. Their objection was couched in terms reminiscent of those recorded by Mark when Jesus was rejected at Nazareth. They knew his earthly antecedents and so bridled at his claim of having come from heaven.

An aside: Royal Ancient Order of Grumblers (verse 43)

God's people had a long history of grumbling. They had grumbled at Moses in the wilderness. 'Why have you brought us out here to die? At least we had food in Egypt!' Sadly, too many church members over the years seem to have taken on a kind of apostolic succession of grumblers! They are never happy and seem incapable of seeing God's blessings now. It becomes an approach to life. A common conversation is: 'How are you, Mrs X?' 'Oh, you know how it is, Vicar. Mustn't grumble!' They go on to grumble at length. Hear the word of the Lord: 'Stop grumbling!'

Explanation (verses 44-50)

Jesus unpacked this teaching in two ways. First, he stated that the initiative and authenticating call was God's. In doing so, he promised personal resurrection (verses 44, 50). This went almost unnoticed at this point. Secondly, he appealed to their spiritual heritage. He referred to Isaiah 54:13 and the promise that God would teach them (verse 45) as well as to the experience of their forefathers (verse 49).

Repetition (verse 51)

Jesus reasserted that he was the bread of life. He developed the thought by saying that this bread was his flesh which he would give for the life of the world.

Conclusion

At this point in John's narrative, major events and themes are being set up – i.e. Jesus dying, institution of the Eucharist/Communion, Resurrection. To be continued!

Proper 15

JOHN 6:51-58
1 Kings 2:10-12, 3:3-14; Ephesians 5:15-20

Introduction
Again, this week the Gospel reading follows on smoothly from the previous week. The passages interlock like tongued and grooved fence panels or floorboards. The discussion and fall-out about Jesus being the bread of life rumbled on.

Caution
The reading contains phrases and terminology that have featured over the years in discussions about the nature of the Eucharist/Communion and the real/symbolic presence of Jesus. Consequently, it is easy to be distracted. That is not the main thrust of this passage of Scripture.

Bread packed with goodness! (verse 51)
Jesus said he was living bread – provision. He had come from heaven – incarnation. He offered eternal life – resurrection. He would give his life for the world – crucifixion, satisfaction.

Tendency to literalism (verse 52)
Jesus' hearers took him literally: 'How can this man give us his flesh to eat?' They should not be judged too harshly by those who have the benefit of hindsight and New Testament teaching at their disposal. Jesus was using familiar language (God's historic provision of bread to his people, Israel) but applying it in a new and mysterious way. However, it is fair to say that the tendency to take things literally when speaking of spiritual realities has always been an obstacle to true understanding.

Flesh and Blood (verses 53-58)
John tells his readers that this is an extract of Jesus' teaching in the synagogue at Capernaum (verse 59). Jesus was clearly determined to

drive his point home. This teaching was fundamental to what would follow. In this regard, he resembles a later 'old school' preacher: 'First I tells them what I am going to tell them. Then I tells them. Then I tells them what I've told them!' Using his favoured term for describing himself, Son of Man, he reiterated his exclusivity (verse 53), the promise of resurrection and eternal life (verse 54), the reality of God's provision (verse 55).

The language, as we have seen, became even more Eucharistic (verse 56). Jesus' reasoning was that those who feed on him will live because he (Jesus) is sent and nourished by the Father (verse 57). He then appealed to their literal and spiritual heritage – in this context, 'bloodline' might even be appropriate (verse 58).

Conclusion

In John's narrative, this extended teaching following the feeding of the five thousand is a pivotal point in Jesus' ministry.

Proper 16

JOHN 6:56-59

Joshua 24:1-2a, 14-18; Ephesians 6:10-20

Introduction

The Gospel reading is very short, only four verses, three of which were in last week's reading! This marks the end of a few weeks spent in John's Gospel, unpacking the significance of Jesus' bread of life teaching following the feeding of the five thousand. Next week the scheme of Gospel readings switches back to Mark. There is a case for majoring on either of the other two principal readings. The Epistle from Ephesians 6 about taking on the whole armour of God works as a stand-alone passage. All-age congregations in successive generations have usually been happy to see a volunteer dressed in armour or cricket/hockey protective clothing. The key teaching point is to wear the *whole* armour rather than getting too quasi-technical about what each piece means!

There is a logical and natural link between the John reading and the Old Testament reading from Joshua. Jesus' teaching about being the bread of life and giving his life for the world was very hard for people to understand. What is more, those who did begin to grasp its meaning found it hard to accept (John 6:60, 66): 'From this time many of his disciples turned back and no longer followed him.'

Make your mind up time (Joshua 24:14-18)

This Old Testament reading records one of many times when God's people, the Jews, had been challenged to make a choice, to be decisive about following God in a way that made a difference to how they lived. Their appointed leader Joshua (Moses' successor) had gathered all the tribes together (verses 1, 2). He knew he was nearing the end of his life (Joshua 23:14) and wanted to prepare them accordingly, much as Jesus did with his disciples. In every age and generation, there is the temptation for God's people to compromise and to be more shaped by the surrounding culture than to shape it! Joshua was as unequivocal in setting out the choice they faced as Jesus was in his day. Joshua framed his challenge in terms of two choices. He exhorted them to choose to serve God without compromise and syncretism. If people were not inclined to serve the Lord, then they should choose whom they would serve. Life cannot be lived in a vacuum. As a Nobel prize-winning song writer and poet once said, 'You're gonna have to serve somebody' (from the *Slow Train Coming* album).

Even though he was nearing the end of his life, Joshua was prepared to lead by example: 'But as for me and my household, we will serve the Lord.' *(Author's note: My son Joshua has this verse tattooed across his back, including the biblical reference!)*

Proper 17

MARK 7:1-8, 14, 15, 21-23
Song of Solomon 2:8-13; James 1:17-end

No one expects the Jerusalem Inquisition (verses 1, 2, 5)

As Jesus' popularity grew, so he and his followers became subject to scrutiny from the establishment, the leaders in Jerusalem. 'Is this guy kosher?' This is something advocates of changes and people who appear not to honour tradition have faced in most walks of life through the ages. Then, when an opinion is reached, attempts to discredit usually follow. Jesus' itinerant band apparently did not observe the customary rituals of hand-washing before meals.

Note: commentary verses (verses 3, 4)

These are aimed at a non-Jewish audience in the early Church, explaining Jewish practices and customs.

Illustration

In many households, people are summoned to the table in these, or similar terms: 'Dinner's ready. Wash your hands and go to the loo if you need to!'

Jesus pulled no punches! (verses 6-8)

Jesus countered their accusatory questions in no uncertain terms. In challenging him over a question of Jewish law, they had given him a stick with which to beat them. He accused them of hypocrisy, quoting the prophet Isaiah. They had lost sight and let go of God's commands in favour of human traditions (verse 8). Worse still, they did this for their own ends.

Internal versus external (verses 14, 15, 20-23)

Attend to internal spiritual issues rather than external matters of show, was a theme that ran through Jesus' encounters with the religious leaders. It remains a challenge to believers today.

Jesus' words to the leaders mostly fell on deaf ears, so he directed his teaching to the ordinary people. At the risk of being basic, he stated emphatically that 'uncleanness' in God's eyes was a matter of the heart, mind and soul. Jesus was no starry-eyed idealist. He was realistic about the thoughts and behaviour of people and the depths to which they could sink.

How much easier to talk about ceremonial details or theological theories than about the nitty-gritty of our private lives, our business practices or our secret thoughts!

Conclusion

Given the note on which the reading ends, it may be wise to allow a little more time for personal reflection before moving on.

Proper 18

MARK 7:24-END

Proverbs 22:1, 2, 8, 9, 22, 23; James 2:1-10, 14-17

Context

Miracles were signs of God's Kingdom in and of themselves. In the Gospel accounts, the placing of particular types of miracle means they take on extra significance. In last week's Gospel, it became clear that most of the Jewish leaders were deaf to Jesus' radical teaching about the way they applied the law. Mark follows that encounter with accounts of Jesus healing a Gentile woman's daughter and a man who was deaf and mute. The Epistle reading from James addresses the issue of favouritism. It obviously connects with Jesus' encounter with the Syro-Phoenician woman.

A faithful and savvy mother (verses 24-30)

Jesus sounds like a modern-day celebrity trying to escape the paparazzi. He could not keep his presence secret even away from his home area (verse 24). Parents of children who are sick and suffering will do anything to get help for their child. It may be hard for some listeners today to understand how a child could be possessed by an evil spirit. Certainly, the symptoms of some described in the Bible might lead modern medics to come to a different diagnosis. However, the little girl was indisputably troubled and her mother begged Jesus for help, based on what she had heard of him (verse 26).

There are not many times when Jesus was hesitant to respond to a request (e.g. the wedding at Cana) and, in this case, it seems strange (verse 27). Jesus did have a sense of his ministry being first to the house of Israel. The woman's quick-wittedness, implying insight that non-Jews could be beneficiaries of his ministry, impressed Jesus (verses 28, 29). She took Jesus at his word and on returning home found her daughter well. Reflecting on how she might have been on her walk/run home may be fruitful for people.

Healed dumb man told to say nothing! (verses 31-36)

There is a delightful irony in this account – worthy of a local newspaper headline writer. Jesus moved on into another area and still the requests for healing kept coming (verses 31, 32). On this occasion, the case history and diagnosis were more straightforward. The way Jesus treated this man is worth noting and holds lessons for caring professions and intercessors alike today. He respected his privacy and took him aside from the crowd. On this occasion, Jesus used actions (touch and spittle) specifically related to the presenting condition. At other times he healed remotely. Jesus sighed deeply which may be taken as a sign of compassion or intensity of prayer. The instruction 'Be opened' is redolent with meaning and significance, literal and metaphorical (verses 33-35). People were predictably amazed and approving. It was almost as if Jesus was employing reverse psychology. The more he told them not to broadcast news of the healing, the more people talked about it.

Application

How ready are people to bring their concerns for those they love to God? How ready are they to talk about good news when it happens?

Proper 19

MARK 8:27-END
Proverbs 1:20-33; James 3:1-12

Background

Peter's confession of faith is a major milestone in Mark's Gospel. From here, the action and Jesus' actual journey headed towards Jerusalem and the denouement of his ministry. Jesus began to speak openly about his impending death. In the course of this reading, Peter goes from hero to zero!

The penny drops for Peter (verses 27-30)

Eager, loyal Peter was given the insight to realise who Jesus was. 'You are the Messiah.' How pleased he must have felt. Often insecure about other disciples, he is the first to answer Jesus' question.

Illustration

Children go through a stage when they are desperate to answer a question. They squirm and squeal with their hand in the air, desperate to answer. As they grow older, they become more cagey and reticent in case they get it wrong. Recognising the identity and status of Jesus was important then and is important now. Jesus wanted the disciples to be clear for themselves about the answer – not simply to go with what the crowds said. Jesus still did not want this spread around at this point.

Reality bites (verses 31-33)

Jesus began to spell out what was going to happen to him. It is not clear whether this followed on immediately from the question about his identity. If not, it was certainly soon after. Peter, having been commended for his earlier response, was stung by Jesus' response to his rebuke. The idea that the Messiah would be rejected and killed was nonsensical, a contradiction in terms from a human point of view. Peter seemed to miss the reference to resurrection.

Raising the bar (verses 34-38)

Up to then, it must have been an attractive prospect to be associated with this popular healer/preacher. Jesus did not hide the cost of discipleship in the small print, any more than God does now. People today are used to the phrase 'Terms and Conditions apply' about competitions, special offers and purchases. Jesus told the crowd that following him meant carrying their own cross. The full significance of that phrase would not have become apparent till later. The paradox of losing one's life to save it is as challenging today as it was then. Similarly, the issue of what really matters is timeless. The reading ends with a reference to being ashamed of Jesus and his teaching. This is even more striking because of Peter's subsequent denial.

Illustration

A local journalist approaches a vicar at the cemetery after the funeral of a well-known very rich man. 'Hey, Vicar, how much did he leave?' 'All of it!' responds the vicar.

Proper 20

MARK 9:30-37

Proverbs 31:10-end; James 3:13–4:3, 7, 8a

Introduction

Internet users are very familiar with quizzes and features asking them to choose their greatest cricket captain, footballer, comedy series, singer, etc. It appears that people love the process of ranking people and items. Similarly, most people are aware of the so-called pecking order in their family, friendship group or place of work. It is an unattractive trait that many use to establish their sense of worth.

Return to base – back to basics! (verses 33, 34)

On returning to Capernaum, which in many ways was their ministry base, Jesus challenged the disciples. He knew they had been arguing as they walked along the road. He probably had a good idea what it had been about but wanted to hear it from their own mouths. Rather pathetically, they had been arguing about who was the disciple with the mostest!

Not a tip for the top! (verse 35)

Although Jesus began by saying, 'if anyone wants to be first', he was not trying to stoke ambition or competition among his trusted band. He wanted them to grasp that the nature of leadership in his upside-down Kingdom would be the opposite of conventional worldly wisdom. True leadership was to be found in a willingness to serve the others. This, of course, was a lesson he hammered away at, right until their last night together.

Making an example of a child . . . in the nicest possible way (verses 36, 37)

Picture the scene – the disciples are sitting down (verse 35) and Jesus places a child standing in their midst. The disciples would have been on a level with the child if not having to look at him/her.

A supplementary (verses 36, 37)

Having made his point about servant leadership, Jesus did something which he often did. He took the opportunity to make an additional related point. Some cultures (e.g. Korea) have a heightened sense of regard for elders – not in itself a bad thing. By stressing the importance of welcoming a child, Jesus is effectively overturning established notions of seniority, honour and worth. He links this directly to welcoming God the Father.

Proper 21

MARK 9:38-END
Numbers 11:4-6, 10-16, 24-29; James 5:13-end

For and against (verses 38-41)

John reports that the disciples had told a man to stop casting out demons in Jesus' name because he was not part of their specific band. This has the ring of a modern-day copyright or franchising dispute. The disciples must have been surprised and possibly even crestfallen to hear Jesus take a pragmatic approach. The 'rogue' exorcist should not be stopped, according to Jesus, because he was using Jesus' name. This was not branding, nor was 'in Jesus' name' an abracadabra magic spell. Instead it showed the intention of the man. Whether the act being done in his name was a dramatic exorcism or simply giving a cup of water, it was to be commended if done in Jesus' name.

Child protection

Verse 42 seems to link back to verses 36 and 37 from last week's reading when Jesus had stood a child among the disciples. It is universally accepted, if not practised, that one should not be hurt. In western culture, there is a widespread sense that children are being deprived of their innocence. It is noteworthy that Jesus' stern warning was aimed at people who might cause children who believed in him to sin.

Take sin seriously (verses 43-48)

Taken out of context and/or applied literally, these verses are harmful. Applied literally, it would mean that most Christians would soon be mutilated wrecks! Of course, it is preferable to emphasise God's love, forgiveness and grace, and yet Jesus made it clear that destructive behaviour and corrosive habits need to be addressed.

Salt and shake (verses 49, 50)

The account of the teaching at Capernaum ends with Jesus making two salt-themed comments. Having issued a warning about judgement, his comment about being 'salted with fire' has the sense that everyone needed refining by fire – an Old Testament theme, as seen in today's related reading from Numbers.

Finally, Jesus refers briefly to salt and how its saltiness can be lost (verse 50), the suggestion in this context being that disputes between people sap the flavour of the salt. This section having begun with Jesus bringing the disciples' argument out into the open (9:33), it closes with Jesus urging them to be at peace with one another.

Proper 22

MARK 10:2-16

Genesis 2:18-24; Hebrews 1:1-4; 2:5-12

Caution – special pastoral sensitivity required

Preachers will need to tread particularly carefully this week. The first part of the Gospel addresses the thorny and painful subject of divorce. Most congregations will include people who have been through the pain of breaking relationships and marriages. Some may well have been made to feel bad by other people, including the Church in the past. Others may still be beating themselves up for their perceived or actual mistakes. The Epistle, especially Hebrews, presents the notion of Christians being in a family relationship with Jesus and each other – a family that, in theory, is better than many earthly families. Sermons are not always the best way for a congregation to explore subjects such as this.

Important background context

It has been suggested that there is evidence of Jewish men abusing the provision of writing a bill of divorce to avoid accusations of adultery. It was a classic case of men circumventing the law by using a loophole. Summarily divorcing the wife before entering a new relationship got them off the hook. The approach to divorce was probably an issue of the day. These Pharisees were using the 'hot potato' topic of divorce to test Jesus' attitude towards the law. Theirs was not a pastoral concern. It is more than likely that they were trying to entice Jesus into making a pronouncement about divorce that could be relayed to Herod. Any discussion about divorce in that region would be interpreted in the light of John the Baptist having been arrested and executed for challenging Herod's marriage to his brother's wife.

Jesus and the divorce test (verses 2-12)

Knowing he was being tested and almost certainly knowing what his questioners believed, Jesus met their question with one of his own.

He often did this (verse 3). The Pharisees immediately quoted the Mosaic provision of divorce. Jesus then pounced on their understanding of how that should be applied, for therein lay the real issue. God is the ultimate realist – so permits divorce because of the frailties of human nature (verse 5). Jesus reminded them of this and then went on to show that God is also the ultimate idealist. His ideal is that covenant relationships such as marriage should last and not be broken. They certainly should not be dismissed and ended lightly on a man's whim. Jesus referred them to the book of Genesis (as per the Old Testament reading) and the foundation there of human relationships (verses 6-9).

Divorce should not be used casually (verses 10-12). The disciples questioned Jesus further. He wanted them to grasp that a bill of divorce did not essentially alter the underlying issue. He was addressing specifically the abusive practice of relying on a piece of paper and a brief legal act to justify wrongful and destructive behaviour – i.e. adultery and cheating on marriage partners.

Children should know their place!! (verses 13-16)

Given the difficulty of the preceding verses, preachers and congregations alike may feel the relief of walking on level ground after slogging up a steep ascent. The place of children is centre stage. Again, Jesus' disciples got it wrong and were reprimanded. The Kingdom belongs to them because it is a legacy to them and because their qualities of uncomplicated trust, innocence and openness are key Kingdom qualities. Jesus made it clear to his adult audience that they needed to learn from children how to receive.

Proper 23

MARK 10:17-31

Amos 5:6, 7, 10-15; Hebrews 4:12-end

Introduction

The Gospel reading is a well-known passage. Over the years, people may have thought that it is anti-riches *per se*. They may fear that authentic discipleship implies a compulsory vow of poverty. In British and American congregations, most people will be able to identify others better off than themselves and quietly excuse themselves! In a global context, most congregations in the developed nations qualify for the tags 'rich' and 'rulers', if not 'young'! All of this is to miss the point. In the case of the rich young ruler the issue was not that he had money – it was that money had him!

This guy is for real (verses 17-20)

Unlike many who approached Jesus to question or trap him, this young man seemed genuine in his request and his desire. Probably having heard Jesus teach about simplicity of faith and life while blessing children, he wants to know how to inherit eternal life ('What must I *do*?'). Jesus picked up on his use of the term 'good' in addressing him. The gaining of eternal life through religious obedience to the law was a live issue of the day. Effectively, Jesus' response is to say: 'Ultimately goodness is unattainable – only God is truly good. If you want to know what to do – look at the laws.' The young man's answer that he had kept the law since he was young seemed to be accepted at face value by Jesus.

Switch currency (verses 21, 22)

Jesus warmed to this man. He invited him to join the band of disciples and follow him – not something he did regularly. However, the young man had to overcome a personalised selection test. He first had to go and sell his belongings and give the proceeds to the poor. This was too great an ask for the young man. His face fell. It is important to note

Jesus did not run after him to offer a sweeter deal. 'Look, old boy, I'm sure we can put your wealth to good use. Have you heard of Gift Aid?' In this man's case, Jesus knew material wealth was an obstacle to radical and wholehearted discipleship.

You cannot be serious! (verses 23-27)

Jesus looked around (verse 23) and the look on his disciples' faces must have said it all. They had just watched Jesus allow a potential key donor to walk away unsigned! Jesus told them not once but twice (verses 23, 24) that wealth carries a spiritual health warning. The root of the disciples' astonishment was the prevailing Jewish understanding that good fortune was a sign of God's blessing, whereas illness or poverty was a sure sign of sin somewhere in the family line. This view was and is materialistic and mechanistic. What is more, it is still prevalent among some Christians in a materialistic culture. Jesus was calling for a massive change of mindset, one that seemed impossible to his hearers (verse 26). They would need God's help (verse 27). The phrase 'All things are possible with God' is a) true, b) a wonderful soundbite, c) sometimes applied out of context so that it becomes a nonsense!

What's in it for us? (verses 28-31)

Peter's observation recorded in verse 28 may have sounded plaintive and had a note of panic. It certainly showed that Jesus' disciples would not find it easy to shrug off their old religious and cultural assumptions. They had already made sacrifices to follow him. More would be required of them in the future. Jesus reassured Peter and the others that they would not feel short-changed. He wanted them to grasp that the old order of things would be overturned in his Kingdom. The last, the lost and the least would come into their own.

Proper 24

MARK 10:35-45
Isaiah 53:4-end; Hebrews 5:1-10

Introduction

One way of beginning today is to ask the congregation which of the following they would choose to express frustration: 'I don't believe it!' in the style of TV character Victor Meldrew in *One Foot in the Grave*, put their head in their hands, or exclaim/motion facepalm? The Gospel begins with Jesus having to deal with James and John making a play for special privilege. Given how often he had spelled out and demonstrated servant leadership, Jesus could be forgiven for resorting to one or all of the above expressions of despair!

A quiet word (verses 35-37)

James and John, members of the inner twelve from day one, approached Jesus quietly. They are looking for special treatment and reward. In Matthew's parallel account, it is their mother who makes the request (Matthew 20:20-28). She might be imagined like a typical Jewish mother in a Woody Allen film. Other people like parents, teachers and sports coaches can sometimes be more ambitious on behalf of someone than the person themself. This can be an unwelcome burden.

Be careful what you ask for! (verses 38, 39a)

Jesus' response seems measured. The disciples generally were prone to trying to run before they could walk. There was so much they yet had to witness, experience and learn. Even though Jesus prefaced his question to them about whether they could share in his sufferings with the observation, 'You don't know what you are asking', the brothers were adamant they could. Their response had echoes of some of the boasts that Peter made. Self-awareness and humility are important traits for followers of Christ.

You will – I can't! (verses 39b, 40)

Although the significance of Jesus' response would have been lost on them at the time, James and John would in time share in his sufferings as predicted. Jesus then made it clear that positions in his Kingdom were not up for grabs to be earned. There would be no post-Ascension honours list!

It's all kicked off again (verses 41-45)

Unsurprisingly, the other ten disciples were angered by the brothers' power-play. It is unlikely that their indignation sprang from a sense of frustration that the pair had not yet learned the lesson about servant leadership. More likely, they were worried that they might have got one over on them. Jesus called for a time-out and sat them down to give them a talking-to. He pressed the same point home in two ways. First, he contrasted notions of power in the world with how he wanted it to be among his followers (verse 42). Then he offered himself as a clear example of servant leadership – 'For even the Son of Man did not come to be served, but to serve, and to give his life as a ransom for many.' This was important leadership training.

Proper 25/
Last Sunday after Trinity

MARK 10:46-END
Jeremiah 31:7-9; Hebrews 7:23-end

Introduction and context

In the immediate prelude to Jesus triumphantly entering Jerusalem (chapter 11), Mark recorded, in what is now chapter 10, different groups of people interacting with Jesus: scheming Pharisees, parents and innocent children, a rich young man and two ambitious disciples. He then ended the section with Jesus healing blind Bartimaeus. He is hoping his readers are opening their eyes.

Obstacles come down where walls once fell! (verses 46-50)

Jesus, his entourage and a large crowd were leaving the historic city of Jericho. A blind beggar named Bartimaeus heard it was Jesus and then did his utmost to be heard by Jesus. 'Jesus, Son of David, have mercy on me!' He may have been blind but apparently he had spiritual insight, judging from the Messianic title he used to address Jesus. People told him to be quiet in no uncertain terms. How could a blind beggar be worthy of Jesus' time? In the same way that he had insisted that children be brought to him for blessing, Jesus commanded that Bartimaeus be brought to him – 'Call him!'

What good news it must have been when suddenly those who were scolding him one minute were telling him to get on his feet the next! Bartimaeus needed no second invitation – the detail that he threw aside his cloak reinforces the sense of this being an eye-witness account (verses 49, 50).

Unnecessary question (verses 51, 52)

Having called Bartimaeus to him, Jesus then asked him what he wanted. One can imagine Peter standing behind him, urging Jesus to look at the man's eyes. It is not as if he was going to hold up his finger and say something like, 'Please can you help with this splinter, I can't see!' Of course, Jesus was being neither slow nor pastorally insensitive. This is another example of Jesus giving people the opportunity to articulate fledgling faith. Jesus responded to Bartimaeus' uncomplicated expression of faith. He healed him and commanded him to go on his way. Unsurprisingly, he chose to follow Jesus.

All Saints' Day

JOHN 11:32-44

Isaiah 25:6-9; Revelation 21:1-6a

Introduction

All Saints' Day is, understandably, a day for looking back and gratefully remembering the faithful souls who have gone before. In doing so, there is an implicit encouragement to look 'up and forward' to heaven. The New Testament reading (Revelation 21) provides a wonderful picture of heaven, where God's presence assures that all is made new. Like the Isaiah reading, it contains the promise that God will one day wipe away every tear. This note of comfort is important on a day when people may bear poignant memories of their own loved ones.

Context

The Gospel reading is a segment of the account of the death of Lazarus at Bethany. It is worth sketching out the first part of this event, not least because Jesus' statement about being 'the resurrection and the life' (John 11:25) is fundamental to the way in which All Saints' Day is commemorated.

Lord, if only . . . (verses 32-37)

The reading takes up the account at the moment when Mary went out to where Jesus had been comforting her sister Martha. Her first words to Jesus were the same as those Martha had used: 'if you had been here, my brother would not have died' (verse 32). It is likely that the sisters had said as much when Lazarus had fallen ill and subsequently died. It is a common expression of early grief to express blame and to rehearse a litany of 'if only's. These are usually directed to other people but sometimes they are turned on the mourner or even on the person who has died. In this case, a similar note of blame was voiced by other mourners and onlookers (verse 37). Even though he knew what he planned to do, Jesus was moved with compassion for his friends (verse 33) and genuinely mourned for Lazarus (verses 35, 36).

Funeral wrecker (verses 38-44)

Jesus disturbed the arrangements for every funeral he ever attended – including his own! The way in which Jesus instructed people to remove the stone from the grave, the details about the grave clothes and the stench of death all deliberately prefigure Jesus' own imminent death and burial. As Jesus implied in his comment to Martha, this was a glimpse of the glory of God. It may be worth reminding people that naturally Lazarus would one day die a second time. This was a miracle of resuscitation, not resurrection. As the final miracle before the entry into Jerusalem, it set things up 'nicely' for the inevitable confrontations with the authorities in the city.

Third Sunday before Advent

MARK 1:14-20
Jonah 3:1-5, 10; Hebrews 9:24-end

Introduction

Today's Gospel reading takes congregations back to the beginning of Jesus' ministry and the call of the first disciples. The weeks following Trinity Sunday have followed, through the Gospel readings, the journey of Jesus and his disciples, particularly their growth in understanding. Today, the readings begin to prepare us for Advent and for marking afresh the birth of Christ.

Taking up the call (verses 14, 15)

Humanly speaking, the arrest of John the Baptist acted as a catalyst to Jesus. Having been baptised by John and tempted in the desert, Jesus now went around Galilee. His message was couched at first in very similar terms to that of John the Baptist. It was a call to repentance and an announcement of good news.

Immediate response (verses 16-18)

At first reading, hearing the alacrity with which Andrew and Simon Peter responded to Jesus' call can seem both inspiring and unrealistic. How unstable does someone have to be to leave their work, home and family instantly to follow a total stranger? Additionally, Jesus himself later told people to count the cost of following him before embarking on something they could not fulfil. Fortunately, John 1:35-42 gives a wider perspective. Andrew was already a disciple of John the Baptist when he met Jesus. Undoubtedly, he and Peter, and probably their wider family group, would have discussed the prospect of the coming Messiah. This was not such a sudden decision as first it seems. Such background does not detract from the obedience of the first disciples. It makes it more authentic.

Two by two (verses 19, 20)

Jesus chose two pairs of brothers to be at the core of his close band of disciples. Later, he sent them out in pairs on their first ministry journeys. God rarely calls his people to be lone rangers operating in isolation. The relatives of the first disciples, and of those who have subsequently over the years responded to a missionary call, should not be overlooked. Often, they have had mixed feelings and experienced a sense of loss.

Final thought

Having clarified that the response of the disciples was not naïve impetuosity, it may be good to note that the disciples responded without delay (verse 20). Fear of the unknown can lead to inaction and missed opportunity. Once the call of God is heard, the direction of people's lives should change.

Second Sunday before Advent

MARK 13:1-8

Daniel 12:1-3; Hebrews 10:11-25

Introduction

The Old Testament reading from Daniel includes the words: 'Those who are wise will shine like stars'. In the approach to, and during, the season of Advent, preachers do well to take these words to heart. Dealing with apocalyptic or 'end times' material always calls for caution as it is all too easy for church members to latch on to one aspect of these teachings without a proper understanding of the context.

Apocalyptic writing in the Bible, like prophecy, usually has two or even three foci: an imminent one related to Jesus' life; one related to the Fall of Jerusalem in AD 70; and a later, unspecified, end-time focus.

Throughout subsequent history, people have sometimes been too quick to identify events as signs of the end of the world.

Jesus has left the building! (verses 1, 2)

The Temple had been an impressive project undertaken through the lifetime of Jesus and his disciples. It was clearly an impressive structure. Jesus used it as a metaphor and identified himself with it. He responded to the comment of one of his disciples with a shocking prophecy. He predicted that this whole edifice would one day be razed to the ground. Making such a comment while walking around a national monument rarely goes down well – National Trust membership can be rescinded!

Timing is crucial! (verses 3, 4)

Soon afterwards, Jesus and some of the disciples were sitting across from the Temple. They were understandably keen to know more about the timing of these events and what would be the signs. Note that, by now, they took Jesus at his word – they believed him.

Alert, not alarmed! (verses 5-8)

Jesus' advice was good then and is good now. World events can be alarming. 'I don't know what the world is coming to!' is a common expression – and probably has been in every era! Modern mass media bring not only news but vivid live coverage of wars, earthquakes and famines. Jesus warned his closest associates that they should be wary of being deceived by impostors. They would hear about and even experience terrible things but these would only be signs of what would come later. In verses after the set reading, Mark records some of the things that Jesus said would need to happen before the end of the world.

Conclusion

It is easy to take life for granted. No one knows how long on earth they will have. Taking each day as it comes, making the most of it and trusting God for the future is an approach that has served Christians well in every age.

Christ the King/
Sunday next before Advent

JOHN 18:33-37
Daniel 7:9, 10, 13, 14; Revelation 1:4b-8

The end of the lectionary year brings a proclamation and celebration of the kingship of Christ – a right royal end to the year! Returning suddenly to the account of Jesus' trial before Pilate might strike people as strange. It will be important to give the context and reasoning behind the selection. The reading from Revelation, set as the Epistle, speaks of Christ the King in glory. Consequently, it contrasts well with the Gospel picture of Jesus under arrest – in human terms brought low. Combining the two may be a good way of heralding the season of Advent.

King Who? (verses 33, 34)

Pilate was the face and expression of Roman rule in Jerusalem. He was duty-bound to determine whether Jesus had made a claim of kingship, which would be a challenge to the rule of Caesar. Parallel accounts about the way his wife had taken an interest in Jesus meant it was also a personal matter. There is an irony that, in only a few weeks' time, the Christmas and Epiphany readings will feature wise men enquiring of a ruler where the King of the Jews had been born!

Jesus characteristically answers a question with a question. It was not hard to guess the terms in which the Jewish leaders had framed their request and complaint to Pilate. In life, many people have views about God, Jesus and the meaning of life that are not really their own!

What have you done? (verse 35)

Pilate wanted straight answers. It is possible to imagine Jesus being tempted to say in reply, 'What have I done? Where would you like me to begin?' By this time, he had a CV or back catalogue packed with miracles, inspired teaching and other wonders.

A true King (verses 36, 37)

Jesus was no mere vassal or political appointee. He told Pilate his Kingdom was other-worldly and therefore outside of Pilate's jurisdiction. He pointed out that his supporters had not resorted to force. He was not the latest in a line of messianic rabble-rousers or insurrectionists. (Resurrectionists?) However, he did not blanch when Pilate said, 'So you are a king.' Jesus expressed his purpose and mission as being to declare the truth. Truth would attract its own audience.

Conclusion

Recognising the Kingship/Lordship of Christ is a big step. Accepting it in such a way that it transforms life is an even greater challenge for all who would follow Christ and take his name.

YEAR C

First Sunday of Advent

LUKE 21:25-36

Jeremiah 33:14-16; 1 Thessalonians 3:9-end

Introduction

Most, but maybe not all, church members will be aware that Advent Sunday marks the beginning of a new year in the Church's calendar. Wishing congregations 'Happy New Year C' will go down better in some places than in others. The season of Advent is traditionally a time of preparing for celebrating the Incarnation. As well as looking ahead to the coming of Christ, there is always an element of anticipating his Second Coming. The Gospel reading is strikingly apocalyptic. Preachers may well want to remind people that when Jesus spoke about the end of the age he sometimes had in mind his current era and sometimes the end of the world as we know it. His words often applied in the first instance in a prophetic way to the destruction of Jerusalem in AD 70.

Context

This passage today comes from towards the end of Jesus' life. He had begun to warn his disciples plainly about his own approaching death and resurrection. The words are spoke in or around the splendid new Temple which was nearing completion. It dominated the skyline and loomed large in people's theology and discussions. See Luke 21:5 for the immediate context of this passage.

Apocalypse Now! (verses 25-28)

Jesus spoke about the end of the age in language and in the style of the traditional apocalyptic literature of the prophets. The imagery was striking. He spoke about it as an event of cosmic significance (sun, moon and stars, etc., verse 25). People would find it terrifying (verse 26). The Son of Man, which was Jesus' preferred title for himself, would appear with clouds and glorious signs. In Jewish thinking, these were classic features of a theophany (verse 27). Notwithstanding their

260

fear, Jesus' followers were to realise that this was also the day of their redemption. They would be rescued from within these dramatic events. 'Your redemption is near' (verse 28).

Parable of the fig tree and trees (verses 29-31)

Jesus slipped in a short simple parable to emphasise the inevitability of these events. When people saw new fresh shoots on the trees they knew that summer was on its way. The natural world is full of repeated signs of a certain coming season. 'When you see these things happening, you know that the kingdom of God is near' (verse 31).

What will not pass away? (verses 32, 33)

The precise meaning of verse 32 has been the cause of much debate through the years. If Jesus is understood to be talking about the events of AD 70, there is not a problem. When, however, it has been taken to refer to the end of the age then it would appear not to have been fulfilled – Jesus' disciples all died in due course. There are alternative readings of the word 'generation'. When read as 'race' – i.e. the Jews – then there is not a problem. Such speculation should not be allowed to detract from the clear promise that Jesus' words will never pass away.

Practical Advice (verses 34-36)

Jesus concluded his discourse on these things by repeating earlier instructions. His words sound in a way like directions from a government guide on how to survive a major disaster. His followers were not to be distracted either by dissolute living or by the worries of everyday life. They should not be caught out by events. They should be on their guard, hoping and praying when the time came that they would escape and face the Son of Man without fear or shame.

Second Sunday of Advent

LUKE 3:1-6
Malachi 3:1-4; Philippians 1:3-11

Context

St Luke was renowned as a physician and as a keen historian. Throughout his Gospel and the sequel Acts, his accounts have special medical detail and reference the wider historical context. The Old Testament reading from Malachi 3 is a clear prophecy about the ministry of John the Baptist.

John the Baptist: Herald and Highway man! (Luke 3:1-6)

Historical context (verses 1, 2a)

Luke gives the historical context for John the Baptist's ministry. He marks it by three measures, almost as though he were triangulating a location. He gives a Roman context (Tiberius Caesar and Pontius Pilate), a Jewish local political one by naming three tetrarchs including Herod in Galilee, and finally a Jewish religious one (high priests).

John the Herald (verses 2b-4)

John was not a self-appointed spokesperson or wannabe prophet. This was his divine destiny. The word of God came to him when he was in the desert. He embarked on an itinerant ministry, calling people to repentance and offering baptism as a mark of forgiveness.

John the Highway man (verses 5, 6)

John's ministry was more than simply announcing the impending arrival of the Messiah. The words from Isaiah 40 speak of preparing a highway, the Royal Highway. People are familiar with road improvement schemes or motorway construction – e.g. giant earthmovers levelling steep slopes. The scope of God's rescue or redemption plan is fully expressed: 'all people will see God's salvation' (verse 6).

Third Sunday of Advent

LUKE 3:7-18

Zephaniah 3:14-end; Philippians 4:4-7

Advent Hope from the other readings

Advent is supposed to be a season of hope, and yet sometimes the dire warnings about the fate of Jerusalem and the end of the age can obscure this fact. Today's Old Testament reading includes wonderful words of forgiveness and the promise of restoration. St Paul's words in Philippians encourage people not to be anxious but rather to rejoice in the knowledge that the Lord is near. Verse 7 speaks of the peace of God guarding our hearts. The word 'guard' there means 'to garrison' or 'to set a guard dog'.

John the Baptist fails audition for church welcome team! (verses 7-9)

Ask people to imagine how they would feel if, having trekked out into the wilderness to be baptised in a muddy river by a wild-looking man, they were met with John's greeting – 'You brood of vipers!' (verse 7). Matthew also recorded John saying these words but, in his Gospel, they were directed at the scribes and Pharisees who came along with the crowds of ordinary people (see Matthew 3:7). John's message was that true repentance would show itself in changed lives (verses 8a, 9). In that sense, the gospel or good news has not changed. Appealing to a historical spiritual ancestry was not enough, notwithstanding God's covenant with Israel (verse 8b). This was a decisive time for individuals and for Israel (verse 9).

John the Baptist passes his audition for the preaching rota! (verses 10-18)

John's preaching hit the target. This account reads like accounts of the apostles in Acts and of revivalist evangelists. The people were clearly affected by his words. They asked him what they should do. There is a close similarity to Jesus' teaching in parts of the Sermon on the Mount.

He spelled out what changed lives would look like for ordinary people (verse 10), for tax collectors (verse 12) and for soldiers (verse 14).

John the Baptist proves himself a true evangelist (verses 15-18)

People wondered if he might be the Christ (verse 15). He was aware of his limitations. He pointed people away from himself towards Jesus who was to come (verse 16). He did not sugar-coat his message. The coming of Christ would be a decisive time, provoking a crisis for some (verse 17). His preaching was challenging but was ultimately good news (verse 18). Proclamation of the gospel should free people from the guilt trap – not put them on a guilt trip.

Fourth Sunday of Advent

LUKE 1:39-45 [46-55]
Micah 5:2-5a; Hebrews 10:5-10

Silly introduction

Q: Why can today be called 'Two Ronnies Sunday'?
A: Because it is 'Four Candles/fork handles Sunday' – the fourth candle on the Advent wreath is lit!

Introduction

This week's Gospel reading from Luke goes back to chapter 1. The destiny of John the Baptist and Jesus was interwoven from the outset. This segment comes immediately after the angel of the Lord had appeared to Mary. During that miraculous encounter, Mary was told that Elizabeth, her older kinswoman, had also become pregnant (Luke 1:35).

Time in the country (verses 39, 40)

In times past, this phrase was often a euphemism for a young girl becoming unexpectedly pregnant. It also reflected a common custom of women being packed off hurriedly to relatives elsewhere to find support and to avoid gossip and shame in the home village. In the light of the angel's words, Mary goes to the home of Zechariah and Elizabeth who were excitedly coming to terms with their own news on the baby front. The Gospel accounts do not give any details about how Mary's own family reacted to her pregnancy. It cannot have been easy for them.

Supernatural Childbirth Trust? (verses 41-45)

The mutual support these two godly women gave each other was a great gift of God and a mark of his provision. It was an emotional and highly spiritual moment when they greeted each other. Elizabeth's baby stirred in her and she pronounced prophetic blessings on Mary (verses 42, 45). Her humble rhetorical question 'why am I so favoured, that the mother of my Lord should come to me?' (verse 43) prefigured the response her son John would give to Jesus some 30 years later.

Mary's response to Elizabeth and to God (verses 46-55)

Mary was inspired to respond. These words are the words of the canticle, the Magnificat. It seems a spontaneous act of worship, unsurprisingly reflecting Old Testament words well known by a devout Jewish woman. If Mary had sat down to compose a song of worship and had begun with an empty page, she might well have asked herself the question: 'What do I know of God to include in a song?' Her words in turn prefigure some of Jesus' words in the Beatitudes.

Christmas Day
(see also Years A and B)

LUKE 2:8-20
Gospel reading from Set 2

Introduction

Christmas comes and goes each year. As people get older, it's sometimes hard for them to distinguish precisely one from another. They remember that Granny nearly choked on a sixpence one year but cannot be certain which year it was. Similarly, they might have been given a wonderfully exciting gift that they remember clearly but they are vague about how old they were exactly. Luke, being a historian, was keen to tie his account of events to other attested historical facts. Note and point out how often he includes direct speech in quotation marks (verses 10-12, 14, 15). He appears to be quoting sources.

In this segment from Luke chapter two, the interaction between the divine and the human, between heaven and earth, stands out.

Comfort and joy

Of course, Christmas is not wonderfully happy for everyone. It is right to acknowledge and have sympathy for pain, suffering and grief in the world and in the lives of people we know *but* Luke's account makes it clear that this was a time of good news, joy and wonder: glory (verse 9), good news of great joy (verse 10), praise (verse 13), glory (verse 14), treasures (verse 19), glorifying and praising (verse 20).

Word of mouth

From day one, the Christian message has been passed on by word of mouth. The gospel has cascaded down through the years as one tells another, and they tell another and so on. An angel spoke to the shepherds (verses 10-12). They took him at his word and decided to go and see what the Lord had told them about (verse 15). Their actual visit and encounter with Jesus is 'reduced' to a one-liner by Luke here (verse 16), although he does stress their urgency. The shepherds immediately 'spread the word concerning what had been told them about this child'(verse 17). The reading ends with further emphasis on the fact that they went on their way praising God because of the things which 'were just as they had been told' (verse 20).

Conclusion – A Saviour for all the people

The positive message passed on by word of mouth that triggered so much joy is for everyone. While recognising that Christmas traditions and celebrations cannot automatically make people happy, the news of a Saviour brings hope for all who are struggling in some way or another in life.

First Sunday of Christmas

LUKE 2:41-END
1 Samuel 2:18-20, 26; Colossians 3:12-17

Introduction
People say that childhood rushes by. It certainly seems like that as Luke's account races forward to an incident when Jesus was 12 years old.

Illustration
Losing track of a child in a crowd is most parents' nightmare. 'Stay close, don't speak to strangers' is time-honoured advice. Many people may also have memories of becoming lost as a child and the sense of panic.

The lost boy (verses 41-45)
Jesus was 12 years old when this event took place. The family were travelling as part of a group of pilgrims to and from Jerusalem. His parents were completely unaware that Jesus had stayed in the city. They were not negligent and he was not being wilful – not one of their finest moments as a family unit, however!

Date with destiny – future promise (verses 46-50)
There are various elements that resonate with significance in the light of later events – Jesus in Jerusalem at Passover, debating in the Temple, in his Father's house with a sense of duty, found by his parents on the third day. All sorts of bells are ringing! Jesus was listening and questioning and amazing people with the depth of his insight (verses 46, 47). His parents remonstrated with him – they had been anxiously searching. Sharp exchanges between parents and adolescent sons and daughters are part of family life. Only one has been able to pull out the 'Because I'm the Son of God' clause by way of excuse and explanation! Although Jesus did not actually use such words, the intimation was there. His parents did not understand what he was saying.

All's well that ends well (verses 51, 52)

Luke concludes the chapter with two summary verses. Jesus was obedient. Mary had plenty more to mull over – use of the word 'treasured' is noteworthy. Jesus matured and grew 'in favour with God and man'.

Second Sunday of Christmas

JOHN 1[1-9], 10-18
Jeremiah 31:7-14; Ephesians 1:3-14

Introduction

Congregations will almost certainly have heard the Christmas Gospel from John 1 (his prologue) at some point in the preceding weeks. Focusing on verses 10-18 may be advisable.

In the world (verse 10)

Christ was at the centre of creation, party to and integral to the Divine creative act (see also verse 3). Preachers may remind people that this is what 'begotten not made' means when they recite the creed.

Unrecognised – unreceived (verse 11)

These are tragic words. There is something desperately sad about people failing to recognise or receive the Messiah. The tragedy is for people, for the human race. The headline is not about an unwelcome child or rejected king; it is about unreceptive, spiritually slow and rebellious people.

Receiving and giving (verses 12, 13)

These two words are more commonly found the other way around (giving and receiving). In these verses, John sets out a contrast with the unreceptive in the previous verse. Those people who received the Christ, who believed in his name, received something important. Christ gave them the right (or authorised them) to become children of God, not by token of being human, but by giving them new (spiritual) birth.

The one and only! (verses 14, 18)

Announcers at sporting or entertainment events still use this phrase to give someone a big build-up. It is nearly always hyperbole. In Jesus' case, it was an accurate statement of fact. He was the one and only, *the* logos or Word of God. He carried and displayed the same glory as God the Father from whom he came and with whom he was one. 'Full of grace and truth' (verse 14b) does not mean that Jesus was a repository for propositional truth. Rather, it means that he epitomised integrity and authenticity: the embodiment of God who is ultimate truth and life.

Grace and truth (verses 15-18)

Although still in his prologue, John set up another contrast – one that would be central to his readers' understanding of the gospel, preached and personified by Jesus and written down by John. It was almost as though John the Evangelist mentioned John the Baptist slightly earlier than he had intended (see verses 19-36). John was setting out to write an account of the life of Christ but he could not help talking about the great blessing they had received from 'the fullness of his grace'. This should almost be subject to a spoiler alert! The contrast is between Moses and Jesus. The law was given through Moses, grace and truth came through Jesus (verse 17). God was made not only visible but knowable (verse 18).

Epiphany Sunday

(See Year A)

First Sunday of Epiphany/
Baptism of Christ

LUKE 3:15-17, 21, 22
Isaiah 43:1-7; Acts 8:14-17

From the other readings

The other two set readings combine the themes of baptism and the witness to the Gentiles. In the Old Testament reading, Isaiah sets out the promise of God's presence and protection through the waters, based on God having created Israel. It goes on to express a promise of redemption and ransom which seems to be given to an international audience. The Epistle is an account of the apostles laying hands on Simon the sorcerer and praying for him to receive the Holy Spirit.

Speculation and clarification (verses 15-17)

Luke describes how there was a widespread sense of expectation. The revival movement of people going to be baptised by John in the Jordan showed the spiritual temperature was on the rise. Consequently, some were speculating that John might be the Messiah (verse 15). John set them right by describing his own unworthiness and by contrasting his water baptism with the baptism of fire that Jesus would bring (verse 16). 'You ain't seen nothing yet!' The coming of Jesus would be decisive and divisive in judgement (verse 17). Although verse 18 is not included in the set reading, it is an important summary verse that makes clear that John was preaching Good News.

Baptism in brief (verses 21, 22)

It is a little surprising, given Luke's customary love of detail, that his account of Jesus' baptism is so concise. The main elements contained in other accounts are all there. Jesus identified with ordinary sinful, repentant people in submitting to John's water baptism, even though he did not need it (verse 21). As he was praying, God the Spirit descended on him and God the Father affirmed him: 'my Son, whom I love'. It is a deeply Trinitarian passage.

Second Sunday of Epiphany

(See also Year A Epiphany 4 and Year B Epiphany 3)

JOHN 2:1-11

1 Corinthians 12:1-11; Isaiah 62:1-5

Blessings and new names (Isaiah 62)

The Old Testament reading is packed with promise and encouragement – a good antidote for winter sadness! God's people are promised a glorious new dawn and season of honour. Israel's name will be changed from 'Deserted and Desolate' to 'Married and Delighted' – Desirée, in effect. The wedding theme links to the Gospel reading.

Spiritual gifts in a season of gifts (1 Corinthians 12)

In the same way as the Magi brought gifts to the infant Jesus, so God blesses and equips his Church with spiritual gifts for everyone for the common good.

Shame about the wedding! (John 2:1-11)

The marriage motif runs throughout the Bible. In both Old and New Testaments, Israel is represented as God's bride. Jesus used the metaphor of the bridegroom in some of his parables, and in Revelation 21 the New Jerusalem is described as a bride coming from heaven. The Church is the bride of Christ. All of which lends additional weight to the setting of Jesus' first miracle being a wedding. It may have been that a need arose (the wine ran out, verse 3) and Mary the Mother of Jesus was eager for her son to demonstrate his powers (verses 4, 5). There are many applications to be made from this reading, notably teaching about the new wine of the Kingdom, the wisdom of turning to Christ when resources run low and the importance of doing 'whatever Jesus tells you' (See Epiphany readings in Years A & B above). Whatever subsidiary themes are drawn out, the most important point is that Jesus revealed his glory in this, the first of his miraculous signs. The wedding couple or their families were not named, perhaps to spare them embarrassment.

In any culture, failing to provide sufficient hospitality brings shame on the hosts. In Middle Eastern culture, that was particularly so. The intervention of Jesus, albeit pressurised by his mother, saved the hosts from lasting shame. They would have been forever known as the family who skimped on the drinks front! Although having enough wine at a wedding is not a matter of life and death, sparing people from shame and dishonour is a gospel and Kingdom sign.

Third Sunday of Epiphany

LUKE 4:14-21

Nehemiah 8:1-3, 5, 6, 8-10; 1 Corinthians 12:12-31a

Water Gate (Nehemiah 8)

Older members of congregations will remember the Watergate scandal in America involving President Nixon and stolen documents. The Old Testament reading from Nehemiah is the account of how the people of Israel assembled at the Water Gate and over a period of five hours heard the law of God read to them. This sparked a time of national repentance and rededication to God.

Illustration

The honeymoon is over! In most walks of life, anyone who starts in a new job is granted a honeymoon period. They are given time to find their feet and get up to speed with the demands of the post and the expectations of their colleagues. For figures in the public eye, politicians, football managers and clergy, to name but a few, such a period of grace may prove to be notoriously short. Sooner, rather than later, opposition and disapproval arrive!

NB. Misleading editing *(preachers may decide to use this as their conclusion)*

The appointed Gospel passage ends at verse 21! Like a redacted sports report or literary review, it can give a false impression. It is a false and misleading break. The subsequent verses show that when Jesus applied the words from Isaiah to himself the people were furious and reacted against him with the threat of violence (verse 22-30).

Promising start (verses 14, 15)

Jesus emerged from his testing in the wilderness and, inspired by the Holy Spirit, began his public ministry, initially to a warm reception. He taught in the synagogues and people loved the freshness and authority of his teaching.

Nazareth Synagogue 'gig'! (verses 16, 17)

Inevitably, the time came for Jesus to teach in his home town. Given how his fame had spread, people may even have been agitated for him to do so. As was his custom, he went to the synagogue, was handed the scroll and expected to read. He had been given the scroll of the prophet Isaiah. He found a specific passage and read it.

Prophesied manifesto (verses 18, 19)

The words Jesus read were in effect his mission statement: inspired good news, a radical message of freedom, healing, wholeness, justice and release. He was going to declare the year of the Lord's favour to the last, the least and the lost.

Anticipation and application (verses 20, 21)

When Jesus finished, it's likely that you could have heard a pin drop. Everyone was looking at him, expecting him to do or say something more. A good Anglican reader might say: 'This is the word of the Lord.' Jesus amazed his hearers by telling them that these words had been fulfilled in their own hearing.

Conclusion

Initially, people were amazed, but the mood changed when Jesus began to unpack the teaching and not accede to their demands for a miracle (verses 23, 24).

Fourth Sunday of Epiphany/ Presentation of Christ in the Temple

LUKE 2:22-40

Ezekiel 43:27–44:4; 1 Corinthians 13

Sounds familiar?

Preachers and congregations may do a double-take when they first read or hear this week's Gospel. This is because it overlaps with the passage of Scripture set for the 1st Sunday of Christmas a few weeks ago.

Other readings

The Old Testament passage from Ezekiel is part of an extended prophecy and instructions about the renewal of the Temple and of worship there. The dominant metaphor is about access, doors being open and locked. The Epistle is St Paul's classic passage on love, so often used/misused (!) in marriage services. It always rewards further meditation. It gives an analysis and description of love, lived out. It celebrates the primacy and durability of love.

Jesus presented in the Temple (Luke 2:22-40)

It would be an enormous surprise if the earthly parents of Jesus were anything other than devout. Clearly, Jesus was not a normal Jewish boy and yet he had a normal Jewish upbringing. He had been circumcised and named on the eighth day in accordance with custom (verse 21). Leviticus 12 gives the background to the regulations about purification following childbirth. Following the birth of a son, a woman would have to wait a total of 41 days (8 plus 33) before making the prescribed offering and being purified. Mary and Joseph offered 'a pair of doves or pigeons' (verse 24). This was the concessionary offering if people were unable to offer a lamb plus a dove/pigeon.

Simeon (verses 25-35)

The description of Simeon was another mark of how God had provided and prepared for the birth/Incarnation of his Son. He was a wise old holy man who was sensitive to the promptings and guiding of the Holy Spirit (verses 25, 26, 27). Luke described the moving event of Simeon taking Jesus in his arms and blessing him. The words he spoke are well-known to many as the words of the canticle the Nunc Dimittis (verses 29-32). They are full of messianic and missiological significance. This child would indeed be the light of the world, for Gentile as for Jew. Joseph and Mary marvelled at the words (verse 33). Simeon then blessed them. Some people use the term 'Ah, bless' in a very light-hearted way. Blessings are good but some are heavy, linked as they are to God's calling on the life of an individual. The words about what lay ahead for Mary and the pain it would cause her must have been disturbing (verses 34, 35).

Anna (verses 36-38)

As soon as Simeon finished blessing the child and prophesying to Joseph and Mary, another of the temple characters appeared on the scene. Anna was a prophetess, old and devout like Simeon. They made quite a ministry of welcome team! She prayed her thanks to God and immediately began to tell other 'seekers' in the Temple about Jesus.

Returning home (verses 39, 40)

The Gospel passage concludes with these summary verses that focus on the years in which Jesus grew up as a boy. Harmonising the account of the family fleeing to Egypt for a period is helped by understanding these verses in that light. Jesus thrived physically, emotionally and spiritually.

Proper 1

LUKE 5:1-11
Isaiah 6:1-8 [9-13];1 Corinthians 15:1-11

The number of 'Sundays before Lent' varies each year depending on the date of Easter. The readings allocated for the 5th, 4th or 3rd Sundays before Lent when these occur are known as 'Propers'. Preachers should check which Proper is allocated to which Sunday in any given year.

Introduction

Reading the call of the first disciples is usually an inspiring reminder to long-standing Christians of how their own faith journey began. It is also challenging to those who are still undecided about what it means for them to follow Christ. The accounts give the main details of events but do not describe the inner wrestling that each of the first disciples felt. In fact, it can seem as though they were unstable men who took a rash decision to go walk-about with Jesus, with little regard for their families and other loved ones. Alternatively, it can seem that they were imbued with such levels of faith that the decision was a no-brainer. Neither of these scenarios is accurate. In most cases, there had been prior exposure to either John the Baptist or to Jesus himself. The men had been party to discussions and in different ways were looking for something. Today's Gospel is a case in point. Luke records (4:38, 39) how Jesus had visited Simon Peter's house and had healed his mother-in-law!

Come in Number 1 – your time is up! (Luke 5:1-3)

By this point in Luke's account, Jesus had already begun his public ministry and was attracting a significant following (verse 1). Jesus borrowed Simon's fishing boat and addressed the people from it. This must have been a striking scene.

Payback time (verses 4, 5)

Having made use of his boat, Jesus wanted to repay Simon in some way and give him a powerful and personal demonstration of the power behind his preaching (verse 4). Initially, Simon questions the wisdom of Jesus' suggestion – the first of many times he would do this – because he had already endured a fruitless night's fishing. It was typical of Simon that he immediately moderated his stance – 'but because you say so, I will let down the nets'. The seeds of faithful obedience were evidently present in his life, alongside his natural impetuosity and scepticism. People are complex!

Boom time (verses 6, 7)

The seasoned fisherman took the landlubber's advice and was rewarded with a bumper catch that required two boats to land at the risk of sinking.

Make your mind up time (verses 8-11)

Despite his simple origins, Simon had spiritual insight and a degree of self-awareness. Having seen what Jesus had done, he instinctively felt unworthy – always a healthy reflex reaction in the presence of God. Simon and his companions were genuinely awe-struck. Using words that were to become familiar after his resurrection, Jesus told them not to be afraid but to follow. They beached their boats, burned their bridges and followed him.

Proper 2

LUKE 6:17-26
Jeremiah 17:5-10; 1 Corinthians 15:12-20

Plain teaching (Luke 6:17-19)

Luke sets this body of teaching from relatively early in Jesus' ministry on a plain, as opposed to the Sermon on the Mount in Matthew's Gospel. It covers similar teaching and is declamatory in style, reminiscent of some Old Testament passages (e.g. psalms and prophecies). Parables were to follow. Jesus' audience on this occasion was mixed, drawn from different regions (verse 17). People were drawn to Jesus by his teaching and his remarkable healing power. They wanted to touch him – they needed his touch (verses 18, 19).

In any gathering of Christians, it is likely that, if asked, people will give a wide range of answers as to what first attracted them to Christ. Preachers may want to give people time to reflect on this, or in some settings to share their answers with their fellow church members.

Blessings (verses 20-23)

Jesus looked at his disciples. His words appeared to be addressed to his disciples, with the crowd able to hear as well (verse 20). The Kingdom of God is sometimes described as the inside-out, upside-down Kingdom. This is one of many places where Jesus challenged the popular and prevailing view of the day – namely, that all success and wealth indicated God's blessing and approval. Suffering and difficulty were attributed to some assumed sinfulness. In speaking these words, Jesus clearly had in mind what lay ahead for his disciples after his death. They also had a current and more general application. It was a message of hope for the poor and the hungry, for all who were hated, rejected and persecuted because of Jesus. One day, there would be a massive reversal of their fortunes (verses 20-22). He wanted them to know that they were the latest in a long and noble line of people who had suffered because of their faith in God (verse 23). The Christian era has seen countless ordinary and extraordinary saints added to that noble fellowship.

Woes (verses 24-26)

There are two sides to every coin. Having declared a promise of blessing on one group, Jesus spoke plainly about the fate of the self-satisfied and privileged. Temporal wealth, happiness and fame are time-limited and ultimately of no lasting value. The comments about human commendation are particularly apposite in an age of approval ratings – not least for Christian leaders!

Proper 3

LUKE 6:27-38

Genesis 45:3-11, 15; 1 Corinthians 15:35-38, 42-50

Note

The radical counter-cultural teaching from last week's reading continues. Jesus' audience was clearly wider than the disciples at this point. 'To you who are listening I say' (verse 27). Having announced blessings and woes immediately before this, Jesus went on to show how his teaching would apply in practical ways. He made it clear that his understanding of showing love to someone had to have tangible expression. It was not about feelings but actions. This, and similar, passages have been the template for people who tried to apply passive, yet positive, resistance to oppressors. The context of the teaching was the Roman occupation. It is both counter-cultural and counter-intuitive.

Love your enemies (verses 27-30)

The instruction flew in the face of reflexes of self-preservation and self-defence. Loving, doing good for and praying for enemies has never been a popular or easy teaching to apply consistently. It felt then as it feels now – namely, 'How to be a wimp or a door mat in four steps.' Jesus wanted his followers to be peacemakers, to model a different way of living.

Do as you would be done by (verse 31)

This has been a popular saying for many years. It is a good rule of thumb for personal attitudes to others. It is not in itself a strong basis upon which to build a personal ethic, focusing as it does on a personal return. Loving God and the people he has made is a deeper foundation. Ultimately, Christians are called to reflect God to the world – 'Be merciful, just as your Father is merciful' (verse 36).

Charity that begins and stays at home is not charity! (verses 32-35)

Most cultures have a strong expectation that people should look after their loved ones. This was very strong in Jewish culture. Jesus always urged people to go above and beyond. He made it clear that there was nothing distinctive about doing good only to their own families. This is what sinners did (verses 32-34). He reiterated that people should love their enemies by giving and lending without strings attached and with no expectation of reward, 'save that of knowing that they do God's will', to paraphrase St Ignatius Loyola. God is kind and loving to the undeserving – his people should follow suit, not least because they are undeserving themselves (verses 35, 36).

Negatives and positives (verses 37, 38)

Living in this radical way meant refraining from judging and condemning others, thereby blessing them and avoiding those things themselves. It also meant being generously proactive and forgiving, attitudes which would bring their own reward.

Illustration/quotation

Mark Twain reportedly once said, 'It ain't those parts of the Bible that I can't understand that bother me, it is the parts that I do understand.' Today's teaching probably falls into that category. For the record, Mark Twain did not appear to be a great fan of the Bible!

Second Sunday before Lent

LUKE 8:22-25

Genesis 2:4b-9, 15-25; Revelation 4

Storm before the calm?

With Lent approaching, the Gospel is Luke's account of Jesus calming the storm. This is a well-known and much-loved episode. Throughout the centuries, Christians have drawn comfort when facing literal and metaphorical storms at sea and in life. This is an instance of Jesus performing a miracle in a nautical setting; there were others. This section marks the beginning of a series of miracles of different types that showed the extent and range of Jesus' authority.

Jesus looking for peace (verses 22, 23a)

Jesus had been ministering to the crowds and dealing with the expectations of his earthly family (see verses 19-21). He was looking for some peace and an opportunity to recharge his energy levels. He quickly fell asleep in the boat.

Unexpected storm – semi-expected response (verses 23, 24)

Weather and sea conditions changed quickly as they are prone to do in that part of the world. The boat was swamped and the disciples were overwhelmed with fear. They woke Jesus; it is hard to tell with what degree of expectation precisely. He stood up, spoke, and the sea calmed down.

Fear exchange (verse 25)

The disciples were amazed. Their fear of physical peril abated with the storm and was replaced by a fear of a supernatural, spiritual nature. The most logical reaction from them might well have been: 'How did he do that?' More tellingly, given the purpose of the Gospel, they speculated about Jesus' identity.

Application

When tough times come in life, most Christians at some point or another wonder whether God might have nodded off and taken his eye and hand off them. Similarly, it is quite common when the storm of life threatens to overwhelm for people to turn away from God and their fellow disciples. In the boat, the disciples did the right thing. They immediately took their concern to their Master. Jesus brings peace, either because he occasionally changes the landscape of people's circumstances or, more commonly, by changing their inner landscape of fear and anxiety.

Sunday next before Lent

LUKE 9:28-36 [37-43A]

Exodus 34:29-end; 2 Corinthians 3:12–4:2

Introduction

The Old Testament reading is the account of Moses' face shining radiantly after he had encountered God. Preachers may also like to emphasise that Jesus' death is referred to in verse 31 of this passage as his 'exodus'. The account of the Transfiguration follows on swiftly from Peter's confession of Christ. In many ways, that event was a pivotal point in Jesus' ministry.

The Transfiguration was an intense supernatural experience for everyone involved, but most notably for Jesus himself. Although he never doubted his identity as the Messiah, the Son of God in human form, he needed encouragement and divine affirmation. When this happened at his baptism and in the Transfiguration, the events emboldened those who witnessed them.

Intense prayer (verses 28, 29)

Jesus took his inner circle with him up the mountain to pray. His rhythm of engagement and withdrawal was well-established. It is always good to follow such a pattern, but so often 'the spirit is willing but the diary is packed!'. As Jesus prayed, he became gloriously radiant. When the earthly and heavenly dimensions intersect, there is invariably some release or expression of physical energy, such as light, thunder, earth tremors.

Look who's here! (verses 30, 31)

Two of the great figures from the Old Testament, Moses and Elijah, appear. Such appearances were traditionally interpreted as a messianic sign. It is likely that Jesus subsequently shared what had been discussed – his departure or exodus.

While you were sleeping (verses 32, 33)

This was not the only time the disciples struggled to stay awake while Jesus laboured in prayer. They woke and saw what was happening. True to form, Peter immediately offered to do something – namely, to build shelters. It was as though he was the sort of man who only processed his experiences but enacting them and doing something. Men of a practical nature will no doubt sympathise. It is natural to want to try and capture the mountain-top moments and hold on to them. They are to be experienced for what they are at that moment.

The voice from the cloud (verses 34-36)

A sudden descent of cloud is not uncommon in mountainous settings. However, the audible voice of God is altogether something else. The disciples were frightened. God the Father affirmed his chosen Son, and added the command that they should listen to him. This was an awesome but deeply unsettling experience for the disciples. Even Peter, usually only too quick to speak, chose to keep this event to himself.

No rest for the . . . righteous! (verses 37-43a)

Even the Son of God had to go back down the mountain to experience the everyday challenges of life in the valley. A father approached him, requesting help for his child. The boy was gripped by seizures that were attributed to an evil spirit. He had already approached the other disciples but they had drawn a blank. Jesus seemed peeved by the low levels of faith among his disciples and the people generally. His rhetorical question hints at his departure which has been uppermost in his mind. Jesus spoke an authoritative word of rebuke and the boy was released from the grip of evil. Once again, people were amazed 'at the greatness of God'. Clearly, more people were revising upwards their view of Jesus and the source of his power.

Ash Wednesday

JOHN 8:1-11

Psalm 51:1-18; 2 Corinthians 5:20b–6:10

See Year B

First Sunday of Lent

LUKE 4:1-13

Deuteronomy 26:1-11; Romans 10:8b-13

Head and heart (Romans 10:8b-9)

Lent and the seasonal disciplines associated with it can help people to grow in devotion to God and knowledge of him. Oliver Cromwell once wrote: 'I had rather have a plain russet-coated captain that knows what he fights for, and loves what he knows, than that which you call a gentleman and is nothing else' (Letter from Cromwell to Sir William Spring, September 1643). St Paul's words in these verses similarly bring head and heart together: 'If you declare with your mouth, "Jesus is Lord", and believe in your heart that God raised him from the dead, you will be saved.'

Jesus tempted in the wilderness (Luke 4:1-13)

In chapter 3 of his Gospel, Luke describes the ministry of John the Baptist, gives a brief account of Jesus' baptism and inserts an extensive genealogy of Jesus. He then recounts the way Jesus was led into the wilderness. It may seem strange to some people to read that Jesus was led by the Holy Spirit into the wilderness to be tempted (verses 1, 2). In the Lord's Prayer, Christians ask that they may not be led into temptation. This was a necessary retreat and training period for Jesus, prior to beginning his ministry. Jesus fasted and prayed, was hungry and therefore vulnerable. Christian discipleship will inevitably bring trials and at times be an uphill struggle. The old hymn 'Father, hear the prayer we offer' includes the lines: 'Not forever in green pastures would we ask our way to be' and 'Not forever by still waters would we idly rest and stay'.

People sometimes speculate on what form Jesus' temptations took. Was it an internal struggle in his mind and spirit? Was he literally taken to a high place and to the Temple in Jerusalem? Various film-makers have presented this in different ways. It is wise not to get bogged down in this – for 'the devil is in the detail'!

Threefold temptation

Questioning his divine identity twice – 'If you are the Son of God' (verses 3, 9); questioning his devotion, allegiance and trust in God – 'If you worship me' (verse 7):

- tempted to use his miraculous power for personal satisfaction (verse 3)

- tempted over personal ambition (verses 6, 7)

- tempted over personal security and safety (verses 9-11).

It is written

On each occasion Jesus resorted to Scripture by way of riposte to the devil, even when Scripture was misused in the temptation itself (verses 4, 8, 12).

Application

Services and gatherings in Lent ideally make more provision than normal for quiet and unhurried reflection. People may appreciate time to think about the ways and the areas in which they are prone to temptation.

Second Sunday of Lent

LUKE 13:31-END
Genesis 15:1-12; Philippians 3:17–4:1

Foundations

The Old Testament reading (Genesis 15) is the account of God making his covenant with Abraham. As such, it provides a foundation for an understanding of God's dealings with his world and people. The Epistle from Philippians includes Paul's delightful description of his fellow Christians as his 'joy and crown who should stand firm' (Philippians 4:1). This resonates with the tender affection Jesus expressed for Jerusalem (see below).

Context

The Gospel reading comes at a point when Jesus was slowly but inexorably making his way towards Jerusalem and the climactic events that lay ahead (see Luke 13:22).

Unexpected warning (verse 31)

Jesus was met on the way by some Pharisees. Usually, confrontation followed such a meeting but, on this occasion, they seemed men of good will without an ulterior motive. They were privy to Herod's plans and had come to warn Jesus to go elsewhere (verse 31).

Blunt response (verses 32, 33)

Jesus always had a keen and clear sense of timing in the purpose of God (verse 33). At this point, he would not be deflected from going to Jerusalem, either by these Pharisees or by his anxious disciples. His response to Herod was testy and determined (verse 32). Paraphrased, it could be: 'I will do what I do; I am coming for you.' There was rueful irony in his words; he mentioned a time span of three days and added a comment that no prophet should die outside of Jerusalem (verse 33).

Tender lament (verse 34)

In a single sentence, Jesus denounced Jerusalem and spoke tenderly of her. The image of a hen protecting her chicks is a striking one. The desire was strong and present but the willingness to be saved was absent on the part of the city and her people.

Solemn prophecy (verse 35)

The reading and the chapter close with Jesus' warning of desolation in the mid-term and an enigmatic statement about his imminent triumphal entry into the city.

Third Sunday of Lent

LUKE 13:1-9

Isaiah 55:1-9; 1 Corinthians 10:1-13

Note

The table of readings goes back in time this week. The Gospel passage is the first part of Luke chapter 13, the last part of which was last week's Gospel.

Invitations and offers (Isaiah 55:1-9)

The Old Testament reading from Isaiah is well-known and greatly loved. The prophet sets out God's gracious invitation to people to come and freely avail themselves of God's generous provision for their physical and spiritual welfare (verses 1-3). The terms of God's loving covenant are set out and people encouraged to turn from evil lives and to seek God while he can be found. Verses 8 and 9 set out most poetically the difference and the contrast between human behaviour and thought with God and his ways.

A call to repentance (Luke 13:1-9)

Making sense of terror and disasters (verses 1-5)

People today are no strangers to reports of terror outrages. They seem to happen all too frequently. Faced with suffering and brutality, people wrestle with their understanding of life and belief in God. Innocent victims are overtaken by awful events. Jesus was living in a time of occupation in which human life must have seemed very cheap. People asked him about Pilate's recent brutality. Jesus answered with a rhetorical question, as he so often did. He challenged the underlying connection that people commonly made between suffering and sin. He pressed home his point by referring to a recent disastrous building collapse. For Jesus, the bottom line was that there is a universal need for people to turn away from wickedness and turn towards God.

A parable about a fig tree in a vineyard (verses 6-9)

Jesus used fig trees by way of illustration on various occasions. The vineyard was a common and well-known symbol for Israel. The parable was one of many that Jesus told to demonstrate that there would be a day of reckoning when God would look for fruitfulness in people's lives and in the national life. A failure to produce fruit led to the fig tree being cut down. It may be fanciful to think that the time span of three years was linked to the length of Jesus' ministry. At the end of the parable, the owner's worker pleads for a stay of execution on the basis that he would till and fertilise the ground around the tree (verses 8, 9). The implication is that the request is granted. This is reminiscent of Abraham bargaining with God over the fate of Sodom (Genesis 18:16-33).

Conclusion

It is always sad if people have an impression of God as capricious and vengeful. He is slow to anger and quick to kindness. He does not want any to perish.

Fourth Sunday of Lent

LUKE 15:1-3, 11B-32

Joshua 5:9-12; 2 Corinthians 5:16-end

Note

The first three verses of Luke 15 introduce a series of Lost and Found parables. Preachers may want to fill in the gap by way of background for their congregations.

You can tell much about a man from the company he keeps (Luke 15:1-3)

Tax collectors, sinners and assorted social outcasts were attracted to Jesus and welcomed by him. He did not hesitate to share meals with them. This led to an outbreak of muttering by judgemental religious leaders. These people considered some of Jesus' associates and friends to be ritually unclean and the rest as undesirables! Jesus was aware of their objections and prejudices. He responded with three parables, each of which stressed the joy of finding that which was lost (sheep, coin, son).

The Parable of the Lost Son (verses 11b-32)

This is one of Jesus' most famous parables. Through the ages people have identified with the prodigal son. Jesus' story seems to strike a chord in every age and culture. It has been adapted and developed in many forms of art, notably Rembrandt's painting 'Return of the Prodigal Son'. Henri Nouwen's book of the same title, inspired by the parable and the picture, is recognised widely as a modern spiritual classic.

The Church of England prayer after Communion containing the line 'Father of all, while we were still far off, you met us in your Son and brought us home' regularly reminds worshippers of the parable. There is a strong argument that the parable could be called the Parable of the Forgiving Father.

The story and characterisation is so vivid, even though in modern terms it would be described as Flash Fiction, that people have analysed each of the characters as though they were real people in a historical account.

Key features:

- The younger son's request to receive his inheritance as an advance would have been recognised as a hurtful action (verse 12). It was tantamount to saying, 'I wish you were dead.'

- Adventure became self-imposed exile. The young man left his roots but found himself destitute, abroad in a famine. Shades of *Down and out in Paris and London* by George Orwell (verses 13-16).

- Jewish listeners would have been shocked by the detail that he tended pigs and ate their food (verse 16).

- He came to his senses and realised that he had sinned against his father and God. This is what true repentance looks like (verses 17-20).

- The father was looking for him and is described as full of compassion (verse 20). The return and reinstatement of the son is cause for celebration (verses 21-24).

- The section of the jealous and resentful older brother is not a postscript (verses 25-32). It is central to Jesus' purpose in telling the story. He has the judgemental Pharisees and teachers of the law in his sights (verses 1, 2).

Fifth Sunday of Lent (Passion Sunday)

JOHN 12:1-8

Isaiah 43:16-21; Philippians 3:4b-14

Background

Jesus being anointed at Bethany became more significant because the circumstances of Jesus' death meant that his body could not receive the customary honour and care.

The setting (verses 1, 2)

Jesus was in his home from home, among friends who loved him. The death and raising of Lazarus is recorded by John in chapter 11. The dinner was given in his honour.

The anointing (verse 3)

Mary anointed Jesus. Her gesture was extravagant, tender and loving. There was a healthy sensuality to it. Mary was offering love and worship.

The objection (verses 4-6)

There always seem to be people in life who are intent on spoiling special events and who criticise the gracious actions of others. Some of them are even to be found in church, as most leaders know only too well! At face value, there was some substance in Judas' objection. The text makes it clear that he did not have a genuine heart for the poor. He was 'dipping his hand in the till' and would come to a sticky end!

The explanation (verses 7, 8)

Jesus immediately leapt to Mary's defence. No wonder women seemed secure in Jesus' presence! Jesus stated categorically that Mary had, in effect, prepared him for burial. His comment about 'always having the poor with you' was almost an aside and not intended to be a significant socio-political comment.

Jesus was now prepared, and the scene was set for the dramatic final days of his ministry and mission on earth.

Palm Sunday

LUKE 19:28-40

Psalm 118:1-2, 19-end; Philippians 2:5-11

The epitome of humility (Philippians 2:5-11)

The reading set as the Epistle is the classic passage in which St Paul urges Christians to try and imitate Jesus' humility. It acts as a commentary on Jesus' entry into Jerusalem – humbly on a donkey.

Context

In Luke's Gospel, the triumphal entry (which may be something of a misnomer – see above) follows Jesus telling the Parable of the Ten Talents. In that story, some of the servants reject their king (see Luke 19:27).

Illustration

There is a football chant that has been sung by crowds for many years when watching a cup tie. 'We're on our way to Wembley, we shall not be moved.' Even footballing minnows sing it in wildly unrealistic hope. From verse 28 onwards, Jesus' disciples could have sung about being on their way to Jerusalem. Indeed, they may well have sung pilgrim psalms and songs.

On the road (verses 28-31)

Jesus very deliberately headed towards Jerusalem. Bethphage and Bethany were natural staging posts and places where he had friends (Lazarus, Mary and Martha). It is not clear whether the availability of the donkey/colt as instructed was due to a prior arrangement, to an assumption on Jesus' part or a supernatural provision.

Needs must (verses 32-34)

The owners were either taken by surprise or did not recognise the disciples. Once they heard the words 'The Lord needs it', they were happy to loan it. At a stroke, their humble beast of burden became one of the most famous and celebrated animals in history.

The crowd's gone wild (verses 35-38)

The response of the crowd to seeing Jesus arriving on a donkey was spontaneous and bore the hallmarks of welcoming a returning king who had been triumphant in battle. As the city came into view, the cries took on a messianic tone.

The moment to shout (verses 39-40)

By this stage of Jesus' ministry, there always seemed to be Pharisees on hand. Effectively, he was under surveillance by the authorities. Scandalised by the cries of the crowd, they asked Jesus to silence them. He may have stilled the storm but he would not/could not silence them. Even if the people were quiet, the stones would cry out!

Postscript (verses 41-44)

These verses are not included in the set reading. However, they do shed light on Jesus' demeanour that day. He was not rabble-rousing – on the contrary, he was moved to tears as he contemplated the reaction and fate of the city.

Maundy Thursday and Good Friday
(See Year A)

Easter Day

JOHN 20:1-18
(see Year B)
OR LUKE 24:1-12
Acts 10:34-43

Note

Luke 24:1-12 is the alternative reading set for Year C.

Missing body (Luke 24:1-3)

A common expression of grief is to be busy in practical things. Get on with the necessary – process the emotions later. Jesus' friends were in shock but they planned to go and prepare his body properly (see Luke 23: 55, 56). He had been put in the tomb in haste without ceremony before the Sabbath. We know from parallel accounts that they wondered whom they could get to roll the stone away for them. It would not have been sealed. They thought someone had beaten them to it – the stone had been rolled aside and the body was gone (verses 2, 3).

He is not here! He is risen! (verses 4-8)

Sometimes grieving people imagine they have seen all sorts of things, including a lost loved one. The detail of the women's exchange with the angels is vivid and has the feel of authentic eye-witness testimony. The angels' opening question is a wonderful one: 'Why do you look for the living among the dead?' (verse 5). They went on to remind the women of what Jesus had told them before his death. His crucifixion had to happen (verses 6-8).

Women's words (verses 9-12)

Luke, the painstaking historian with an eye for detail, names the group of women who returned with the extraordinary news of the empty tomb (verses 9, 10). It was a remarkable tale and perhaps the disciples should not be judged too harshly for not believing the women. But then again, maybe they were fulfilling a gender stereotype after all! Peter, ever the action man, ran to the tomb. He looked into the tomb, saw the discarded graveclothes and went away wondering to himself (verse 12)! This was not a 'whodunit?' – more a case of 'what was it?'

Jesus' body was never found. There is no final resting place for devotees to visit. Before his death, Jesus had repeatedly said that his rising again would be proof positive of his divinity and of his power to defeat death. Christianity stands or falls on the fact of the Resurrection. For countless Christians through the intervening years, the empty tomb has provided hope when confronted with the death of their loved ones or their own mortality.

Conclusion

When Jesus was born, angels announced 'News of great joy – a saviour has been born.' Outside his empty tomb, the angelic message was: 'Why do you look for the living among the dead? He is not here; he has risen!' Good news of great joy indeed.

Second Sunday of Easter

JOHN 20:19-END

Exodus 14:10-end, 15:20, 21; Acts 5:27-32

Introduction

This Gospel reading primarily concerns events one week after the resurrection of Jesus. Preachers might begin by asking people to reflect on the celebration a week ago, and on what they have done in the intervening period. They might like to imagine how the first week after Jesus' resurrection might have felt for his followers.

Fear and tears turned to joy (verses 19-23)

Jesus' disciples knew that they would be prime suspects when the authorities discovered the empty tomb. A guard had been set specifically to prevent any attempts to fabricate Jesus rising from the dead as he had promised. Consequently, they were hiding behind locked doors for fear of being locked up (verse 19a)! Jesus suddenly appeared among them, greeted them with words of peace and showed them his wounds by way of proof. They were overjoyed (verse 20). To say that Jesus' appearance gave them food for thought is an understatement! No wonder that Jesus repeated his greeting of peace.

Thomas – doubting or honest? (verses 24-29)

Nicknames stick and are hard to shrug off. Thomas has gone down in history as the arch-doubter. This seems unfair. He was absent, the reason for his absence not given, when Jesus first appeared. The others told him what he had missed: 'We have seen the Lord.' He must have been feeling all sorts of emotions. He stated categorically that he would not believe unless he could touch Jesus' wounds for himself. When Jesus appeared a week later, he wasted no time in addressing Thomas' doubts. This was not like an unkind teacher shaming the boy who has missed a lesson and has not done his homework! Rather, it was a compassionate act, bringing Thomas back in step with the others. For his part, Thomas was quick to respond to Jesus' instruction to stop doubting (verse 27). His response was unequivocal and succinct: 'My Lord and my God!' (verse 28). Jesus' response to Thomas was to give a blessing to all those who would have faith in him without the benefit of seeing him in the flesh or in his resurrection body!

And there's more! (verses 30, 31)

John makes it clear that there were many other appearances accompanied by miraculous signs that did not get recorded. He reiterates his purpose in writing: 'that you may believe that Jesus is the Messiah, the Son of God, and that by believing you may have life in his name'. In some manuscripts, an alternative reading is 'so that you may *continue* to believe'. If, as is quite likely, some of the early Christians were beginning to have doubts, the account of Thomas' confession of Christ would carry additional weight.

Third Sunday of Easter

JOHN 21:1-19
Zephaniah 3:14-end; Acts 9:1-6 [7-20]

Introduction

Preachers may want to remind people that John's Gospel contains insights relating particularly to the experience of Peter. The account of Jesus appearing to the disciples back at the Sea of Galilee provides a symmetry to the accounts of Jesus' ministry. The account in today's Gospel passage is packed with echoes of earlier events.

Going fishing or slinging his hook? (verses 1-6)

This episode is sometimes presented as Peter simply going back to his old life. Such a view fails to consider that the Risen Christ had told them to return to where they had first met. He had promised to meet them there. The nocturnal expedition turned out to be unrewarding, in the same way as when they were first called by Jesus and had witnessed a miraculous catch. Jesus reprised his actions of that fateful first encounter with the same dramatic result (verses 5, 6). The disciples did not realise it was him (verse 4).

Breakfast invitation (verses 7-14)

John is generally accepted to be 'the disciple whom Jesus loved'. It was he who first recognised Jesus. He told Peter who, true to form and notwithstanding his recent failure, jumps into the water to greet Jesus. He was not sheepish or slow in coming forward. Eventually, the fish were landed, counted and brought to Jesus (echoes of the Feeding of the Multitudes?). An interesting detail concerns the word John chose to describe the fire Jesus had made. He used the word 'anthrakia' (older church members may remember buying anthracite coal!). This meant charcoal fire. The only other place this term is used is in John 18:18 where it describes the fire in the courtyard, by the light of which Peter denied Jesus. Coincidence or intentional? The language used to describe the way Jesus distributed the bread and fish strongly echoes the description of the distribution of bread and wine both in the Upper Room and in the meal on the Emmaus road.

One to one (verses 15-19)

Most people can relate to Peter's experience of knowing there is a conversation that needs to take place after a falling out or some other awkwardness. It might almost have been a relief when Jesus suggested he and Peter take a little walk. There was unlikely to have been much small talk! Jesus asked Peter three times if he loved him. The same number of times Peter had denied him. Peter responded: 'You know I love you!' It stung him that Jesus felt he had to ask three times. Different words for love are used in the exchange. It was also telling that Jesus called him 'Simon, son of John' rather than Peter. Jesus commanded Peter to feed and take care of his flock, which he would have understood to mean his people and followers. Peter would go on to play a major role in founding and leading the Church. His epistles show how much he took this lesson to heart. Jesus' prophetic words about how he would end his life were salutary. Peter's life and death would glorify God. The reading ends with the simple but profound repetition of Jesus' call to discipleship: 'Follow me'.

Application

The loving and purposeful way in which Jesus reinstated Peter provides hope and encouragement for Christians who feel they are failed disciples, who have denied Jesus in some way. Peter was not only forgiven but recommissioned.

Fourth Sunday of Easter

JOHN 10:22-30

Genesis 7:1-5, 11-18; 8:6-18; 9:8-13; Acts 9:36-end

Word for widows (Acts 9:36-end)

Sometimes the Church does not always care for widows as well as it should. Ageism and sexism sometimes combine to make older women on their own feel second class – unless required for a rota. The reading from Acts is the account of Peter raising Dorcas to life. This encouraged the widows then and might do the same today.

Winter wondering (John 10:22, 23, 24)

Jesus was in Jerusalem for the winter feast of Dedication. People and religious leaders in the city were wondering about him. There was much speculation concerning his identity. They asked him to tell them plainly (verse 24).

Illustration

Most people recognise the scenario of being introduced to someone at a party or meeting, being told their name and immediately having to say, 'Sorry, I didn't get your name.' Psychologists tell us that this is because people are preoccupied with checking that the person doing the introduction gets their own name correct. Also, many people are poor listeners. Jesus told his questioners that he had already told them that he was the Christ and had backed up the claim with his actions (verse 25).

Sheepish (verses 25, 26)

The people had told Jesus they wanted him to spell things out, so he did! He told them plainly that the reason they did not recognise or accept his miracles for what they were (i.e. proof positive that he was from God) was because they were not his sheep. He returned to the metaphor he had used before about being the shepherd to his flock (John 10:1-18.)

Secure sheep (verses 27-30)

Jesus then appeared to take the conversation in a slightly different direction. Members of his flock listen to him, are known by him and follow him (verse 27). They have eternal life and are totally secure in his care. They are the Father's flock and cannot be snatched from the Father who is greater than all. Jesus finished by making a statement that showed he was the Christ: 'I and the Father are one' (verse 30). Some of his listeners understood what he was saying. This is evident because the next verse says that they went to stone Jesus for blasphemy (verse 31).

Fifth Sunday of Easter

JOHN 13:31-35
Genesis 22:1-18; Acts 11:1-18

Child protection issue (Genesis 22:1-18)

The account of Abraham being tested by God jars on the modern ear. What sort of person would be prepared to kill their son on an altar? Abraham obviously lived in a very different time. He was called by God to forsake the pagan worship of his day. The most important feature of that event was that God spared the child. The sweep of Scripture is that children should be valued and protected. Jesus was especially clear that people who harmed children in any way were committing great evil and must be held accountable.

Breaking down cultural barriers (Acts 11:1-18)

The mandatory reading from Acts is about Peter defending the way he had broken the Jewish law by eating with Gentiles. This signalled a hugely significant shift in the understanding of the first Christians. They realised that the Gospel of Jesus was for everyone. This was a new move of God – not simply a renewal movement in Judaism.

Children, don't fight! (John 13:31-35)

Probably from time immemorial, parents have given the same advice to their children: 'I'm popping out, children, don't fight while I'm gone.' Earlier in this chapter, John records how Jesus had washed his disciples' feet and modelled humility and servant leadership to them (John 13:1-20). Jesus spoke the words in this reading immediately after Judas Iscariot had left the Upper Room to go and betray him. Perhaps acutely aware of the way in which people can lose their way and stoop to such depths, he gave his remaining disciples this new commandment (verses 34, 35). Jesus spoke about 'the Son of Man' being 'glorified', not because he could only speak about his death euphemistically. He had not shrunk from spelling out what was about to happen. Here, he wanted them to understand something of the full significance of what God was doing in him through his death (verses 31, 32). He addressed them tenderly as 'little children' in the way a mother might. He told them that this was something he had to do alone, without them accompanying him. He was about to fulfil his mission, the very thing he had come to do (verse 33). By calling his instruction a new commandment, Jesus was underlining how important this was. It would be a hallmark of his followers and of the early Church. Jesus was on the point of giving his life for them out of love for them and for his Father. They were to love one another in the same way that he had loved them. The full weight of this command would be felt only after his death and resurrection (verses 34, 35).

Church history has plenty of examples of Christians showing sacrificial love for their fellow believers.

Sixth Sunday of Easter

JOHN 14:23-29 *OR* JOHN 5:1-9
Ezekiel 37:1-14; Acts 16:9-15

Spoiled for choice!

Preachers have plenty of options this week as they decide on their principle focus.

Valley of dry bones (Ezekiel 37:1-14)

The Old Testament passage is the striking vision of God breathing life into the battleground of dry bones. It was a message for exiled Israel but also speaks of resurrection and renewal in subsequent ages. It is a passage full of hope and promise. 'Our bones are dried up and our hope is gone; we are cut off' (verse 11).

Expanding mission – night vision! (Acts 16:9-15)

The reading from Acts records how St Paul had a vision in the night in which a Macedonian was calling him to come and help in what was new territory on Paul's missionary journey. The Gospel was spreading west to what is now modern Europe. The first event on this venture was the conversion of the successful business woman, Lydia. She was godly and a strategic leader.

More from the Upper Room Discourse – Parting Shots (John 14:23-29)

Binary responses (verses 23, 24)

The word 'if' is only small but it can be used in various ways. In some settings, it can denote uncertainty. People sometimes speak of things being 'iffy'! On other occasions, such as in these verses, it can assume a positive response. Jesus was assuming love on the part of his disciples. Such love would lead to obedience. The Father and the Son would dwell in such people. A lack of love would result in, and be shown by, disobedience.

Promises, promises! (verses 25-27)

Jesus knew his disciples would be initially shocked and devastated by his death and departure. He wanted to reassure and equip them. As sure as he was speaking to them then, the Holy Spirit would come to them and teach them. This is another clear Trinitarian passage. The presence of the Holy Spirit would also give them a deep sense of peace in the face of trouble from the world. The world cannot replicate God's love.

Coming and going! (verses 28, 29)

When people feel harassed they sometimes say, 'I don't know whether I'm coming or going!' By contrast, Jesus knew precisely what was going to happen and what he was doing (verse 28). Assuming again that his disciples loved him, Jesus told them that they should be glad he was returning to the Father. They would see him die, rise again, appear repeatedly and then go to the Father. They would not be left alone. He did not want them to lose faith because they were unprepared. Forewarned was forearmed.

Alternative reading: Healing at the pool (John 5:1-9)

This is an account of healing packed with drama. Jesus was in Jerusalem for a festival – he was never a stranger to the city (verse 1). For many years, people questioned the existence of this pool with the distinctive detail about the five porticoes or colonnades (verse 2) – it was discovered by archaeologists in the late nineteenth century. Like the pool of Siloam (discovered in 2005), it is thought to have been a pool for ritual Jewish washing.

The exchange between the man and Jesus was central to the episode. The man had been there for 38 years (verse 5) so it was not altogether surprising for Jesus to ask if he really wanted to be healed (verse 6). 'First one in gets healed – last one in is a sissy!' Additional controversy was added by the fact that this miracle was performed on the Sabbath.

Ascension Day

(See Year A)

Seventh Sunday of Easter

JOHN 17:20-END

Ezekiel 36:24-28; Acts 16:16-34

A case in point (Acts 16:16-34)

The Gospel reading is part of Jesus' high-priestly prayer in which he prayed for protection for his followers. The New Testament reading is the account of Paul and Silas in prison in Philippi. Luke recorded how they prayed and worshipped after being unfairly detained. They had the chance to escape following an earthquake but stayed put. They saw their suicidal jailer come to faith and baptised him and his household.

Illustration

Often when people ring their doctor's surgery they are offered appointments with one of the team of doctors. Most people when given a choice would prefer to see their own doctor – not least because she or he knows them best. Similarly, if facing difficulty and in need of prayer, Christians might think that it would be better to be prayed for by a seasoned intercessor or skilled minister. Prayer is prayer but people's preference is understandable. The Gospel reading shows Jesus praying for all believers. Coupled with the promise that the Holy Spirit intercedes for people, it is encouraging for people to know that they are being prayed for by the best!

Jesus praying for all believers (John 17:20-end)

This is the third section of Jesus' prayer. In it he prayed for those who would become Christians because of the apostles' ministry. It is remarkable that it was written down to inspire people over the centuries. Jesus prayed several specific things:

- that they would be present with and rooted in God (verse 21)
- for unity among believers, a one-ness of mind and purpose (verses 21-23)
- that they would be a witness to the world, reflecting the unity and love of God (verses 21, 23)
- that they would be with Jesus and see his glory (verse 24)
- that they would know God's love and the presence of Jesus living in them (verses 25, 26).

Pentecost

JOHN 14:8-17
Genesis 11:1-9; Acts 2:1-21

Introduction

Jesus promised the Holy Spirit to his disciples on many occasions, increasingly as he neared Jerusalem towards the end of his earthly ministry. His disciples often found it hard to understand Jesus' teaching about what lay ahead. They were also often apprehensive, battling doubt and feeling unworthy of their call. Christians who feel like that are in good company. It may be worth noting that, although the set Gospel reading begins with a question from Philip, it follows on directly from Thomas very honestly saying they did not know the way Jesus was talking about. Jesus responded with his famous words: 'I am the way and the truth and the life' (John 14:6).

Father and Son (verses 8-11)

Philip asked Jesus to show them the Father (verse 8). That would be enough for them. It was almost as though he were saying: 'That's not too much to ask, is it?' His request saddens Jesus. This is another of those occasions where Jesus seemed disappointed and frustrated that the disciples were so slow to grasp basic truths (verse 9). He wanted them to realise that, by seeing him and getting to know him, they had seen and known what God was like. He pointed to his words (verse 10) which were the Father's words and to his miracles (verse 11).

Do as I say AND as I do (verses 12-14)

In the same way that having the Father dwelling in him inspired his words and shaped his actions, Jesus expected his disciples to speak and do as he had done. The implication being that they could only do this if he was in them, that's where the Holy Spirit came in. Because Jesus was returning to his Father, this would signal a new era in which they would be able to do remarkable things and to ask God for anything, in his name. Of course, this does not reduce God to being an automated dispenser of goodies.

The Holy Spirit promised (verses 15-17)

When Jesus said, 'if you love me' he was assuming that they did and was showing what would follow because of their loving obedience. The three Persons of the Godhead are at work. Jesus asked the Father to send the Counsellor. It is unhelpful if people have a mental image of an analyst or agony aunt. The Holy Spirit leads believers into understanding truth. He is the one Comforter, the one who comes alongside and brings strength. Recognising and receiving the Holy Spirit was impossible for people in the world who were not equipped or able to see him. Those who were united to Jesus (see above) could know him.

Trinity Sunday

JOHN 16:12-15

Proverbs 8:1-4, 22-31; Romans 5:1-5

Ordinary Time resumes on the Monday following the Day of Pentecost. The readings set for each Sunday after Trinity Sunday are known as 'Propers'. They are numbered 4–25. Because the number of 'Sundays after Trinity' varies each year depending on the date of Easter, preachers should check which Proper is allocated to which Sunday in any given year.

Introduction

The mindset of preachers on Trinity Sunday can sometimes be akin to a rock climber contemplating a testing over-hang or a tricky traverse. Explaining the mystery of the Holy and Indivisible Trinity can seem daunting, which can lead to dry and convoluted theological argument. Alternatively, it can be viewed as an opportunity to declare the wonderful mystery and glorious workings of God, Father, Son and Holy Spirit. The New Testament reading from Romans 5 is richly Trinitarian and full of encouragement for those facing trials and in need of hope.

What's mine is yours! What's mine is ours! (John 16:12-15)

Today's reading is short (four verses) but it is like a superb string quartet. It is a fragment of Jesus' words of encouragement to his disciples as he was preparing them for his imminent 'departure'. Jesus did not want to overburden his followers (verse 12). Discipleship is essentially a process. God teaches his people throughout their lives. He follows a syllabus individually tailored to each person. This is the work of the Holy Spirit, promised here by Jesus (verse 13).

He teaches what he hears and brings understanding of what will be. Father, Son and Holy Spirit are of one mind (verse 13).

Illustration

The Spirit is not a glorified version of Google or Wikipedia. He is more like an active personal coach. (NB. All analogies are inadequate!)

He glorifies Jesus by taking his teaching, reminding people of it and helping them to apply it. All of this is with the purpose of bringing glory to the Son. Everything that the Son has is the Father's (verses 14, 15).

Illustration

A mother had three sons. They went to the same school. She sewed identical name labels into all their clothes. The label only showed their family name.

Conclusion

People sometimes get in a tangle because they like to be clear about which one of the Trinity does what! The danger of this is modalism, of using language as though describing an old-fashioned industrial dispute about the demarcation of duties! Similarly, people have been known to fret over to whom they should address their prayers. It may be helpful to remind people that when anyone says, 'Father, Son and Holy Spirit' they are using shorthand for God the Father, God the Son and God the Holy Spirit. One in three, three in one. No hierarchy.

Proper 4

LUKE 7:1-10

1 Kings 8:22, 23, 41-43; Galatians 1:1-12

Introduction

For churches that like to follow a sequential exposition in one book, it is worth noting that a new series in Galatians begins today. In an era when there is much talk about the pros and cons of immigration and when the spectre of racism raises its ugly head all too often, the reading from 1 Kings 8 combines with the Gospel to make a positive statement.

A pressing need (Luke 7:1-3)

Jesus came to Capernaum, very much his ministry base. A valued servant belonging to a centurion was on the point of death. The centurion had heard about Jesus and was sufficiently desperate/impressed to enlist the help of his Jewish friends. He wanted Jesus to come and heal his servant, a sign that he believed Jesus could do so.

A deserving case (verses 4-6a)

The centurion's friends did not hesitate to make representations to Jesus. The man clearly had a love for the Jewish nation and had expressed this in practical terms by building the synagogue. It appears to have been a sincere gesture – more than a canny 'hearts and minds' charm offensive. At this stage of Jesus' ministry, people did not have much of a grasp of the notion of undeserved grace. People were operating under a system of merit. Jesus regularly addressed this, though people found it hard to shrug off the ingrained sense of all good things being a blessing and all bad things being a curse or punishment from God (see Galatians 1:6). Discovering the wonder of God's grace is, and always has been, liberating. Jesus responded to the need and the seed of belief in the centurion and set off with them to his house (verse 6a).

A personal request (verses 6b-8)

The centurion came to meet Jesus face to face. His friends had made a strong case on his behalf but he felt unworthy of receiving Jesus in his home (verses 6b, 7a). He went on to show the extent of his faith in Jesus' power to heal. He had recognised that Jesus had authority and knew from his military experience how authority worked (verses 7b, 8).

An amazing example (verses 9, 10)

People were usually amazed at Jesus. On this occasion, Jesus was amazed at the faith of the centurion. He took the opportunity of highlighting the fact that he had not even seen such faith among his own Jewish people. Here was a Gentile setting the bar higher! The men who had brought the initial message went back to the house and found the servant well. The implication is that the centurion stayed to spend time with Jesus.

Proper 5

LUKE 7:11-17
1 Kings 17:17-end; Galatians 1:11-end

Introduction

Jesus upset the arrangements for every funeral he ever attended or came across. The raising of the widow of Nain's son is a case in point.

Another town – another need (Luke 7:11-13)

This episode followed hard on the heels of the healing of the centurion's slave. People were flocking round him (verse 11) and as they entered Nain they came across a funeral procession (verse 12). When confronted with suffering and grief, Jesus responded with compassion. 'His heart went out to her' (verse 13). Even though able to heal people and raise the dead, Jesus never trivialised the grief people felt. He shared their common humanity and felt their pain. When he told the mother not to cry, it was by way of comfort, knowing what he was going to do.

The power to 'wake' teenage boys! (verses 14-17)

Picture the drama of this scene. Having spoken to the mother, Jesus approached the coffin which was being carried by mourners. Jesus was accompanied by a crowd who had followed him. The widow was similarly supported by a crowd from the town. The coffin bearers stopped and stood still (verse 14); everyone was watching. Jesus addressed the young man directly, telling him to get up. The son sat up and began to talk. The crowd would start to buzz, people craning to see what was going on. The pall-bearers would have had to lower the coffin and let the erstwhile deceased step out. 'Jesus gave him back to his mother' is the most remarkable understatement (verse 15). The word 'awesome' is used liberally by young people today, to the extent that it has almost become devoid of meaning. On this occasion, the crowd were struck with awe. Word spread. People speculated that a great prophet had appeared. Others even went so far as to say: 'God has come to help his people' (verse 16).

News spreads (verse 17)

Luke ends this account with a summary verse. Word began to spread further afield about Jesus and his remarkable ministry.

Conclusion

A reading like this is very positive. Everybody loves a happy ending. For some, however, hearing these words will be a bitter-sweet experience. Most churches include people who have had to face bereavement in their families. Many Christians pray for miracles, and those are few and far between. Preachers may choose to address this head-on. Every individual that Jesus brought back to life had to die again. It is the nature of this life. We are not meant to live on earth for ever. When Jesus brought the dead back to life he was giving a foretaste, an example of his authority over death. When he was raised to new life by God the Father, he opened the way to eternal life for everyone.

Proper 6

LUKE 7:36–8:3

2 Samuel 11:26–12:10; Galatians 2:15-end

Introduction

Many of the Gospel readings feature Jesus' parables. It may be worth noting that today's Old Testament reading from 2 Samuel includes the parable that the prophet Nathan told David to challenge him about his affair with Bathsheba and the murder of Uriah. The Epistle from Galatians chapter 2 is part of Paul's account of his debate/dispute with Peter over the application, or not, of Jewish law to Gentile believers. The inclusion of passages that do not reflect well on God's people adds weight to the authenticity of the Scriptures!

Jesus anointed by a sinful woman – public rebuke for a Pharisee (Luke 7:36–8:3)

A beautiful gesture (verses 36-38)

Jesus was in the home of Simon the Pharisee. There was a wide spread of views of Jesus among that religious party, ranging from the deeply hostile, to the cautiously curious, through to the sympathetic. Ultimately, a majority decided against Jesus and plotted to destroy him. The woman, whose reputation appeared to be common knowledge, anointed his feet with costly perfume. Her tears, almost certainly of repentance and regret, were even more precious, especially in Jesus' eyes. Kissing his feet and wiping them with her hair was sensuous and intimate. It is not inconceivable that some of the men present may have felt a little jealous!

Thinly veiled disapproval (verse 39)

Simon the host did not voice his outrage. However, it can be assumed that Jesus picked up the vibes, read his thoughts and heard the words he may have muttered under his breath. Simon made a double judgement. It was not hard to write off the woman as a sinful person.

Because Jesus accepted her worshipful act, he concluded that Jesus was not a genuine prophet.

Pointed parable (verses 40-47)

Jesus was a guest in Simon's home. Consequently, he corrected him courteously, giving him an opportunity to learn an important lesson for himself. The burden of debt and the attendant worry it brings is a well-known scenario across the ages. Jesus asked Simon to say which of two debtors in his story was the more grateful. He answered correctly that, naturally, the person who had been let off the larger debt would be the more grateful. Jesus then applied the story in a pointed way and which showed Simon in a bad light. Apparently, Simon had not accorded Jesus the welcome normally associated with an invitation to a meal in one's house. He had not provided water for Jesus to wash his dusty feet, nor had he offered the customary kiss of greeting. Jesus contrasted Simon unfavourably with the woman. Her sinfulness was indisputable, but so now was her forgiveness.

Personal touch (verses 48-50)

Having made his point to Simon and the other guests, Jesus then turned his attention to the woman. He spoke pardon to her (verse 48). The guests mutter and question his identity (verse 49). Only God could forgive sins. Jesus sent her on her way, her head held high, secure in the knowledge that she was restored to society with a clean slate.

Women welcome! (8:1-3)

The last section of the reading spells out the fact that women were drawn to Jesus by his treatment of them.

Key thought

'Her many sins have been forgiven – as her great love has shown. But whoever has been forgiven little loves little' (verse 47). Jesus rammed home his message of forgiveness. 'Forgive us our sins, as we forgive those who sin against us' (Lord's Prayer).

Proper 7

LUKE 8:26-39
Isaiah 65:1-9; Galatians 3:23-end

Pastoral note

Modern society has a very different understanding of mental health issues from that of Jesus' day. There are accounts in the New Testament of distressed and troubled people which might make the modern reader uncomfortable. At the time, such emotional, mental and spiritual disturbance was unapologetically attributed to evil spirits. It is tempting to take a more 'sophisticated' view and dismiss such claims. Interestingly, many people today remain fascinated by concepts and expressions of evil in films, horror stories and computer games. The twentieth-century Christian writer, C.S. Lewis, highlighted the equal and opposite errors of dismissing evil power on the one hand and being preoccupied with it on the other. The Gospel accounts show Jesus exercising authority over evil spirits and showing compassion towards their victims.

Context

This encounter occurred immediately after Jesus had calmed a storm on the voyage over the lake to Gerasa, Gentile territory (verses 22-26).

Presenting problem (verses 27-29)

As soon as Jesus landed, a demon-possessed man confronted him. He was dirty, dishevelled and distressed. He had slept rough for a long time among the tombs. He had been manacled and yet had often escaped to solitary places (verse 29). His reaction to Jesus was extreme. Jesus had immediately commanded the evil spirit to leave him. The spirit caused the man to shout at Jesus, asking what he wanted with him and correctly identifying him as Son of the Most High God (verse 28).

Probing question (verses 30, 31)

Jesus in turn asked what his name was. 'Legion' was the response, indicating that many spirits were involved. (Those less inclined to accept such a diagnosis would be hard-pressed to deny that this unfortunate individual had multiple issues.) The spirits begged Jesus not to send them to a place of destruction (verse 31).

Be gone, you swine! (verses 32-35a)

Jesus cast out the demons who, with his permission, entered a large herd of swine who promptly stampeded and rushed headlong into the lake and a watery death (verses 32-34). This was good news for the man but bad news for the local pig farmers (verse 35a).

Dressed and in his right mind (verses 35b-37)

The man was transformed. When the locals came to see what had happened, they found him with Jesus, safe, sane and sound. All of this was too much for people in the area. They begged him to leave because they were frightened (verse 37), whereas on other occasions crowds were reluctant to let Jesus go. Not one to out-stay his welcome, Jesus sailed away (verse 37).

Bloom locally (verses 38-39)

As Jesus was about to go, the man begged to accompany him. There were times when Jesus called people he had healed to follow him and at other times he told them to keep quiet. This time he told the man to stay in the area and to tell his story widely so people would know what God had done for him. It must have been a powerful testimony for some time to come!

Final word

'And deliver us from evil' (Lord's Prayer).

Proper 8

LUKE 9:51-END

1 Kings 19:15, 16, 19-end; Galatians 5:1, 13-25

Context

Last week's Gospel was about Jesus healing a demon-possessed man and destroying a herd of pigs in the process in Gentile territory. This week continues to feature reaction to Jesus in Samaria. In the verses immediately preceding this reading, the disciples asked Jesus if they should stop people who were not part of their group from performing exorcisms in Jesus' name. The disciples seemed to be gaining confidence and becoming slightly combative as time went by.

Verse from Galatians Chapter 5

'You were running a good race. Who cut in on you and kept you from obeying the truth?' (verse 7). The sort of verse it is good to apply by way of personal review from time to time.

Scorched earth? (verses 51-56)

Jesus gave James and John the nickname 'Sons of thunder' (see Mark 3:17). It seems they were firebrands. Jesus always had a keen sense of God's timing within his mission and ministry. At this point he deliberately headed towards Jerusalem. Apparently, people they met on the way became aware of this or recognised them as a band of pilgrims bound for their Holy City (verses 51, 53). As was his custom, Jesus sent a few of his followers ahead to sort out arrangements – a sensible strategic move. Word came back that they would not be welcome. On hearing this news, James and John asked Jesus if he wanted them to call down fire from heaven and destroy the place. Rather like Peter on other occasions, they might have expected a word of approval from the Master. However, they found themselves on the end of a stinging rebuke (verse 55). Another village had the privilege of welcoming them.

Walk the walk. Weigh the cost! (verses 57-62)

Walking the way of the Cross was never meant to be, and rarely is, a stroll in the park. The second half of the Gospel reading shows three brief encounters between Jesus and would-be disciples.

- **No fixed abode.** In the first exchange a man approached Jesus and declared he was ready to follow him wherever he went. Jesus responded enigmatically that, unlike foxes and birds, the Son of Man was of no fixed abode! It is not clear whether the man then followed Jesus or not (verses 57, 58).

- **Dead and buried.** The next exchange is one in which Jesus appeared to make the first move by calling a man to follow him. His response seems reasonable, unless he meant he would follow at some future indeterminate point after his father had died. Jesus responded again slightly mysteriously, apparently making a point about spiritual life and death. It seems that Jesus told this man to proclaim the Kingdom of God in the context of family grief in which he found himself (verses 59-61).

- **Goodbye to farewells!** In the last exchange, the request by the man to say goodbye to his family was not unreasonable. Jesus responded famously about the importance of not looking back when ploughing. People who like neatly striped lawns will understand this more than some! Again, it was not clear whether the person did follow Jesus.

Proper 9

LUKE 10:1-11

Isaiah 66:10-14; Galatians 6: [1-6] 7-16

From the Old Testament

Descriptions of the character and works of God based on aspects of femininity are few and far between. The reading from Isaiah (66:10-14) expresses the caring and nurturing aspect of God in clear female terms. It is a passage that promises peace and comfort.

Seventy-two sent two by two (Luke 10:1-3)

Jesus trained his disciples by letting them see what he did, explaining it and then sending them out to do it. He did this on various occasions. This sending out of 36 pairs of disciples happened immediately after Jesus had been teaching about the cost of following him (verse 1). The fact that he sent them out in pairs modelled collaborative/shared ministry from the very outset of mission. His followers are not meant to be lone rangers. St Paul followed this example in planting churches. He worked with teams of co-workers, training them on the job as Jesus had done. Jesus' disciples were being sent ahead of Jesus, acting both as heralds and reconnaissance. Jesus' words about praying for additional workers in the harvest fields have been particularly relevant to missionary societies (verse 2). God still calls workers. There is no shortage of opportunity or need. He warned the disciples that they would encounter opposition and danger (verse 3).

Marks of mission (verses 4-11):

- Travel light, unencumbered with too many possessions (verse 4a).

- Be focused. Being friendly and talking to strangers can be a good thing in mission. In this instance, Jesus wanted them to go to where they had been sent (verse 4b).

- Be ambassadors of peace. They were to speak peace and to have a peaceable mindset (verses 5, 6).

- Accept hospitality freely and graciously. Do not be greedy or picky. Do not take advantage of the offers (verses 7, 8).

- Offer healing to the sick and in so doing proclaim the Kingdom of God (verse 9).

- When unwelcome, do not waste time. Move on and warn the people about the nearness of the Kingdom of God and the implications of rejecting it (verses 10-12).

Conclusion

Throughout the subsequent ages, the Church has been called to go out in mission, balancing boldness with gentleness, hoping for fruit but not being surprised by rejection.

Proper 10

LUKE 10:25-37

Deuteronomy 30:9-14; Colossians 1:1-14

Note

The New Testament reading today begins a series in Colossians.

The Parable of the Good Samaritan (Luke 10:25-37)

Rather like the Parable of the Prodigal Son, this parable is so vivid and well-loved that people sometimes forget that it is a story and not a historical account. However, one of the reasons Jesus' stories struck a chord with his hearers was that they were firmly rooted in their everyday experience. There were sections of roads which were notorious for robbers. The story may even have been loosely based on recent events at the time.

Activity/introduction

The term 'Good Samaritan' is widely known and used. The French highway code has a Good Samaritan clause – compelling drivers to stop and offer assistance at an accident. Preachers might ask people if they can think of a time when they were grateful for a good Samaritan, the kindness of strangers.

The context (verses 25-29)

Jesus told this parable as a direct result of being challenged by an expert in Jewish law. It seems likely that there was some general debate at the time about the nature of eternal life and how it could be gained (verse 25). The assumption was that it involved doing something on the part of the individual. Some groups at the time emphasised obeying the law in every detail, others emphasised doing works of charity. Therefore, unlike some of the questions brought to Jesus by the scribes and Pharisees, this was not a trick question. As so often, Jesus' first reaction was to answer the question with a question. He put the man on the spot by asking him what his understanding was of what was written in the law (verse 26). The man gave an orthodox answer by quoting verses from Deuteronomy 6 and Leviticus 19. These verses linked together wholehearted love for God with a love for neighbours, practically expressed (verse 27). There were vertical and horizontal dimensions. It was a good answer and Jesus commended him for it. Jesus, perhaps detecting a reticence, encouraged him to apply his own thinking (verse 28). Luke tells us that the man was trying to justify himself and was looking for 'wriggle room' by debating what was meant by the term 'neighbour' (verse 29). Should charity not only begin at home but also stay at home? Jesus had already shown a propensity for ignoring the limitations and barriers of the law when it came to relating to Gentiles.

Compare and contrast (verses 30-35)
This is one of Jesus' parables in which he set up a situation in which there was an obvious contrast. The victim of the mugging needed help. Three people came upon the scene. Two religious people, a priest (verse 31) and a Levite (verse 32), representatives of two expressions of keeping the law, passed by without helping. The third person, a Samaritan (shock horror), not only stopped but went the extra mile in his care of the unfortunate man (verses 33-35).

There's your answer! (verses 36, 37)
The expert in the law had asked for a definition of 'neighbour'. Jesus had given him one, but pressed him to pronounce his ruling (verse 37). It was a no-brainer as the man had to concede. The exchange ended with Jesus repeating his advice that the man should go and do likewise (verse 37b).

Proper 11

LUKE 10:38-END
Genesis 18:1-10a, Colossians 1:15-28

Introduction

Users of social media are regularly invited to do basic personality tests online. Today's Gospel reading shows the contrast between two sisters. One was a busy activist, the other more of a contemplative. Most churches have both sorts of people. Preachers may invite people to think about which they are more inclined to be. It is hard to balance both aspects but is something good to aim at. Many members of congregations will have childhood memories of squabbling with siblings over who was, or was not, doing their fair share of chores.

Location (verse 38)

We know from other accounts that Martha and Mary lived with their brother Lazarus in a village called Bethany. It was on Jesus' most frequent route to Jerusalem. Jesus treated it as a home from home. On this occasion, it appeared to be described as Martha's house. At the very least, it was Martha who took the initiative in offering Jesus hospitality (verse 38).

You treat this place like a . . . synagogue! (verses 39, 40)

Martha busied herself to the point of distraction being a good hostess who wanted to honour Jesus with customary hospitality (verse 40). Mary, by contrast, sat at Jesus' feet, eager to learn from him. It may not be fanciful to at least wonder if she were also attracted to him. As a woman, she would probably have appreciated being able to be close to the teacher in an informal setting, unlike the segregation she must have experienced in the synagogue. It does not detract from the central message of the passage to speculate whether there was a little jealousy at play in the exchanges! Martha was clearly indignant with Mary and Jesus. 'Don't you care, etc.?'

Calm down, calm down! (verses 41, 42)

The way in which Jesus repeated Martha's name suggests a gentle rebuke and an encouragement to calm down. Jesus pointed out to her that she was in a proper tizzy, upset about so many things (verse 41). This suggests that perhaps Martha may have been inclined to being distracted more widely in life. There is a saying: 'The main thing is to keep the main thing, the main thing.' While open to the charge of being a typical man who expected meals to prepare themselves, Jesus was reminding Martha about her priorities. Mary's decision to sit and learn from Jesus was the better decision and one which would have longer-lasting benefits (verse 42).

Conclusion

There is a contemporary move in western society encouraging people to discover the benefits of *mindfulness*. It is sad that so many people have been unaware of the rich tradition of meditation and contemplation in Christianity. Most people would benefit from being more of a Mary than a Martha!

Proper 12

LUKE 11:1-13

Genesis 18:20-32; Colossians 2:6-15 [16-19]

Illustration and introductory activity

The disciples asked Jesus to teach them to pray. Older church members may recall a song by the American crooner Jim Reeves, entitled 'Daddy, my daddy, teach me how to pray.' Although verging on sentimentality, the song was popular in its day. It was a ballad in which a young boy asked his father to teach him how to pray. In the last line, the father leaves the boy's room with tears in his eyes as he realises he had forgotten how to pray! In most homes, bedtime prayers are a thing of the past. It may be interesting to ask people: a) who taught them to pray, and b) whom they have taught to pray?

Show us how to do that (verse 1)

Jesus had an ingrained habit of setting aside time to pray privately. His disciples watched him pray regularly in this way. Although they would have been used to the set prayers of synagogue worship, which drew deeply on the Psalms, they did not know how to pray like Jesus did. They knew John the Baptist had taught his disciples to pray. At least two of them had been followers of John.

A prayer AND a pattern for prayer (verses 2-4)

There has been debate over the years about whether Jesus intended the disciples to pray his words as a prayer or as a pattern for prayer. The answer may be both! When Jesus prayed in the Garden of Gethsemane on the night of his arrest, he followed the pattern he had taught: 'he looked up to heaven and said, "Father, the hour has come; glorify your Son so that the Son may glorify you"' (John 17:1, NRSV). He went on to pray that God's will would be done on earth as in heaven, that the disciples would be protected from temptation and in trials. The prayer which has become known as the Lord's Prayer is a Kingdom prayer, a prayer of forgiveness and a prayer for provision and protection.

After the How to Pray the Why pray! (verses 5-13)

Jesus knew that the disciples would be hesitant or reluctant to pray. That is human nature. Try and sort it out on your own and then as a last resort in emergency – pray! He used three pictures or mini-parables to encourage them to pray:

The midnight caller (verses 5-8)

If the phone or doorbell rings very late at night, the natural reaction is to look at a clock and exclaim, 'Who's calling at this time of night?' The scenario Jesus painted was plausible but probably not common. Someone surprised by an unexpected visitor knocks on a friend's door and asks to borrow three loaves of bread. Even if the friend is less than chuffed to be disturbed, he will get up and help his friend because of his boldness. Jesus was not teaching that God was disinclined to help. Rather, he was encouraging his disciples to be bold.

Ask, seek, knock (verses 9, 10)

Jesus persisted with the analogy of knocking on doors (think of Bob Dylan's 'Knock, knock, knocking on heaven's door'). This is one of Jesus' most memorable sayings. All who ask, seek and knock will receive, find and be let in. It is a wonderful three-part promise.

Fathers – trustworthy, not tricksters (verses 11-13)

Knowing that some of his disciples were already fathers, Jesus used a simple everyday analogy. When their sons asked for a fish or an egg, they were hardly likely to give them a snake or stone instead (verse 12). They would not deceive, disappoint or harm their child. If flawed earthly parents behaved like that then they should know that their Heavenly Father would be all the readier to give them good things. As Jesus drew nearer to the end of his time on earth, he told his disciples more and more about the gift of the Holy Spirit who would come to them (verse 13).

Proper 13

LUKE 12:13-21

Ecclesiastes 1:2, 12-14; 2:18-23; Colossians 3:1-11

Old Testament reading

The reading from Ecclesiastes stands as a counterpoint to Jesus' parable. On its own it reads as a bleak analysis of life. Toil and strife in life without some sense of higher purpose is terribly depressing. The parable is a stark warning in similar vein but points people towards a deeper sense of wealth and purpose.

The Parable of the Rich Fool (Luke 12:13-21)

There is a saying: 'Where there's a will there's a family!' Dispute over legacies are as old as the hills. Jesus was perceived as a wise teacher and consequently people approached him for authoritative advice (verse 13). This was not a trick question. Jesus' question to the man about who he thought had appointed Jesus as judge was, of course, a loaded one (verse 14). Jesus must have detected a love of money and possessions in this man. Instead of giving a ruling in this case, he told a parable by way of warning. Sometimes Jesus left the application till after the parable, and sometimes he left the story hanging like a riddle for people to solve for themselves. Here, he gave a stark warning as a prologue – life is not about possessions. Greed is insidious (verse 15).

Attitude and actions (verses 16-19)

Jesus' story was about a prosperous landowner. Deciding that he needed more storage space for his crops was not, in itself, bad or foolish. The problem was his attitude. Success and wealth dazzled him and he lost his way. He thought he was self-sufficient and so opted for the easy life. He lost sight of the bigger picture and of God. It is a familiar story – not only with celebrities but also for ordinary people.

Final demand! (verses 20, 21)

Wealth itself is not the problem. It brings opportunity and responsibility and comes with a spiritual health warning. Life hangs by a slender thread. No one knows when their time will be up. God surprised the man. He called the man a fool, and given the question that prompted the parable, asks who will inherit everything he must leave behind (verse 20). Jesus said it was folly to build up material wealth but not be rich towards God. He deals in a different currency.

Final word

Sit light to wealth, do not let money stick to your fingers because one day it will not be required on the journey!

Proper 14

LUKE 12:32-40

Genesis 15:1-6; Hebrews 11:1-3, 8-16

Introduction

This week's Gospel picks up the theme from last week and the Parable of the Rich Fool. It develops the warning about the perils of wealth and encourages radical generosity. The theme of watchfulness means that it is similar in tone and content to some of the readings for Advent. Immediately before, Jesus had warned his followers not to worry. Echoing words from the Sermon on the Mount, he told the crowds to trust God who clothed the lilies of the field and cared for the birds of the air.

Heavenly deposits, not earthly treasure (verses 32-34)

Contrasting his followers with worldly pagans, Jesus told them not to be afraid because God had given them the greater, lasting wealth of his Kingdom (verse 32). Clergy used to be fond of saying that their pay was lousy but the fringe benefits were out of this world. Jesus' followers were expected to have a radical view of possessions and material wealth. They were to sell their goods and give money to the poor. In so doing, they were building up their spiritual inheritance – a legacy that was safe and secure (verse 33). Jesus' saying, 'For where your treasure is, there your heart will be also' was well-known and widely quoted in the past. In a materialistic culture, it is still important for people to ask themselves what it is they really value. Whatever their answer, that will be their motivation and driver (verse 34).

Watch out! (verses 35-40)

It seems that Jesus used similar analogies regularly to impress on people the importance of being ready and watchful. Here he used two related scenarios. The first was of servants watching out for their master who was returning from a wedding banquet. They needed to have their lamps trimmed, be clothed and ready to open the door to him and serve him any time of the night (verses 35, 36, 38). Such servants would find themselves rewarded in a delightful manner. Their master would swap roles with them and serve them (verses 37, 38)! Jesus then underlined his teaching by using another of his favourite pictures. Thieves and robbers used an element of surprise to get what they wanted. If homeowners knew when they were coming – burglary timetable posted in the market square on Mondays! – they would not let their houses be broken into. In the same way, the Son of Man would take the world by surprise. His followers needed to be ready (verses 39, 40).

Application

It is all too easy to become distracted by the busyness of doing life, yearning and earning. Remaining alert spiritually requires a conscious effort.

Proper 15

LUKE 12:49-56
Jeremiah 23:23-29; Hebrews 11:29–12:2

Long division (verses 49-53)

Jesus' coming to earth, his death and resurrection were decisive events (verse 49). Jesus described his imminent passion and death as a baptism (verse 50). He provoked crisis and was divisive. This was not God's purpose but, because people were free to respond to the message of the Kingdom, it resulted in differences of opinion and division (verses 52, 53). It was ever thus. It is important that people understand that verse 51 is a clear example of where effect is expressed as though it were purpose. Ultimately, God wanted people to know peace in every aspect of their lives.

Preachers will need to exercise pastoral sensitivity. In some families, the sense of sadness and failure when young people appear to turn their back on their faith and upbringing is very strong.

Times tables! (verses 54-57)

Jesus' earthly ministry was exercised against the backdrop of turbulent times for Israel. Roman occupation combined with a sense of spiritual and political unrest was the context into which he spoke. The response to John the Baptist and other self-proclaimed prophets and leaders demonstrated a rising tide of spiritual and nationalist hopes. Jesus used meteorological and legal analogies to make people realise that they were in danger of failing to understand what was happening. There was a note of impatience and frustration in his words (verse 56). He reminded the crowds that they were adept at reading the local weather. It was eminently predictable (verses 54, 55). Jesus asked them a rhetorical question. What was stopping them from interpreting spiritual signs?

Illustration

Encourage people to remember sayings they know about the weather. 'Red sky at night, shepherd's delight', etc.

He was encouraging them to be decisive and to use their critical faculties (verse 57). Putting things off and inactivity often had negative consequences. He gave the example of resolving a legal dispute. The longer it was allowed to run, the greater the chance that it would end badly (verses 58, 59). This is a theme that will be revisited in Advent in a few weeks' time.

Final thought

In every age, people have struggled to understand great events and difficult times. Wise women and men will always be in demand. *'Men of Issachar, who understood the times and knew what Israel should do' (1 Chronicles 12:32).*

Proper 16

LUKE 13:10-17
Isaiah 58:9b-end; Hebrews 12:18-end

Sabbath issues – the rest is history!

Attitudes to Sunday observance in the west have changed massively within a lifetime, even among Christians. Older church members will remember shops not opening and strict limitations on what children could do on Sundays. Undoubtedly, some of those customs seem quaint and legalistic. However, as society becomes open all hours, 24/7, so there is a growing realisation that the change of pace and chance to rest have been lost. In Jesus' day, there were issues about how the Sabbath was observed. He confronted legalism on the basis that people were missing the point of why God had enshrined the principle of rest within creation.

Sabbath observance and healing (verses 10-13)

It was the Sabbath and Jesus, as was his custom, went to a synagogue with his disciples and began to teach. He saw a woman there who had been bent double for 18 years. There is no suggestion in the account that she approached him. Filled with compassion, he took the initiative. It was almost an impossibility for him to declare the Kingdom of God and to leave this woman bound by her disability. He spoke an authoritative word of freedom to her and laid hands on her. She was healed instantly and understandably began to praise God.

Sabbath observation and squealing! (verse 14)

The synagogue ruler saw what Jesus had done and was indignant. His response verges on the 'Pythonesque'! Instead of remonstrating with Jesus, he turned on the people, presumably including the woman. 'How dare you come to God's house and be healed on his day! This should be done in the working week.' Put like that it sounds ridiculous, but custom and sensibilities had been offended. The woman's spine was healed but toes had been trodden on.

Ass! (verses 15, 16)

Of course, it was probably purely incidental that Jesus chose beasts of burden to highlight the ruler's error, but there is a delicious irony at play. Jesus did not hold back. Whenever he encountered hypocrisy, he named it for what it was. He reminded the ruler and those who shared his views that even they would untie their ox or donkey and lead them to water on the Sabbath. That was not deemed as work. It was common sense and basic kindness, both of which trumped Sabbath observance. They were permissible acts. That being the case, Jesus argued, how could it be wrong for a woman to be unbound on the Sabbath?

Humiliation and jubilation (verse 17)

His opponents were shamed into silence. Undoubtedly, they must have withdrawn and grumbled in private. The ordinary people, by contrast, were thrilled at what Jesus had done. They loved his actions and his attitude.

Proper 17

LUKE 14:1, 7-14
Proverbs 25:6, 7; Hebrews 13:1-8, 15, 16

Note

This week's Gospel reading does not include verses 2-6 of Luke chapter 14 which describe how Jesus healed a man in a Pharisee's house. Jesus used a rhetorical question about helping an animal on the Sabbath in the same way as he did when healing a woman in a synagogue (see last week's Gospel from Luke 13). It was such an effective argument that it is no surprise that he employed it on numerous occasions to make the same point. The very brief Old Testament reading from Proverbs 25 is advice about not exalting oneself in the presence of a king. Better to wait and be summoned higher.

Sabbath surveillance (verse 1)

By this stage of his ministry, Jesus had become accustomed to having his every word and action scrutinised by religious leaders who wanted to gather evidence and catch him out. He was in the house of a prominent Pharisee and was being closely watched.

Table plan – table talk (verses 7-11)

Jesus himself was keenly observant. He noticed how other guests were almost falling over one another in their attempts to get the best seats, those close to their host. Even as they were taking their places, Jesus told them a parable. It was simple and pointed. It reads rather like advice on social deportment from magazines for young ladies and gentlemen in the 1950s! Jesus told the assembled guests that, if they wanted to avoid the humiliation of being demoted down the table, they would do better to choose lowly positions. This way, they might enjoy being invited to take a more elevated place. At the end of the parable, he spelled out its meaning. Self-promotion would lead to humiliation whereas humility would bring its own reward.

Benefit lunch (verses 12-14)

Ladies who lunch know the rule of reciprocity. In some social circles, accepting an invitation implies that there will be a return offer! This seems to have been the case in Jesus' day. He followed up his parable about choosing where to sit with direct advice on whom to invite for lunch. Jesus told his host not to limit his hospitality to family, friends and neighbours – all of whom would invite him back. He told him to invite the down and outs and outcasts. Such radical hospitality, like humility, would bring its own reward on resurrection day.

Application

This passage raises uncomfortable questions for churches: Is there an in-crowd? Do the activities of the church only cater for one social or income group? How open is the hospitality offered by church members?

Proper 18

LUKE 14:25-33
Deuteronomy 30:15-end; Philemon 1-21

The cost of being a disciple

By this stage in his ministry, Jesus had attracted a huge following of ordinary people. In this passage, he was at pains to make sure that people were aware of the seriousness and cost of becoming one of his followers. Christians have never been able to claim that they were not shown the small print terms and conditions before making their choice.

We all have our cross to bear! (verses 26, 27)

The saying 'You can choose your friends but not your family!' reflects the fact that sometimes family life can be hard graft. In the Jewish society in which Jesus lived, family was hugely important. It was not an era of great social mobility and so most people lived in extended family groups. Jesus' words were shocking then and now. The word 'hate' is extreme (verse 26). Preachers may want to remind congregations that one rule of biblical interpretation is to 'allow scripture to shed light on scripture'. This saying of Jesus is an apparent contradiction of his teaching elsewhere – e.g., 'honour your father and your mother', etc. This is another of example of Jesus using the language of hyperbole to make a point forcibly. He wanted to make his would-be followers aware that he would expect them to be loyal to him above all else. He did not want them to be distracted by family business. That is not to say he wanted them to be neglectful of family. At the very end of his life, when dying on the Cross, he made provision for his mother and for his closest friend. He was yet to carry his cross but it is interesting that he chose that term to express personal discipleship (verse 27). It was even more poignant in hindsight that Jesus needed the help of Simon of Cyrene to carry his cross.

Do the maths (verses 28-33)

The accounts of the calling of his first disciples can at times make it look like they followed on an impulse, recklessly. In nearly every case, there had been prior knowledge or spiritual searching. In this reading, Jesus used two scenarios by way of short parables to teach the importance of weighing the cost before following him. There may have been a well-known example of an unfinished tower in the region (verses 28-30). During the most recent economic recession, there have been many examples of stalled building projects where funds have run dry. Jesus spelled out that people ridicule those who do not do their estimates well. The second example was of a king who has not prepared properly to face an enemy. Knowing the size and strength of forces at his disposal should have shaped his strategy. A wise king knew whether he could fight or should plead or negotiate for peace.

Application

Becoming a disciple of Jesus is not something one does as a hobby. It involves sacrifice. Sometimes it is described as all-consuming. All-encompassing might be more appropriate.

Proper 19

LUKE 15:1-10
Exodus 32:7-14; 1 Timothy 1:12-17

Note

Churches that particularly value sequential series may like to note that the Epistle is the first of a number from 1 Timothy.

Lost sheep and coins

Having given time and attention to the cost of being a disciple, Jesus then began a series of parables on aspects of being lost and found.

The lost sheep (verses 1-7)

Jesus had to endure much muttering. Some clergy may sympathise! Outcasts and undesirables were drawn to Jesus like moths to a flame. This did not go unnoticed by the religious leaders. This was another occasion when Jesus heard their stage-whisper complaints (verse 1). Jesus welcomed sinners and was happy to share meals with them. The old saying 'You can know a man by the company he keeps' certainly applied to Jesus but in a slightly different way. He was in every way 'Friend of Sinners', he told them. It should be remembered that Pharisees and teachers were meant to be the spiritual *shepherds* of Israel. There is an element of humour in this parable that is probably intentional. Shepherds were often figures of amusement – too many hours in the fields talking to their flock! Part of the humour is that the shepherd begins the day with one hundred sheep, loses one, goes hunting for it leaving ninety-nine alone. The story ends with him standing with one sheep on his shoulders inviting people to celebrate with him. Looking for the sheep was no chore for the shepherd. On the contrary, it was a cause of joy, joy that he wanted others to share in. Some parables were left hanging. This one was direct and explained. His words would have sounded confrontational and offensive to his critics (verse 7).

The lost coin (verses 8-10)

Jesus barely seemed to pause for breath before embarking on a second parable. This reiterated his point. A woman lost a coin. She immediately did everything necessary to find it. She mounted a proper search. There was no sense of 'Oh, I expect it will turn up!' Like the shepherd in the previous parable, on finding it she wanted to share her delight with her neighbours. Again, Jesus applied it in identical manner.

Conclusion

In both these parables, the loser goes to considerable lengths to find that which was missing. The key point is not that Jesus came to seek and to save the lost (which he did), but that the finding of the lost is cause for celebration.

Proper 20

LUKE 16:1-13
Amos 8:4-7; 1 Timothy 2:1-7

Parable of the Bright Manager!

Introduction

In addition to expounding the main message of Jesus' parable, today's reading gives preachers the chance to pass on an important lesson about understanding parables. Many people grow up with, or adopt, a simplistic approach to the parables, in which they automatically identify one character with God. Every element is then 'decoded' in the light of that assumption. This can lead down many a blind alley to a wrong conclusion. This parable is not encouraging people to falsify their business returns. Jesus often taught by nonsensical comparison!

Stewardship and accountability (verses 1, 2)

Jesus often taught about the importance of being faithful and fruitful stewards. Linked inevitably to this was the sense of being accountable to God. The manager in the story was asked to give account to his master because he had been accused of wastefulness of his master's possessions.

Creative accounting (verses 3-7)

The manager encouraged his master's debtors to rewrite their bills not out of an attempt to trick his master or to save his job. He assumed he would lose his job, could not dig, would not beg, so decided to curry favour with business people so they would invite him to their homes when he fell on hard times (verse 4).

Applications (verses 8-13):

- Shrewdness is not in itself a bad thing (verse 8)
- Worldly wealth should be used in a way that leads to heavenly benefits (verse 9)

- The way people handle the small things affects whether they are trusted with big things (verses 10-12)

- No one can serve two masters – it's either God or money (verse 13).

The bottom line (verses 14, 15)

These two verses are not included in the lectionary Gospel reading but they are critical to a proper understanding of the whole passage. Luke comments that the Pharisees loved money and were sneering at Jesus. The 'killer' bottom line is the way that Jesus states: 'What people value highly is detestable in God's sight.' This tempers and clarifies the apparently worldly advice of verse 9.

Proper 21

LUKE 16:19-END
Amos 6:1a, 4-7; 1 Timothy 6:6-19

The rich man and Lazarus

Preachers need to remember that this parable comes hard on the heels of Jesus teaching that people cannot serve God and money (16:13) and Luke commenting that the Pharisees loved money (16:14). It is not about being charitable to the poor, fine thing though that is. The parable follows a traditional pattern, known in that time throughout the Middle East. It has a sting in the tail, a twist unique to Jesus.

'The rich man in his castle – the poor man at his gate' (verses 19-21)

The basic set-up of the story is familiar and graphic. The rich man and Lazarus were at opposite ends of the wealth spectrum. They were Mr Have and Mr Have-not.

Separation and just deserts (verses 22-26)

Jesus followed the traditional view of the afterlife. In time both men died. Lazarus was carried by the angels to Abraham's side whereas the rich man found himself tormented in hell. In western culture, there is a similar sub-genre of Pearly Gates jokes. Jesus' listeners would not have been surprised by the way the story had developed. However, they would have expected the request for the now elevated poor man to go and help the rich man to have been granted. In Jesus' version, no one can cross the great divide in the afterlife. This was the first messianic hint in the story (verse 26).

Request for a final warning (verses 27-31)

The rich man begs Abraham to send Lazarus back to earth to warn his brothers to do all they can to avoid sharing his fate (verse 27). It was a reasonable and altruistic request. Abraham responded that they had Moses (giver of the law) and the prophets to warn them. These were the authors of the scriptures that the Pharisees claimed to base their teaching on. This is the twist that Jesus used to make a powerful point. The main messianic point was made when the rich man said that, if someone from the dead went, they would be bound to repent. Abraham did not grant this request, uttering in the story the prophetic words: 'they will not be convinced even if someone rises from the dead' (verse 31).

Proper 22

LUKE 17:5-10
Habakkuk 1:1-4; 2:1-4; 2 Timothy 1:1-14

Obedient servant

Increase our faith (verse 5)

In the few verses immediately preceding this reading, Jesus challenged his disciples about obedience and offering forgiveness. It seems that they recognised that this was more easily said than done. They asked Jesus to increase their faith (verse 5).

Little faith can have great effect (verse 6)

The disciples thought they did not have enough faith. Jesus wanted them to grasp that even a little faith had greater potential than they realised. When speaking about the faith like a mustard seed, Jesus was focusing on the effect not the literal activity!

Call of duty (verses 7-10)

'I solemnly swear that I will do my duty to God and the Queen/King' is a promise that ex-service personnel and even Scouts and Guides have taken in the past. Some church members may still remember the words of their promises off by heart. Jesus painted a scenario that his listeners would recognise. People in service or employment were expected to do their duty. They did not expect to be especially thanked or waited on hand and foot by their boss. They expected to do what was expected of them. Jesus was teaching that so it was/is with God. The expectations of his disciples were reasonable. They did not require great acts of faith.

PS.

The focus of this parable should not in any way justify employers failing to express appreciation of their staff or surprising them occasionally with a bonus!

Proper 23

LUKE 17:11-19

2 Kings 5:1-3, 7-15c; 2 Timothy 2:8-15

Ten Lepers Healed

Borders and margins (verse 11)

This encounter took place as Jesus was travelling along the border between Samaria and Galilee, clean and unclean country. It involved people who were marginalised by disease and the prevailing religious attitudes towards it.

Keep your distance (verses 12, 13)

Drivers on motorways are regularly told to keep their distance, in case the vehicle in front stops suddenly. Lepers and others who were considered unclean were told to keep their distance in Jesus' day. These ten lepers called to Jesus from a distance. This is another of those encounters in the Gospels which has great resonance with the Prayer after Communion – 'when we were still far off, you met us in your Son'. The lepers' plea to Jesus was one for mercy. They had obviously heard of him. They appealed to him by name and recognised him as Master.

Healing *en route* (verse 14)

On this occasion Jesus apparently did not touch them, make paste with spittle or anything like that. He did not have one set method or model for healing people. Sometimes people get too preoccupied with the 'mechanics' of healing. He directed them to go and present themselves to the priests which is what someone who thought they were healed was expected to do by law. In this way, he was teasing out faith, testing their belief in his ability to heal. Effectively, he was saying 'act now as though you have been healed'. They set off and while *en route* realised that they had indeed been healed.

'I am the one in ten' (verses 15, 16)

It is important to remember that this was an actual event. It is not a parable in the 'Good Samaritan' mould. Only one of the ten from that small colony of lepers came back to thank Jesus. He was jubilant in his gratitude. In mitigation for the other nine, it can be said that they were only doing what Jesus had told them to do. Perhaps they were frightened they might lose their healing. However, Jesus made a point of asking whether the others had been cleansed (verse 17). He highlighted the fact that it was a foreigner who had bothered to come and thank him (verse 18). He sent the man on his way, blessing him with a word of healing (verse 19). Some might argue that, although all ten were cleansed, only this one man was truly healed.

Final word

It is good in life to know where to go for help and whom to thank.

Proper 24

LUKE 18:1-8

Genesis 32:22-31; 2 Timothy 3:14–4:5

From the other readings

The Old Testament reading (Genesis 32) is the wonderful account of Jacob wrestling with God. It is a timeless reminder that sometimes the spiritual life involves bouts of wrestling with doubt and difficulty. Some Christians need permission to be honest about their struggles – this reading gives it. Sometimes people need to be more tenacious in seeking God's blessings. The New Testament reading from 2 Timothy includes the famous (and, for some, infamous!) verse about all Scripture being God-breathed or inspired, useful for training, shaping and equipping God's people. St Paul goes on to encourage timid Timothy in his preaching.

The Persistent Widow – or nagging brings its own reward! (Luke 18:1-8)

Introduction

Question: When does persistence become nagging? Wives, parents of teenagers and workplace managers will know the answer to this! From social media: 'Ladies, when a man says he'll fix something he will get it done. There's no need to remind him every six months!'

This is another parable where people need to be reminded to avoid a simplistic interpretation of the story. God is not an unjust judge! Jesus was teaching by contrast – 'if that's what a bad judge does, think how more readily God will answer'. It is also a parable where the purpose is stated at the outset. Jesus was encouraging persistence in prayer (verse 1).

As the widow said to the judge! (verses 2-4)

It is possible that people may have smiled when they heard Jesus' first line of this story. Perhaps there was a notorious judge in the area. The judge in the story had nothing to commend him – he 'neither feared

God nor cared what people thought' (verse 2). A local widow kept coming to him asking for justice and a ruling in a long-running dispute (verse 3). The judge refused her request but, in the end, she wore him down. She persisted in her claim to the point that he relented, if only to prevent himself from being worn out by her (verse 4). Eventually, she received justice (verse 5).

Thus, said the Lord (verses 6-8)

Jesus then spelled out the contrast and applied the parable. His rhetorical questions in verse 7 anticipate the resounding answer 'No!' The disciples were being encouraged to be persistent in prayer ('his chosen ones, who cry out to him day and night', verse 7). Having made his point plainly, Jesus concluded with another question about whether the Son of Man will find faith on earth when he comes (verse 8b). This linked the teaching on persistence to the parallel theme of readiness.

Final note

Most congregations include people who have prayed over a long period about an issue and have yet to see an answer. They may even have ceased to pray. A brief recognition of that may honour and encourage them in equal measure.

Proper 25/
Last Sunday after Trinity

LUKE 18:9-14
Jeremiah 14:7-10, 19-end; 2 Timothy 4:6-8, 16-18

The Parable of the Pharisee and the Tax Collector (Luke 18:9-14)

Six short verses on a huge topic. Discovering and keeping a proper view of one's own standing before God is a constant challenge for most Christians. Perhaps this is particularly so for leaders who have usually made sacrifices in response to a sense of vocation. Beginning with grace it is all too easy to slip into merit! The previous parable (Luke 18:1-8) was told to his disciples, while this one was directed to people who were 'confident of their own righteousness and looked down on everybody else' (verse 9). It features a Pharisee – enough said!

A one-liner introduction/scene-setter for older people

Children used to play a little game that involved twisting their hands: 'Here's the church, here's the steeple, open the doors and there's the people.' Here's the temple – look inside, see two people, is how Jesus set the scene (verse 10).

Worshipper #1 – a Pharisee (verses 11, 12)

He stood up. The implication was that he was somewhere near the front (near the Holy of Holies?) or at least very visible. He rehearsed a self-congratulatory litany based on the premise that he was better than other people. He looked down on robbers, evil doers and adulterers. He even made an instant value judgement on the tax collector, his fellow-worshipper. He fasted and even tithed – he was keen!

Worshipper #2 – a tax collector (verse 13)

Jesus' listeners had a fixed idea of the second character. Tax collectors were unlikely to win the popularity stakes. They made money from their local community by collaborating with the occupying forces and collecting taxes that were resented. They took their own cut. They were social pariahs. Jesus' tax collector was under no illusions. His self-esteem was not high! He knew he was a sinner. He stood at a distance, beat his chest and begged for mercy.

It's the way you tell 'em! (verse 14)

Jesus' application may be obvious to modern audiences but would have been shocking when he delivered it. The upstanding religious leader did not go home having received God's approval. It was the tax collector who went home justified because whoever 'humbles themselves will be exalted'.

A contemporary version (on a slightly different topic!)

The parable of the frontbenchers and backbenchers! The former are regularly on their feet making speeches and being in the headlines. Backbenchers are not well-known – they get on with the job of serving their constituents! Making a difference locally. Church, take note.

Final thought

As with the Holy of Holies, so with holiness – those who think they are nearest to attaining it are probably furthest away!

Fourth Sunday before Advent

LUKE 19:1-10

Isaiah 1:10-18; 2 Thessalonians 1

Note

The New Testament reading is 2 Thessalonians 1, a three-part mini-series running up to Advent.

Introduction: Zacchaeus the Tax Collector (verse 1-10)

If the National Association of Tax Collectors held an annual awards night, Jesus might well have been invited to be the after-dinner speaker! Following the parable of the Tax Collector and the Pharisee last week, this week's Gospel reading is the delightful and famous account of Zacchaeus and Jesus.

Location! Location! (verse 1)

This encounter took place in Jericho. Jesus was passing through, not expecting to stay. It was renowned for the battle in which Joshua and the Israelites saw the city walls collapse. In addition to the significance in Jesus' time, there is a contemporary irony of Jericho being a designated Palestinian West Bank town! It is one of the oldest cities of habitation in the world, famous for one of the oldest city walls!

Zacchaeus (verses 2-4)

He was a chief tax collector, wealthy and successful. Professionally, he had made it to the top of the . . . tree! He was short. He wanted to see Jesus. He was resourceful. He ran ahead and shinned up a tree.

Illustration

Sports coverage from large cricket or football matches in some parts of the world often includes shots of local spectators hanging precariously from branches to get a view of the action inside packed stadia.

Jesus (verses 5, 6)

Jesus stopped at the tree and looked up. Someone may have pointed out Zacchaeus to him. Zacchaeus may have looked incongruous and therefore conspicuous in his fine clothes. Or Jesus may have known supernaturally that an honest seeker had gone out on a limb! Like with a tax collector: You pay your money and . . . ! Jesus' invitation was the most significant thing. He called Zacchaeus by name and told him that he needed to stay at his house. Some people dread unexpected, self-invited guests. In this case, Zacchaeus was probably shocked, affirmed and excited in equal measure. He could have been forgiven for falling from his perch from shock, but Zacchaeus came down instantly, in full view of the crowd and welcomed Jesus enthusiastically into his home. There are echoes here of Revelation 3:20: 'I stand at the door and knock. If anyone hears my voice and opens the door, I will come in and eat with that person, and they with me.'

Local mutterers! (verse 7)

This was another occasion when the local judgemental mutterers had a field day. 'How dare he!' go and eat with a sinner. Sadly, there seems to have been a long chain of apostolic succession for this group. Christians do well to avoid membership.

Repentance and reparation (verse 8)

This sequence of events was clearly deeply significant for Zacchaeus. His change of heart and direction was very public. His sincerity was evidenced by his declaration to give away half his wealth and to pay back his erstwhile victims four-fold.

Public declaration (verses 9, 10)

Jesus was always concerned that people should be made whole. This went beyond mere physical healing and/or forgiveness. Whether it was a woman healed from gynaecological problems, lepers, adulterers or tax collectors, he made sure they were restored to their proper place in society. They were rescued from the margins. Therefore, on this occasion, Jesus pronounced forgiveness and salvation on Zacchaeus and his household. Despite his background, his profession and personal history, Zacchaeus was declared to be a 'son of Abraham' – a child of the covenant.

Third Sunday before Advent

LUKE 20:27-38

Job 19:23-27a; 2 Thessalonians 2:1-5, 13-17

Background

In most versions of the Bible this passage (Luke 20:27-38) is entitled 'Resurrection and Marriage'. It was a puzzle then and the teaching that there is no marriage in heaven is an unpopular notion now, assuming the marriage was a happy one! Clergy on a bereavement visit to a widow or widower are advised not to recommend this as a funeral reading. The Sadducees were rivals to the Pharisees and were distinguished from them by, among other things, their lack of belief in a general resurrection (verse 27). The Old Testament passage for today from the Book of Job includes the key verse of that whole book: 'I know that my redeemer lives, and that in the end he will stand on the earth' (Job 19:25).

Pitfall to avoid

Preachers should be aware that the 1954 film (and recently revived musical) *Seven Brides for Seven Brothers* is *not* related to this passage. That is based on a story called *The Sobbin' Women* which in turn was based on a Roman legend, *The Rape of the Sabine Women*.

The question (verse 27-33)

The Sadducees brought Jesus a trick question/test case. They appealed to the Law of Moses, which stated that men should marry their brother's widow if no heir had been produced. Their example was deliberately absurd as they wished to ridicule the notion of resurrection. After seven brothers in succession died childless, the woman finally died as well – probably from exhaustion! It is easy to imagine the smugness with which they delivered their question, 'Whose wife will she be?' (verse 33).

The answer (verses 34-38)

Jesus employed a technique straight from the instruction manual for media training. People preparing to be interviewed are advised to 'answer and offer'. Give a brief answer to the question posed and follow it with a comment that may take the interview on to territory of your choosing. He stated that marriage was for this life (verse 34) not for the life to come (verse 35). He went on to state categorically his belief in resurrection (verse 36). Jesus then went on to speak about Moses' encounter at the burning bush in which he addressed God as the God of Abraham, Isaac and Jacob and used the present tense. To God, all those patriarchs were alive (verses 38, 39). He had turned a classic passage of Scripture on them to win the argument.

Postscript

Verse 39 is not in the set Gospel reading but in it Luke recorded that teachers of the law looking on admired his style and people did not dare to ask any more trick questions.

Pastoral footnote

If anyone is wrong-footed and upset by the idea that there is no marriage in heaven, preachers may reassure them that the general understanding of life after death is one of there being no disappointment. There will be reunion with those we have committed to God's safe-keeping. Heavenly closeness with God and other people will supersede any earthly relationship. Marriage at its best is a foretaste of heaven!

Second Sunday before Advent

LUKE 21:5-19

Malachi 4:1-2a; 2 Thessalonians 3:6-13

Introduction

As Advent draws closer, preachers face the challenge of preaching on apocalyptic passages (such as today's reading) in such a way as to raise awareness without over-heating! It can never be assumed that people know that Jesus appeared to have had the Fall of Jerusalem in AD 70 in mind when speaking. Apocalyptic, being a form of prophecy, often has more than one focal point.

The action in this part of Luke's Gospel is in Jerusalem.

The Temple loomed large (verses 5, 6)

The Temple stood out and dominated the skyline and drew people's gaze. (Examples: London Eye, the Shard, Eiffel Tower, Millennium Stadium in Cardiff, etc.) It had been built over several lifetimes and was probably not finished in every detail. It stood for so much spiritually and nationally. It was a mark of the presence of God even in a time when the country was occupied and governed by the Romans and their vassals. Jesus' disciples were dazzled by it (verse 5). Jesus' words that one day it would be razed to the ground would have been shocking and almost incomprehensible (verse 6).

Know the times (verses 7-11)

Not unreasonably, the disciples asked Jesus to tell them when these things would happen. Jesus told them there was a little while yet and warned them not to be deceived by people claiming to be messiahs or that the end was nigh. Through the ages, especially in unsettling times, people have gone back to verse 9: 'When you hear of wars and uprisings, do not be frightened.' People, especially the elderly, watch the news and regularly exclaim or ask themselves: 'Whatever next? Where's it all going to end?'

Closer to home (verses 12-16)

In the UK there is a mini-industry built around reclaiming premiums for PPI, insurance policies that were mis-sold. Jesus could never be accused of not being upfront about the cost of following him. The first disciples and their successors were warned in no uncertain terms that a decision to follow Christ might be very costly. In these verses, he warned that they would be betrayed by family members, imprisoned and hated for his sake (verses 12, 16). He encouraged them not to worry in advance. When the time came, they would find that they would be given the words to say (verses 13-15). The Book of Acts gives clear examples of this in the lives of the apostles.

Bottom line (verses 17-19)

Such graphic warnings could frighten and demotivate the disciples. The Gospel reading ends on a reassuring note: by standing firm you will gain life (verse 19).

Final word

In the light of the Gospel reading, it may be appropriate to pray for the persecuted Church in various places across the world and for any church members struggling to deal with opposition or antipathy within their family.

Christ the King/ Sunday next before Advent

LUKE 23:33-43
Jeremiah 23:1-6; Colossians 1:11-20

Introduction

On the last Sunday of a Lectionary year the Church celebrates Christ as King. People who are asked to read the Gospel reading may be forgiven for thinking that there is a typo on the rota as they find themselves confronted with an account of the crucifixion.

Activity

It may be interesting to hear whether any church members have met the Queen or any other monarch. If so, under what circumstances? Contrast a ceremonial investiture with a king's visit to troops on a battlefield.

From the Old Testament reading

This Lectionary year ends appropriately on a note of promise. The verses from Jeremiah 23 include God's promise that he will one day gather his remnant of people scattered widely. From a preacher's point of view, in the indictment of bad shepherds there is the implicit reminder that shepherds of God's people must tend them faithfully and lovingly.

Crucified King (verses 33-38)

A crucified Messiah was a literal nonsense. The Old Testament spoke of anyone being hanged or crucified on a tree being under a curse. On the battlefield, armies would look to kill the king (or his general) and take their enemies' standard. Barbarically, the heads of defeated kings have been displayed in different eras and cultures. Therefore, reading the account of Jesus' death is deliberately done so that the extraordinary nature of his kingship can be declared. In his apparent defeat on the Cross and rising from the dead, he was achieving his great victory.

The cross, an instrument of torture and execution, is the most unlikely of religious symbols.

There is much that is terribly ironic in this account of Jesus' death. The juxtaposition of death and life are striking: the Place of the Skull; an innocent man between two convicted criminals, one on the right and one on the left (verse 33); Jesus asking for forgiveness for his tormentors (verse 34); the cries of the people: 'He saved others; let him save himself if he is God's Messiah, the Chosen One' (verse 35).

At the heart of this reading are the mocking questions from the crowd and the soldiers: 'If you are the king of the Jews, save yourself' (verse 37). Jesus died beneath a sign that read: 'This is the King of the Jews.' This was the question Pontius Pilate had asked Jesus (23:3).

Two criminals (verses 39-43)

As had been prophesied, Jesus divided opinion until the very end of his life. Flanked by criminals, it shows the cruel slow nature of crucifixion that there was a point at which conversation was possible. One of them, speaking from within his agony, insulted Jesus, telling him mockingly to save them and himself (verse 39). In stark contrast, the other criminal reprimanded his doomed companion. This second man knew that Jesus was innocent and recognised the injustice of Jesus being crucified (verses 40, 41). He then made possibly the most famous last wish of a condemned man in history: 'Jesus, remember me when you come into your kingdom' (verse 42). 'Ask, and it will be given to you,' Jesus had said. One of his last acts on earth was granting this request: 'Truly I tell you, today you will be with me in paradise' (verse 43).

Conclusion

In the next few weeks the focus will shift on to the Christmas story. Today's readings remind people of the journey from heaven to earth and back, from the manger to the tomb via the Cross. The journey of the King. The Royal Procession.

Table of Lectionary years ABC

2016 / 2017	A
2017 / 2018	B
2018 / 2019	C
2019 / 2020	A
2020 / 2021	B
2021 / 2022	C
2022 / 2023	A
2023 / 2024	B
2024 / 2025	C
2025 / 2026	A
2026 / 2027	B
2027 / 2028	C
2028 / 2029	A
2029 / 2030	B

Index of Gospel Readings